Contents

Preface

We are proud to present this book on intercultural dialogue as a joint effort by the International Association of Universities (IAU) and the Council of Europe. This co-operation – between an international university organisation with global scope and a European intergovernmental organisation with important activities in higher education policy as part of its focus on democracy, human rights and the rule of law – underlines how important the ability to conduct intercultural dialogue is to our societies. It also underlines the fundamental role of higher education in developing and maintaining this ability.

The book is based on close co-operation between our two organisations around two events: a conference organised by the Council of Europe's Steering Committee on Higher Education and Research (CDESR) at the Peoples' Friendship University of Russia in June 2009 and the IAU International Conference at Notre Dame University – Louaize in Lebanon in November 2009. Each organisation contributed decisively to the conference of the other: the IAU provided the rapporteur for the conference in Moscow whereas the Council of Europe gave one of the plenary presentations in Lebanon. The idea of a joint book grew out of this co-operation, and the book is edited by those who were the strongest advocates of the co-operation: Hilligje van't Land of the IAU, who was rapporteur to the Moscow conference and one of the main organisers of the conference in Lebanon, and Sjur Bergan of the Council of Europe, who was the main organiser of the Moscow conference and spoke at the conference in Lebanon.

As President of the IAU and Chair of the CDESR at the time the foundation for this book was laid, we are convinced that a tolerant and respectful dialogue is both necessary and unavoidable for the recognition of diversity and multiculturality in the world in which we live. We hope this joint book will serve as a window and a mirror to overcome our cultural ignorance, will help prepare its readers not only to debate but to listen, will help foster the emancipating powers of cultural diversity and will help us learn how to use them more effectively in our responsibilities as educators and researchers.

As the world moves closer together, a vital skill for nations, communities – including the higher education community – and individuals will be the ability to deal positively with otherness. In this context, cross-cultural education and education for dialogue represent one of the best options for the future of our societies. The internationalisation of higher education cannot be understood without this cross-cultural component. It is not just a matter of having more foreign students or having more foreign faculty. That will help, but it is not enough. It is a matter of understanding and accepting each other, and that is where education comes in. That is where dialogue, tolerance and democracy come in.

As our world becomes ever more globalised and knowledge-based, education and science themselves have also become more knowledge-intensive. It does not require great elucidation: more and more knowledge will be produced – it has been estimated that the amount of knowledge doubles in less than every five years – and the average levels of education are rising – not with equity, not with even quality, but they are rising.

While the whole concept of education is shifting as a result of this knowledge growth, the main aim of education as well as research is to contribute to the next generation of locally rooted, well-informed global citizens capable of jointly ensuring peace, progress, freedom and democracy. We are therefore increasingly confronted with questions about the direction which education and science must take on a number of crucial issues, and one of those issues is cultural diversity and the ability of those with different cultural backgrounds to relate constructively to each other. Education and research of course play an important role in developing our economy but their role cannot and should not be limited to that. Education and research are equally vital in preparing for democratic citizenship, in enhancing the personal development of learners and in enabling our societies to develop and maintain a broad and advanced knowledge base.

In our diverse and interconnected world we have many neighbours – nearby and faraway, neighbours who come from very diverse backgrounds. It is essential to increase and improve our knowledge, information and understanding about other people, other cultures and other societies. It is vital that we understand that what is different is not necessarily less worthy of esteem. To achieve this, we must be prepared to engage actively in dialogue, unconditionally and with a truly open mind.

Increasing knowledge, awareness and understanding is, then, the main aim of this book. It aims to explore the role of higher education – institutions, faculty, students and policy makers – in enabling our societies to function in an interconnected world in which contact with those of different backgrounds is a given and not an option. This book aims to be a small contribution to ensuring that such contacts will lead to co-operation and not to antagonism. The book aims to enable its readers not to win a debate but to try to understand the other by listening carefully – and, to do so, it will be necessary at times to remain silent as well.

We hope this book will inspire its readers to initiate dialogue in their own institutions and societies, to explore how they as well as their institutions can be actors in intercultural dialogue and to help further develop the role of higher education as a crucial actor in modern societies, not only in implementing the political agenda of our societies but in setting that political agenda in the first place.

Professor Juan Ramón de la Fuente   *Professor Radu Mircea Damian*
President, IAU   *Chair CDESR, 2007-2010*

Message from the rectors of the Peoples' Friendship University of Russia and Notre Dame University – Louaize

Our universities both hosted one of the conferences from which the articles in this book are drawn. We are proud to be associated with this publication, and the backgrounds of our institutions help explain why we both feel that intercultural dialogue should be a key concern of modern universities, regardless of where they are located.

The Russian Peoples' Friendship University was established fifty years ago to provide education opportunities for students from Africa, Asia and Latin America, in particular. It was therefore an international institution from its inception and intercultural contacts were part of its daily life from its first day. Over the past twenty years it has faced the unusual challenge of transforming itself from an institution for foreign students only to one where half the students are foreigners and the other half are Russians. This has not made intercultural dialogue a less pressing concern: rather, the new situation has highlighted the relationship between the host country and its culture and the highly diverse cultural background of its students. It has pinpointed the need for students to be fluent in the host country's language and at least one foreign language and it has underlined the openness to other cultures that should follow from being fluent in several languages. Based on its experience in promoting intercultural dialogue among its students, as well as its research and experience with intercultural dialogue in internationalising higher education, the Russian Peoples' Friendship University has made dialogue on campus an important part of its institutional policy and also plays an active role in fostering dialogue in broader society.

Notre Dame University – Louaize, Lebanon is also a young university, founded in 1987. It has a confessional identity in a society of many faiths and persuasions. On the foundation of its own identity and heritage, the university remains open to the cultural and religious diversity of the society and the region of which it is a part, and its student body reflects that diversity. It stresses the importance of fluency in Arabic, as the language of the country and the region, as well as in foreign languages, particularly English and French. Notre Dame University – Louaize is convinced that it cannot fulfil its mission of preparing future citizens of Lebanon unless it seeks to instil in its students and faculty respect for the dignity of others, regardless of their cultural background and religious or political persuasion. Notre Dame University – Louaize aims to develop a culture of dialogue in all its students so that the intercultural dialogue conducted on campus will be pursued in the broader society of which the university is a part.

Both our universities illustrate why higher education needs to be highly sensitive to intercultural dialogue and why developing the ability and desire to engage with those whose background and convictions are different from our own is an integral part of the mission of higher education, just as much as the more traditional concepts of specific academic disciplines. Dialogue requires knowledge of other cultures and societies, but knowledge alone is not enough. After all, if knowledge of the other is treated as the puzzled discovery of the exotic, there is little basis for dialogue based on respect. Universities must develop knowledge but also a deeper understanding of other cultures and they must foster the attitudes that lead to open minds treating others with respect and never putting the basic human dignity of others in doubt. This also means that those who talk must sometimes raise their voices when the basic condition of respect for human dignity is disregarded, whether by members of their own institution or by outside actors.

Engaging in dialogue does not mean giving up one's own traditions and convictions, but being open to those of others. Engaging in dialogue does not mean saying our own views are wrong, but being open to the possibility that those of others may be right. Engaging in dialogue does not mean giving up teaching, but remaining open to the possibility of learning in all circumstances. Not least, engaging in dialogue means being open to the possibilities that while some truths are self-evident, there is often more than one side to an issue. These are not only attitudes and values on which democratic, pluralistic societies must build: they are also part and parcel of the heritage of higher education.

As leaders of higher education institutions, we are proud to have offered the possibility for academics, students and civil servants from a variety of backgrounds to exchange views on the role of higher education in helping our societies grow in wisdom and maturity. We are also proud to be associated with a book published jointly by the International Association of Universities and the Council of Europe, and we find it fitting that this book should be published jointly by an organisation of higher education institutions with global membership and an intergovernmental organisation that, while its membership is European, has demonstrated its openness to the world by adopting a White Paper on Intercultural Dialogue.

We hope this book will not only demonstrate why intercultural dialogue is essential to higher education but also illustrate some ways in which higher education may take the dialogue forward, on campuses but also far beyond.

Our institutions demonstrate, through their origins and present circumstances, why intercultural dialogue is important. Through their polices and practice, they also illustrate how dialogue can be made a pervasive reality. We hope that our examples as well as the many views and ideas presented in this book will provide inspiration for institutions and governments, faculty and students to make intercultural dialogue a reality on campus and an essential element of the societies we aim to build and develop.

Professor Vladimir M. Filippov   *Fr Walid Moussa, OMM*
Rector   *President*
Russian Peoples' Friendship University   Notre Dame University – Louaize, Lebanon

A word from the editors

Sjur Bergan and Hilligje van 't Land

The book you are about to read bears the title *Speaking across borders*. Had we lived in an age in which sound bites were longer, we would have made a point of including listening in the title because true dialogue requires the will and the ability to both listen and speak. One of the main aims of this book is to make the case for the role and responsibility of higher education in developing the competences and attitudes that will help its graduates further intercultural dialogue in our societies. The contribution of individual academics and graduates is one aspect of the role of higher education in furthering intercultural dialogue; but equally institutions, as important actors in society, share that role.

The second part of the title – across borders – may seem obvious. If we speak about intercultural dialogue, we speak about dialogue across national borders. We do, but the issue is a little more complicated than that. State borders are not the only ones – though history provides a long list of examples where better dialogue across political borders could have meant less armed conflict. Luckily, history also provides many examples of successful dialogue and co-operation across national borders, of which the European construction is perhaps the most spectacular.

When referring to intercultural dialogue, however, borders between political systems are not the only borders. Few if any countries are entirely monocultural and even less so in an age in which international migration is the rule rather than the exception. Of course, immigration is far from a new phenomenon. The countries of North and South America were built on immigration from Europe and elsewhere, and co-existence with the original population was rarely easy and seldom charac- terised by dialogue. As has been remarked, to decide the contentious issue of who discovered America, one would need to ask the people who stood on the shore to greet the discoverers. Immigration to and within Europe has also been the historical rule rather than the exception, to the extent that a period of the early Middle Ages in Europe has come to be referred to as the Period of Migration.[1]

Borders are not only international. Cultural borders also exist within countries, regions and local communities, and in many cases these borders determine with whom one socialises, what kind of work one does, where and how one worships and how one is considered in the community. The Dutch-American political scientist Arend Lijphart coined the term *verzuiling* (literally "pillarisation" but the Dutch rather than the English term is used for good reason) to describe communities in which all or most interaction is between individuals belonging to the same group.

---

1. The equivalent term in German is perhaps even more poignant: *Völkerwanderung* means literally "the wandering of peoples".

Needless to say, *verzuiling* is not a prescription for cohesive societies, and one important purpose in furthering intercultural dialogue is to promote cohesion and prevent *verzuiling*: the division of society into comfort zones that are almost mutually exclusive and between which interaction is limited as far as possible.

Democratic societies have abolished formal borders between easily identifiable groups in society, as exemplified by the legal provisions that not so many generations ago institutionalised discrimination against Blacks in the US Deep South, Sámi in northern Norway or all but the indisputably white in apartheid South Africa. Nevertheless, informal borders remain and may have almost as strong effects as formal borders. The symbolic border of the railway tracks can be almost as powerful as the physical borders manned by immigration officers. If the prevailing mood in a community is strongly isolationist or exclusionist, only the most persistent individuals will be able to break the mould. Borders may also exist in people's thoughts and habits, even without undue pressure from their immediate surroundings. For a variety of reasons, individuals may be reluctant or uncomfortable engaging in dialogue or co-operation with people who have a different background, speak another language, dress differently or hold different values.

That physical, international boundaries between states – which are, after all, political constructs – are not the only borders is also underlined by the UNESCO Constitution, which states that "since wars begin in the minds of men, it is in the minds of men that the defences of peace must be constructed" (UNESCO 1945: Preamble). Open minds and open-mindedness are ideals which are often talked about, but less often practised. When closed, minds may be our most important borders and the most difficult to open. Yet, without open minds, dialogue is impossible and borders cannot be crossed. We may experience this in our everyday lives when new ideas are too often met with the "argument" that, since things have always been done in a certain way, they should continue to be done that way. Had that been nature's way, humankind would not have existed and the animal kingdom would have been entirely amphibious. We may also experience the effect of closed minds in the big issues of our times, when we fail to rise to the challenge of climate change or the need to cross our personal borders as well as those of our countries and cultures.

Whatever the reasons may be that make individuals, groups or societies reluctant to cross formal or informal borders, the result is often suspicion and lack of co-operation. Sometimes the results can be dramatically worse, for societies and individuals. Even if improved knowledge and better acquaintance with the values and backgrounds of others do not automatically lead to more respect and, to borrow the title of the recent Council of Europe White Paper (Council of Europe 2008), living together as equals in dignity, one of the key tasks of education, at all levels, in modern society must be to prepare citizens to live and work in a world in which contacts across borders – international borders as well as those within our own societies and our own minds – will occur frequently, and the ability to handle such contacts will be crucial.

This is the conviction that led an international global non-governmental organisation devoted to higher education – the International Association of Universities (IAU)

– and a European intergovernmental organisation devoted to democracy, human rights and the rule of law – the Council of Europe – to co-operate on a book on the role of higher education in furthering intercultural dialogue. The book builds on two conferences: one organised by the Council of Europe in Moscow in June 2009, in which the IAU played a key role, and one organised by the International Association of Universities in Lebanon in November 2009, to which the Council of Europe contributed one of the main presentations. Both conferences were held at universities – the Peoples' Friendship University of Russia and Notre Dame University – Louaize – and each brought together the main stakeholder groups in higher education: institutions, staff, students and public authorities.

Beyond the two conferences, which provide the immediate background for the book, this joint venture also builds on the long-standing commitment of both organisations to intercultural dialogue. This has always been an important dimension of the Council of Europe's work, but its importance has been made particularly clear through the White Paper adopted by its Committee of Ministers in May 2008. More specifically, the Council of Europe's Steering Committee for Higher Education and Research (CDESR) has adopted a statement on the contribution of higher education to intercultural dialogue (CDESR 2006) and in March 2008 it organised a conference on intercultural dialogue on campus (Bergan and Restoueix 2009).

As an international representative of the universities of the world, one of the IAU's primary functions is to identify and research issues that are of concern and interest to its members and beyond. Convinced of the key role that higher education has to play in fostering intercultural dialogue and understanding, the IAU selected this topic as one of its thematic priorities and created an international task force in 2002. This led to the organisation of an expert seminar in Budapest in 2005, the outcomes of which were published in the IAU review *Higher Education Policy* (van't Land 2005). Since then, the association has regularly devoted special sessions to this topic at its international events, and it was chosen as the theme of the 2009 international conference at Notre Dame University – Louaize in Lebanon. The international nature of the association has contributed to the diversity of voices that have been involved in these events and related publications. The IAU also maintains a series of fairly comprehensive websites providing case studies, bibliographical data, links to higher education institutions and more.[2]

This book is organised around four main themes of intercultural dialogue: its political context; on campus and in society; higher education as an actor; and the roles it can play in practice.

The first theme places intercultural dialogue in its proper political context, where it plays an important role in seeking to develop and maintain a humane society. This part of the book is made up of three weighty contributions from key actors in international education and work for intercultural dialogue. UNESCO's former

---

2. See www.iau-aiu.net.

Director-General **Federico Mayor** explores the role of higher education in fostering a culture of peace and understanding. His starting point is the city of Beirut, which hosted the IAU conference and, earlier on, a UNESCO general conference. On the basis of its history as well as of its present, Beirut aspires to dialogue rather than confrontation. Beirut illustrates the need for a new beginning, which is reflected in UNESCO's constitution as well as in numerous United Nations initiatives. Mayor emphasises that education goes well beyond the technical transmission of knowledge: education also develops personalities and attitudes. Higher education has a key role to play in developing a culture of dialogue and understanding, and Mayor regrets the fact that this positive role of universities draws insufficient attention from the media, for which the important and peaceful role of universities does not seem to be newsworthy. Higher education must be a major actor in a transition from using force to using words, in a profound rethinking of our priorities and actions as individuals and as societies.

Gabriella Battaini-Dragoni, the Council of Europe's Director General of Education, Culture and Heritage, Youth and Sport as well as its Co-ordinator for Intercultural Dialogue, analyses the White Paper drafted under her leadership. She underlines the two key messages in its short title – Living together as Equals in Dignity. First, living together implies much more than co-existence or simply living side by side: it presupposes close contacts and interaction between individuals of different cultures. Second, we do not speak only of the equality of rights but also of equality of dignity: we are all of equal value as human beings. Even if the White Paper encompasses all areas of the Council of Europe's activities, education plays a particularly important role in making intercultural dialogue not only a right but a reality in our daily lives.

In exploring the background to the conference in Lebanon, **Eva Egron-Polak** – Secretary-General of the IAU and an accomplished international educational policy maker – makes the case for putting intercultural dialogue high on the agenda of universities, but she argues from another point of view: that of educators and institutional policy makers. She underlines the fact that the world faces not only a financial crisis but also a crisis of values, an environmental crisis and a social crisis, and she maintains that higher education must be a key contributor to finding our way out of these multiple crises. Echoing Mayor's views, Egron-Polak observes that the issue is not a lack of declarations or intentions but the transformation of these into action. Higher education must help develop individuals who are locally rooted and at the same time educated to be informed global citizens, able to make sound choices, recognise what they do not know and learn how to learn continually about and from others – without prejudice or preconceptions. To do so, those in higher education must, among other things, recognise fully the contributions of all civilisations, all cultures, all religions and faiths, and create conditions of equality and dignity in dialogue, ensuring that we empower especially those who are most marginalised to take part in the dialogue.

The second part of the book sets the scene by linking dialogue on campus and the role of higher education in furthering dialogue in broader society. **Bernd Wächter**, drawing on his report from the Council of Europe conference in March 2008, shows the need for intercultural dialogue on campus. Higher education has been international from its inception and international mobility is a key policy goal in the European Higher Education Area – as it is in many other parts of the world – but that does not mean that the university campus is automatically intercultural. Too often, foreign students are isolated on campus and their contacts are mainly with other foreign students, especially those from the same home country or region. Also, higher education institutions often do not have policies for integrating foreign students and for taking advantage of the resource they represent. Nevertheless, there are promising examples of good practice and Wächter makes a number of suggestions for improving institutional policy and practice.

Hilligje van't Land, who is in charge of developing projects on intercultural dialogue for the IAU, draws on her experience at the IAU (Blasi and van't Land 2005), as rapporteur of the Council of Europe's Moscow conference and as organiser of the IAU conference in Lebanon. Universities are communities in themselves, and diversity on campus is a reality that needs to be fully seized and valued. At the same time, universities are key actors in the broader society. To fulfil this role, the institutions must of course make this a priority but so must public authorities. Staff and students, collectively and individually, NGOs (non-governmental organisations) and university networks all have important roles to play. Policy makers and practitioners need to value all the major purposes of higher education, not just its role in preparing for the labour market. Developing the kind of society in which people can live together as equals in dignity, and in which all citizens are fluent in intercultural dialogue, is an important purpose in higher education and it must be among the goals of higher education reform – in particular in the context of the European Higher Education Area. Intercultural competences should form an integral part of higher education learning outcomes; frameworks for implementation of the principles of intercultural learning and dialogue should be developed, and norms and values adopted, to ensure proper intercultural teaching and learning and to favour dialogue.

The third part of the book examines the role of higher education as an actor in intercultural dialogue. **Edward Alam** maintains that, if higher education is to play a role in fostering intercultural dialogue, higher education itself needs to be transformed into a culture of dialogue. There is much talk about the need for dialogue between disciplines, but there is more talk than practice; and increasing specialisation within disciplines means that even intradisciplinary dialogue can be a formidable challenge. Higher education needs to search for "holiness" – not in a religious sense, but in the sense of searching for the whole truth. Alam makes the point that, unless we start with a unity and wholeness in the curriculum that facilitates genuine dialogue among members of the faculty from the same disciplines, there can never be the kind of interdisciplinary and intercultural dialogue that is so urgent in our global age. It is easy to see why today's strong disciplinary specialisation has come about – so easy, in fact, that one needs to be reminded that this was not the only possible development of research and learning. Alam believes that the success of interdisciplinary education depends directly on the success of intercultural education, and vice versa, and this needs to be understood by policy makers and academics, as well as by religious leaders. The current emphasis on natural sciences must be complemented by research in philosophy and other areas that emphasise a holistic view of human and natural development. One example mentioned by Alam is the success that phenomenology has already had in the way it has cultivated a more robust and unified sense of reason in natural law theory. Dialogue must not be turned into another industry, nor should it be conducted for its own sake: higher education should develop attitudes that make dialogue natural and the preferred way of approaching those from other backgrounds.

Sjur Bergan makes the point that, even when potential interlocutors have the physical or technical means to communicate, they also need to have a frame of mind that will make dialogue possible. Education is about changing attitudes and helping develop our frames of mind. In an age when contact with individuals from very different cultural backgrounds is not an option but an everyday reality, education cannot remain indifferent to this basic fact of human existence. Higher education should be particularly well suited to furthering intercultural dialogue because it is committed to assessing ideas not on the basis of their origin but on the basis of their intrinsic merit, even if there are numerous examples of higher education institutions, staff and students who have acted differently. Higher education must take a comprehensive view of its purposes, and the plural is used here with emphasis. Institutions must aim to develop a practice of dialogue, on campus and beyond, bearing in mind that the ability and will for dialogue cannot be developed solely by listening to lectures. Higher education institutions are excellent at training highly competent subject specialists but they are perhaps less good at educating intellectuals – graduates with a good general culture and the ability to see their own academic discipline in a broader context, able to assess advantages and disadvantages not simply in terms of their own discipline but also in terms of their effects on broader societal goals and in the longer term, people able to take account of knowledge and understanding from several academic fields. It is essential that our higher education institutions produce intellectuals as well as subject specialists.

Darla Deardorff discusses the competences required for intercultural dialogue and the role of higher education in developing these competences in students. Her own recent work suggests that the competences may be categorised into attitudes, knowledge, skills and internal and external outcomes. They may be placed in a visual framework that illustrates how intercultural competence is a lifelong process and how there is no single point at which an individual becomes completely interculturally competent. She also notes that intercultural scholars in the United States do not agree on the role of language in intercultural competence development. Another important point is that intercultural competence does not just happen; for most learners, it must be intentionally developed. Deardorff stresses that the model she presents is based primarily on experience from the United States; it should be tested against and complemented by experience from other parts of the world.

Writing from a student perspective, **Olav Øye and Andrea Blättler** argue that intercultural dialogue must be more than just talk. For most students, intercultural dialogue means occasional chats with international students at their own institutions. When these contacts develop into more substantial discussions, intercultural dialogue begins in earnest. Opportunities for intercultural dialogue are strengthened by organised mobility, and the authors recall that the European Students Union played an important role in establishing 20% mobility by 2020 as a goal of the European Higher Education Area. It is important that mobile students be offered language courses and that these courses also address issues of intercultural communication. Integration of international students into the life of their host institution – and even more so into the life of their host community – remains a challenge, even if some institutions have policies for integration. Øye and Blättler see student organisations as particularly important in providing a space where students can work side by side and discuss freely. At international level, student organisations are faced with many of the same issues of dialogue between people from different backgrounds that challenge other parts of our societies. Nevertheless, in recent experience it has proved less difficult than expected to bring student representatives to agree on key student issues, which seem to be largely the same in most parts of the world, though totalitarian societies present some particular challenges for student participation.

Germain Dondelinger writes from the perspective of another key actor, viz. public authorities. He maintains that we can see why intercultural dialogue is important if we look at the changing nature of our societies. Migration, globalisation, international and domestic security issues and increasingly multicultural societies make the development of intercultural competences and the promotion of intercultural dialogue fundamental. It contributes to a number of strategic priorities, such as respecting and promoting cultural diversity, solidarity, social justice and cohesion. Dondelinger also points to possible tensions, but maintains that individual rights prevail over collective rights in intercultural dialogue contexts. He explores different approaches and the contributions of various actors, concluding that public authorities must develop strategies for provision, staff, curriculum and language policies. Intercultural dialogue should be seen as a way of coming to terms with other world views, traditions and lifestyles through empathy, non-violence and creativity; but the concept of "identity", on which intercultural dialogue hinges, is not static and should not automatically be seen in Manichean terms.

Yazmín Cruz and Cristina Escrigas emphasise that higher education must train professionals but even more it must educate responsible citizens. This requires graduates to have a vision of reality that extends well beyond their own discipline. Higher education must contribute to positive social transformation, taking into account the challenge of intercultural understanding. This corresponds to the mission of the Global University Network for Innovation (GUNI), which seeks to strengthen the role of higher education in society by reforming and innovating higher education policies across the world according to the principles of public service, relevance and social responsibility. For higher education to play its rightful role, universities need to reappraise their purposes, functions and practices through critical engagement in dialogue and discourse with the citizenry on the problematic issues of our societies. This, Cruz and Escrigas argue, requires institutions to overcome the inertia of their current model, moving beyond the outdated paradigms of the ivory tower or the market-oriented university, and reorient higher education so it can better respond to society's challenges. They make the point that we live in interconnected worlds and our global society is faced by two major conflicts: the relationship between humans – that is, co-existence – and the relationship between humans and nature. Recovering the human capacity to evaluate, compare, choose, decide and act is therefore more crucial now than ever before. The authors believe that education is the key to this endeavour, but that a new world calls for a new kind of university, one that creatively redefines its missions and functions, that reinvents itself if necessary so it can continue to serve as a space for reflection and creativity, one that provides the tools needed for social analysis, critical thinking and sustainability.

The fourth part of this book provides examples of the roles education can play in developing intercultural dialogue. **Barasby S. Karamurzov** describes north Caucasus, which is a plural region in various respects – linguistic, ethnic and religious – often in a kind of duality between the native cultures, which are themselves diverse, and the culture of broader Russian society. The fact that the region is relatively less developed in its economy adds to the challenge. The values and norms that dominate a society's culture determine the behaviour and social practices of individuals. In north Caucasus, societies as a whole, and young generations especially, are being influenced by mass culture, which is devoid of national content or symbols; but they are also influenced by the traditional "indigenous" cultural forms, which are being revived at present and are characterised by ethnic and religious exceptionalism. Karamurzov maintains that the opportunities to realise any rational strategy will depend on an adequate knowledge of the structure of identities, variable patterns of value orientations and social action among the younger generations, whence the crucial importance of education.

Drawing on the particular circumstances of Lebanon. **Michel Nehme** underlines the responsibility of universities for creating conditions that allow the promotion and construction of a civilisation based on intercultural dialogue and respect for cultural diversity, thus contributing to the prevention of violent conflict, the management and control of conflicts and post-conflict reconciliation. At times in history, religious and cultural factors have led to conflict and war; at other times, they have prevented or moderated violence. It is, however, too simplistic to describe the Lebanese conflict solely as one of religion, since economic and other factors also play a role. Nehme suggests that the major intellectual contribution should be to arrive at a proposed national political structure based on living together in a harmoniously interactive manner, recognising the heterogeneous nature of Lebanese society as well as the need for a common destiny.

16

Is-haq O. Oloyede analyses the role of higher education in the culturally highly diverse context of Nigeria. The increasing importance of cultural background and affiliation within Nigerian society has had negative impacts on higher education. The competition for control of universities derives from the assumption that universities play significant roles in forming and recruiting the elite as well as generating local employment and economic development. Hence, the location of universities, the appointment of their vice chancellors, recruitment of staff and admission of students become vital issues of contention. However, there are also initiatives that seek to counteract polarisation based on ethnic, religious and cultural background. One is the Nigeria Inter-religious Council, which Oloyede heads and which attempts to educate Christians and Muslims about the background and beliefs of the other group. Within higher education, legislation aims to promote equity in the location of higher education institutions and in the admission of students, but without reserving or earmarking any quotas for any designated ethnic groups. This leads to considerable strife and suspicion as each group tries to obtain as high a share of the national resources in this area as possible. There is, however, hope that a relatively complex admissions policy as well as in hiring staff as well as some targeted programmes of teaching and learning will help turn Nigerian universities into a microcosm of Nigerian society. Students from different parts of the country will be forced to live side by side in student hostels, work together in class and discuss the problems of their country; there is good hope that those measures will also help foster better dialogue and understanding.

Georges Nahas explores the role of higher education in promoting a culture of dialogue and understanding on the basis of his own experience as a Lebanese university leader. Lebanon recognises 18 confessions, Christian and Muslim. Since 1922, the constitution has given specific rights to these recognised groups and it is very difficult for a citizen not to belong to one of them. All Lebanese universities except one are private and many of them have a confessional basis. This been accentuated over the past generation, in particular as a consequence of the Lebanese civil war and the developments that led to the war. The University of Balamand is in northern Lebanon, whereas most higher education institutions are in the Beirut area. Founded in 1988 by merging several existing institutions, it made an effort to recruit staff and students broadly and managed to gain the trust and support of the different groups represented in northern Lebanon. The university implements its vision of non-discrimination and nation-building across confessional lines on three complementary levels – academic planning, institutional rules and regulations, and national and international relations – and it has adopted action plans for each. Over the past two decades, the University of Balamand has established an atmosphere of trust and co-operation within the university and has gained recognition as a site of dialogue. At the same time, it faces a challenge in developing its role as an actor of dialogue in broader society.

Zixin Hou and Qinghua Liu present the Chinese experience of internationalisation and intercultural understanding. They see universities playing a crucial role in educating citizens of the world for the 21st century and they maintain that international understanding is a long-term bilateral understanding implying exchange and interaction, the goal of which is to understand the politics, economics and culture of other countries, while seeking understanding from them in return. Different cultures make the world richer and more colourful, and we should respect and understand the cultural traditions of each country. China has made great efforts to open up its higher education internationally and has shown a very impressive increase in the number of students it sends abroad as well as the number of students it hosts over the past 30 years. The authors illustrate these efforts by the example of Nankai University and its "Nankai-Aichi pattern" in co-operation with Aichi University of Japan and the expansion of the Confucius Institutes, which aim to advance the dialogue between different cultures, further mutual understanding and enhance understanding of Chinese language and culture.

Alf Rasmussen provides an example of public policy specifically devised to improve the internationalisation of education. The Norwegian White Paper on internationalisation encompasses all levels of education, but higher education plays an important role. The Norwegian White Paper is noteworthy for making intercultural dialogue an explicit part of the internationalisation strategy; it sees international success in education and research collaboration and competition as depending on how successful Norwegian society is in intercultural dialogue and understanding. Public policy therefore aims to prepare everyone to be intercultural citizens in this society from early childhood. Norway also finds it needs to enlarge its traditional circle of co-operation with its Nordic neighbours, a few other European countries and North America, which again increases demands for intercultural understanding and awareness, as well as greater and more diverse linguistic competence. The White Paper underlines the fact that international perspectives, languages and cultural awareness are increasingly important competences for those seeking employment. Internationalisation of education must therefore not only focus on students and staff spending semesters or years abroad, but also ensure that education in Norway is international in character and internationally competitive in its quality standards.

We would like to express our appreciation of the work of the authors, who have managed to fit the writing of their articles and answering our sometimes quite detailed editorial questions into their very busy schedules. It is precisely the richness and diversity of the authors' experiences and backgrounds that, we hope, will make this book an interesting and relevant source for further work on intercultural dialogue in higher education. We would also like to put on record our appreciation of the help we received from **Anna Győry**, who was an intern with the IAU for part of the period when this book was being edited, in verifying references and chasing up those that might have been missing.

As editors, we are of course aware that a single book is by itself unlikely to dramatically improve intercultural dialogue. By definition, a book is an instrument of one-way communication, even when it is a collection of essays by different authors in which a variety of views meet within the confines of a single volume. However, it is our hope that this book will help stimulate reflection and that you – our readers

– will then initiate further discussion and dialogue on the responsibility of higher education in further intercultural dialogue.

This book is not an end in itself; nor should it be seen as the final summary of a debate. Through the joint efforts of the International Association of Universities and the Council of Europe, the book is one step on a road that we hope and trust has been only partly travelled, a step which will lead higher education to play its strong and natural role in rising to one of the most important challenges that we face: how, as societies and as citizens, we can communicate respectfully with those whose backgrounds differ strongly from our own, how we can generate a meeting of open minds and how we can live together in equal dignity. We are convinced that our future will depend in part on the ability of higher education to find satisfactory answers to this seemingly simple, yet extraordinarily complex question.

References

Bergan, Sjur and Jean-Philippe Restoueix (eds) (2009): *Intercultural Dialogue on Campus*, Higher Education Series No. 11, Strasbourg: Council of Europe.

Blasi, Paolo and Hilligje van't Land (eds) (2005): Intercultural Learning And Dialogue, *Higher Education Policy*, Vol. 18, No. 4, December 2005 (www.palgrave-journals.com/hep/journal/v18/n4/index.html, accessed on 7 July 2010).

CDESR (Steering Committee for Higher Education and Research of the Council of Europe) (2006): "Statement on the contribution of higher education to intercultural dialogue". Strasbourg: Council of Europe.

Council of Europe (2001): Recommendation Rec(2001)15 of the Committee of Ministers to member states on history teaching in twenty-first-century Europe.

Council of Europe (2008): *Living Together as Equals in Dignity*, White Paper on Intercultural Dialogue, Strasbourg: Council of Europe.

UNESCO (1945): Constitution of the United Nations Educational, Scientific and Cultural Organization.

van't Land, Hilligje (2005): "The IAU Institutional Survey on 'Promoting inter cultural learning and dialogue across the institution: some major challenges for the university'", in Blasi and van't Land (eds), Intercultural Learning And Dialogue, *Higher Education Policy*, Vol. 18, No. 4, December 2005, pp. 437-443.

I. The political context: intercultural dialogue for a humane society

The role of higher education in fostering a culture of peace and understanding

Federico Mayor Zaragoza

Beirut is the city where one of the founding general conferences of UNESCO was held, where many lessons were learned and have since been learned again. All the city claims is dialogue instead of confrontation – words instead of violence. Beirut is the symbol of the future of which we dream, an example for the transition from force to word.

As the first paragraph of the Earth Charter says:

> We stand at a critical moment in Earth's history, a time when humanity must choose its future. As the world becomes increasingly interdependent and fragile, the future at once holds great peril and great promise. To move forward we must recognize that in the midst of a magnificent diversity of cultures and life forms we are one human family and one Earth community with a common destiny. We must join together to bring forth a sustainable global society founded on respect for nature, universal human rights, economic justice, and a culture of peace. Towards this end, it is imperative that we, the peoples of Earth, declare our responsibility to one another, to the greater community of life, and to future generations. (Earth Charter 2000)

At the end of the Charter, in "The Way Forward" section, it states:

> As never before in history, common destiny beckons us to seek a new beginning. This requires a change of mind and heart. It requires a new sense of global interdependence and universal responsibility … Our cultural diversity is a precious heritage and different cultures will find their own distinctive ways to realize the vision … In order to build a sustainable global community, the nations of the world must renew their commitment to the United Nations. Let ours be a time remembered for the awakening of a new reverence for life, the firm resolve to achieve sustainability, the quickening of the struggle for justice and peace, and the joyful celebration of life. (ibid.)

"A new beginning" – that is the key notion we have to retain and consider, and the only way to make this true is through education, culture, science and communication. Education is to build peace, foster dialogue and enhance understanding in order "to build peace in the minds of men" as enshrined in UNESCO's Constitution (UNESCO 1945).

Education is much more than information, formation and training. Education is also about being oneself, behaving according to one's own reflections, choosing according to one's own decisions. To be educated is to learn and to be able to feel free of any kind of dependence, submission or fear. It is to be able to create, to think, to imagine, to dream – all distinctive and decisive capacities of the human condition. According to the Delors Commission, which I appointed in 1992 in my capacity as Director-General of UNESCO, there are four pillars in the education process (Delors et al. 1996):

– learn to know;
– learn to do;
– learn to be;
– learn to live together;

and I would add that the education process is also about learning to dare and learning to share.

For many years, UNESCO's Education Programme was geared to supporting "literacy and basic education". At the request of President Nyerere, Mwalimu ('teacher') of Tanzania, we were able – in a joint venture with UNICEF, UNDP and the World Bank – at the World Congress held in Jomtien, Thailand in 1990 to change it to "Education for all throughout life" (UNESCO 1990a, 1990b).

Higher education is not just a higher level of the education process. Higher education institutions have the capacity and the responsibility to provide advice to, and make a positive impact on, society, governments, parliaments, municipalities and other establishments of the state. Even more, as was emphasised in the First World Conference on Higher Education that took place in 1998 at UNESCO headquarters (UNESCO 1998), higher education institutions have the capacity to be watch towers: to anticipate, to prevent.

It is only with this kind of higher education that we can envisage promoting a culture of dialogue and understanding. And universities can overcome the immense power of the media, which by contrast prevents or reduces substantially the dissemination and impact which our declarations, recommendations and resolutions should have. For instance, in July 2009, when UNESCO celebrated ten years of the World Conference on Higher Education, there was not a single reference to it in the newspapers or the media at large. We are not news, because we often disagree and because we are too silent too often.

Yet higher education is necessary in facing the danger of progressive uniformisation. To be all different, all unique in each moment of our life, is our richness. On the other hand, to be united by universal values is our force. We should be permanently aware of our infinite culture of diversity, alongside the same ethical references of a humanity committed to its common destiny.

Dialogue means to fully express our views (as Article 1 of the UNESCO Constitution says) and to listen to those of others. Dialogue is to respect and to show respect for views completely opposite to our own ideas, to interact with all partners, with only one exception: that of fanaticism, dogmatism, imposition, violence.

All different, holding hands, joining our voices, as a demonstration of brotherhood, otherness and fraternity, so lucidly set out in Article I of the Universal Declaration of Human Rights (United Nations 1948). All together, all educated, all committed to future generations. Higher education must tirelessly favour intercultural and inter-religious dialogue: encounter, conversation, conciliation, alliance.

Let us recover the basic principles of the United Nations: "We, the peoples … have resolved to save the succeeding generations from the scourge of war" (United Nations 1945). Which means that 'we', the civil society, have governance capacity, through a genuine democratic system, to "avoid war", which means: to build peace. The question is how to build peace? The answer again is found in UNESCO's Constitution, approved in London only four months after the Charter of the UN was adopted in San Francisco: "As war begins in the minds of men it is in the minds of men that the defenses of peace must be built" (UNESCO 1945). Peace is built through education, culture, science and communication, in order to provide all humans with free wings to fly in the unlimited space of the spirit.

In UNESCO's Constitution, the key concept of equal human dignity is one of the basic pillars of the "democratic principles" of justice, equality and solidarity – "intellectual and moral solidarity" – that are established in UNESCO's constitution, in order to be able to ensure that educated human beings are "free and responsible" (UNESCO 1945: Article I).

The Universal Declaration of Human Rights, adopted by the General Assembly of the United Nations on 10 December 1948, provides directions on how to behave in order to respect human dignity and equality. It is indispensable therefore to better share not only material goods, but knowledge and experience and most of all – wisdom. In order to better share, the concept of development was progressively introduced into United Nations discussions and debates: in the 1960s, it was decided that development should be social as well as economic, and it should be integral; in the 1970s it appeared it should be endogenous as well, and in October 1974 an agreement was reached that the most prosperous countries should provide 0.7% of their GNP for the development of countries in need; in the 1980s, the commission chaired by Gro Harlem Brundtland introduced the concept of sustainability; and, at last, in 1998, publication of the book *Development with a Human Face* (Mehrotra and Jolly 1998), emphasised the main feature of development: it must be human, because human beings are not only the beneficiaries of but the main actors in development for equal quality of life.

Regretfully, today's societies favour states instead of "peoples", loans instead of aid, exploitation instead of co-operation, plutocracy instead of democracy, and market laws instead of values.

Even if marginalised and weakened, the United Nations system has been a permanent guide aiming to promote understanding and conciliation, and facilitate the transition from a culture of imposition, domination, violence and war to a culture of dialogue, alliance, peace. In sum a transition from force to word.

Yes, from force to word …

The recommendations, declarations, resolutions and initiatives put forward by the United Nations system have been manifold. I consider it essential to summarise and list the UN's contributions since 1990 because, in what could be called the age of globalisation, in which plutocrats have tried to take over from "We, the peoples", the UN has given us key milestones:

- 1990: Education for All
- 1993: Agenda 21 for the Environment
    - World Plan of Action for Education on Human Rights and Democracy
    - Vienna Conference on Human Rights
- 1994: The Contribution by Religions to the Culture of Peace
- 1995: Declaration of Principles on Tolerance
    - Copenhagen Declaration on Social Development
    - Fourth World Conference on Women, Beijing Declaration
- 1998: International Decade for a Culture of Peace and Non-violence for the Children of the World
- 1999: Declaration and Programme of Action on a Culture of Peace
- 2000: UN Millenium Declaration
    - The Earth Charter (Amsterdam)
- 2001: Universal Declaration on Cultural Diversity (UNESCO)
- 2003: Declaration on Dialogue among Civilizations (AG-NU)

At the 2005 United Nations Summit, the heads of state and government unanimously decided to implement the Declaration and Programme of Action on a Culture of Peace and welcomed the creation of the Alliance of Civilizations. More recently, the United Nations and the major UN institutions have also contributed to the debate with key recommendations, such as:

- A/Res/63/113 on a Culture of Peace of 26 February 2005
- The Hague Agenda on City Diplomacy (2008)
- Charter for a World without Violence (2009)
- European Council of Religious Leaders encounters
- European Council of Religious Leaders/Lille Declaration on a Culture of Peace (2009)
- Adopting a consensus resolution, the General Assembly affirms mutual under-standing and inter-religious dialogue as important dimensions of culture of peace[3]

Now that we have all these excellent resolutions and declarations, now is the time to act. We have all the diagnoses and we have to follow up on them – without waiting any longer.

---

3. Consensus resolution adopted by the 63rd UN General Assembly – GA/10784, 13 November 2008.

Globalisation has led to an unprecedented, very worrisome and complex crisis situation (financial, environmental, democratic, ethical, food and more). Without regulatory measures, the multiplication of fiscal paradises, the 'globalisers' and plutocrats have led the world into a situation of social disruption and extreme poverty. On top of this, these people have lied and invaded countries in order to further increase the gigantic and aggressive development of industries which consequently, today and every day, absorb armament expenditure of 3 billion dollars or more when at the same time 60 000 human beings die of hunger each day, most of whom are children. This is an unbearable collective shame.

Any crisis can be seen as a true opportunity to instigate change. Indeed all crises can and should lead us all to rethink the world in which we live and to change it – sometimes also leading to radical transformation – as a response and in-depth reaction to the incoherent behaviour of world governance. There was, for instance, no money in the year 2000 for the Millennium Development Goals (United Nations 2000) for food, for AIDS treatment and more, yet suddenly hundreds of billions of dollars have appeared to "rescue" the same institutions that – because of their greed and irresponsibility, in the words of President Obama (Obama 2009) – led to the present situation. But we cannot remain silent, obedient and indifferent any more. We have to be participatory actors and no longer spectators; we have to behave as aware, committed and involved citizens and not as receptors; we have to stop being dormant and be very alive.

We have been submissive to the point of offering our lives to the designs of the powers in place. Now, for the first time in history, we have the possibility of distance participation, through information technologies such as the Internet and SMS texting. Universities, the scientific community, intellectuals, artists and writers must all lead this new era of freedom, of emancipation, of genuine democracy. They must be at the forefront of citizenship mobilisation to ensure the transition from force to dialogue and understanding.

This is a new beginning. A new era can start.

References

Delors, Jacques et al. (1996): *Learning: The Treasure Within*, UNESCO report on Education for the 21st Century, Paris: UNESCO Publishing.

Earth Charter (2000): available at www.earthcharterinaction.org/content/pages/The-Earth-Charter.html (accessed on 1 July 2010).

Mehrotra, Sandtosh and Richard Jolly (eds) (1998): *Development with a Human Face*, Oxford: Clarendon Press.

Obama, Barack (2009): Inaugural Address, 21 January 2009, available at www.whitehouse.gov/blog/inaugural-address/ (accessed on 1 July 2010).

UNESCO (1945): Constitution of the United Nations Educational, Scientific and Cultural Organization.

UNESCO (1990a): Education for All: The Requirements. World Conference on Education for All (Thailand, 5-9 March 1990). Monograph III. Roundtable Themes III, Paris: UNESCO Publishing.

UNESCO (1990b) World Declaration on Education for All – Meeting Basic Learning Needs, the Jomtien Declaration, available at www.unesco.org/education/efa/ed_for_all/background/jomtien_declaration.shtml (accessed on 2 July 2010).

UNESCO (1998): World Declaration on Higher Education for the Twenty-First Century: Vision and Action, available at www.unesco.org/education/educprog/wche/declaration_eng.htm (accessed on 1 July 2010).

United Nations (1945): Charter of the United Nations, available at www.un.org/en/documents/charter/index.shtml (accessed on 1 July 2010).

United Nations (1948): The Universal Declaration of Human Rights, available at www.un.org/en/documents/udhr/index.shtml (accessed on 1 July 2010).

United Nations (2000): UN Millennium Development Goals, available at www.un.org/millenniumgoals/bkgd.shtml (accessed on 1 July 2010).

Intercultural dialogue and higher education: a Council of Europe view

Gabriella Battaini-Dragoni

Introduction

The Council of Europe's strong commitment to intercultural dialogue is shown above all by the White Paper on Intercultural Dialogue adopted by the Committee of Ministers in May 2008, but it is also shown through a high number of activities, all of them relevant to intercultural dialogue. There is hardly any area of our activities more important to intercultural dialogue than education because it is above all through education that we develop a culture of dialogue.

Culture is, in this sense, a mindset and a behavioural pattern, and these cannot be imposed by legislation nor by political declarations. They must be developed through regular practice along with awareness and attitudes which, like skills and knowledge, come through education. If possible, they should be developed from an early age but they must be practised and maintained throughout life. This means that developing people's ability to engage in intercultural dialogue is not only a matter for primary and secondary schools. Higher education has an obvious role to play, in the same way that higher education has strong relevance to the overarching political goals of the Council of Europe: democracy, human rights and the rule of law. In our diverse European societies, these values cannot be a reality unless we, as societies and individuals, are proficient in intercultural dialogue. Higher education is of key importance in this endeavour.

This is illustrated by the two universities that hosted the two conferences from which many of the articles in this book arose: the Russian University of Peoples' Friendship in Moscow and Notre Dame University in Lebanon. In both universities, dialogue is a fact of everyday life. That sounds simple, and part of their achievement is to make dialogue appear simple, but this achievement relies on a very conscious institutional policy.

The importance of dialogue at these two universities is not limited to intercultural dialogue on campus. Both institutions are very much aware of their roles as actors in society, based on the values of their international and intercultural profiles. They prepare their graduates to be active citizens – in the case of the Russian University of Peoples' Friendship, where students come from well over 100 countries, active in their home countries – to carry with them the experience of dialogue on campus and apply the same principles as citizens of broader society.

It is also significant that this book is published jointly by the Council of Europe and the International Association of Universities. We have different profiles, as an intergovernmental organisation and a non-governmental organisation whose membership is made up of universities, respectively – but we are both committed to intercultural dialogue and to furthering the role of higher education in this respect.

Living together as equals in dignity

Any Council of Europe view of intercultural dialogue will take as its starting point the White Paper adopted by the Committee of Ministers in May 2008. It is now well known and I will not present it in any great detail here. I will, however, underline certain aspects of the White Paper that I consider important for higher education.

The first of these is the title: Living Together as Equals in Dignity. The title is short but it contains two key elements without which intercultural dialogue is impossible.

Firstly, living together. This is far more than co-existence or living side by side. It is also more than mere internationalisation or simply speaking to each other from opposite sides of a mental or physical border. Living together presupposes close contacts and interaction between individuals of different cultures and it is an important challenge to our European societies.

I wonder if it is not also quite a challenge to universities, even if universities are often thought of as international institutions per se. The issue is not just whether we have foreign students and staff on campus. The issue is really whether foreign students and staff are integrated into university life. Are they part of the academic community or are they left to themselves and their own community? If they are, what does this mean for the role of the university in promoting dialogue in broader society, and what does it mean for the way these foreign students and staff will themselves act as citizens?

Secondly, equals in dignity. It is important to underline that we do not speak only of equality of rights – even if the Council of Europe is a human rights organisation – but also equality of dignity. That is, basically, saying that we are all of equal value as human beings. This has profound implications for our societies, and there is no shortage of historical examples of what happens when societies deny the funda-mental value of human beings. It is also worth remembering that some political parties, in many European countries, have based their electoral programme on the assumption that humans are not quite equal if they are "too different". Recognising the humanity of "the other" in practice is far more difficult than doing so intellec-tually. The fact that these parties receive votes is in itself an important argument for intercultural dialogue. Our equal dignity can be denied, but it cannot be abolished, and higher education should play an important role in creating awareness of it. Higher education, an eminently intercultural domain and one committed to intel-lectual curiosity, cannot remain at a distance from this endeavour.

Five policy areas

The White Paper focuses on five broad policy areas:

1. democratic governance of cultural diversity;
2. democratic citizenship and participation;
3. learning and teaching intercultural competences;
4. spaces for intercultural dialogue;
5. intercultural dialogue in international relations.

This is not the place to explain these concepts in detail, but I would like to make the general point that the cornerstones of a political culture valuing diversity are the common values of democracy, human rights and fundamental freedoms, the rule of law, pluralism, tolerance, non-discrimination and mutual respect. Democratic governance does not simply mean that the views of a majority must always prevail: a balance must be achieved that ensures fair and proper treatment of persons belonging to minorities and avoids any abuse of a dominant position. On the other hand, citizenship is, in the widest sense, a right (and indeed a responsibility) to participate in the cultural, social and economic life and the public affairs of the community together with others. This is key to intercultural dialogue, because it invites us to think of others not in a stereotypical way – as "the Other" – but as fellow citizens and equals.

Let us, then, look at the policy areas outlined in the White Paper from the vantage point of higher education.

At first glance, what is immediately of concern to higher education would seem to be learning and teaching intercultural competences. If one way of looking at education is as a process leading to a set of competences, it is indeed difficult to see how or why these competences would not include those needed for intercultural dialogue.

We often hear that today's world is flat – not in the sense this statement would have had 500 years ago, but in the sense that modern technology and modern means of communication have made all parts of Earth so intimately connected that they all depend on each other. This is not the place to discuss whether Earth is really flat or whether the particularities of our cultural heritage represent mountains and valleys. The point is that relating to the world beyond one's immediate horizon is not an option – it is a given and a must. Trying to hide from the broader world makes about as much sense as sticking one's head in the sand. Whether we aim to work internationally or whether we rather aim to work in our home country or even our home region or community, we need to understand those who have different cultural backgrounds and who either live and work in our countries or communities or who visit for purposes of work or leisure.

To put it bluntly: whatever our line of work or our place of residence, it is highly unlikely that we will spend our entire lives avoiding foreigners. All parts of the education system, including higher education, must help learners to gain the competences they need, not only to deal with this complex reality of diverse cultural background, but to thrive in and benefit from this environment. We will be much richer for the effort.

Competences for intercultural dialogue

What, then, are these competences? Competences or qualifications are often referred to as what a person knows, understands and is able to do. I would add that our view of competences should also include attitudes. Do we see opportunities – challenges that can be met – or only insurmountable problems? Do we see cultural diversity as a challenge that can enrich us or a problem from which we must either hide or run?

Beyond the competences that higher education will give learners in their field of study – whether engineering, history or law – higher education must give all graduates a set of generic competences, such as analytical ability, communication skills and the ability to make decisions, often on the basis of incomplete information.

Without aiming to give a complete list of intercultural competences, I would at least venture to say that higher education should provide all its graduates with a world view that does not stop at national borders or even at the borders of Europe; nor should it be limited to the northern hemisphere.

Higher education should provide its graduates with competence in a foreign language – or, even better, in more than one foreign language. This is not only because we need foreign language skills in order to communicate with people from other cultures – and that is important enough in itself – but also because learning a foreign language means understanding and accepting that a concept can be expressed in different ways.

Universities are important in increasing our understanding and knowledge of less widely spoken languages and the cultures they carry, of the history and societies that are less well known to us and of how majorities and minorities relate to each other. Are there situations that tend to make majorities more aggressive and less understanding towards minorities? If yes, how can these situations be counteracted? We know that economic distress tends to make people less understanding of those who have a different background, and that makes the need for intercultural dialogue and awareness even more important in times of economic crisis, like the one we are going through at the time of writing.

Higher education must also build on secondary education to improve its graduates' understanding of history, not only to improve their understanding of where their own countries and cultures come from but also to understand how other countries and cultures have evolved through history. An understanding of history may also help graduates get a better perspective on time. Above all, it may help learners understand the need to understand the views of others. The Council of Europe has been a pioneer in developing methods for history teaching, in particular through the concept of multiperspectivity. This concept has much in common with intercultural dialogue. It emphasises the need to look at historical events from different points of view and to understand how and why others may have very different views on one's own history. Multiperspectivity does not mean that all views are equally acceptable. It does not free historians from the need to look at the evidence, and it does not offer shelter to those who deny basic human dignity or who deny crimes against humanity. Like intercultural dialogue itself, multiperspectivity is open-minded but not mind-less.

The Council of Europe is also a leading organisation in citizenship education. Although democratic citizenship and intercultural dialogue are not the same thing, many of the competences we need for one we also need for the other. The ability to think both critically and constructively is essential for a culture of citizenship: critically, because not all solutions put forward by public authorities are of benefit to citizens; constructively, because for citizens to take ownership of their societies, they must not only be able to block unacceptable proposals but even more importantly participate in developing viable alternatives. Criticising is often the easy part, whereas coming up with viable alternatives may be far more difficult.

It is difficult to imagine how a society can be fully democratic if it cannot conduct intercultural dialogue, and it is equally difficult to imagine how intercultural dialogue can be conducted in societies that stray far from the ideals and practices of democracy. The competences needed for intercultural dialogue are therefore also largely those needed to develop and maintain a culture of democracy, and this culture cannot exist without education.

A particularly difficult point for many Europeans to understand is the role of religion. In many societies as well as in many cultural groups, religion plays a fundamental role, as a belief system and as a cultural reference, and this is often difficult to fathom for those whose background is in more secularised societies. It may be worth remembering that European societies are in many ways atypical in the relatively low visibility of religion, even if here also there are differences between individuals and cultures. The point is not whether one is a believer or not but whether one can understand the role that religion plays in many people's lives, value systems, cultural background and personal attitudes. Higher education should play an important role in developing this kind of understanding. This is why education is the main topic of the Council of Europe encounters on inter-religious dialogue, two of which have already been held in Strasbourg, with the third being held in Ohrid in 2010.

Higher education for intercultural dialogue

So much for the obvious role of higher education in developing the competences needed to make intercultural dialogue possible. As we often hear, competences are what we need to get a job. This is right, and the importance of getting a job should not be underestimated. We hardly need to be reminded of that in a world that is in the middle of an economic crisis – and we can only hope that we are at least in the middle of the crisis and not just at the beginning of it.

What we need to be reminded of is that we need competences not only to get a job, but also for our other roles as citizens and human beings. I cannot resist the temptation here to refer to the Council of Europe's important work on defining public responsibility for higher education and research. This led to a political recommendation by our Committee of Ministers,[4] which also spelled out the main purposes of higher education. As you would expect, preparing for employment is one of those purposes, but it is one of four:

1. preparation for sustainable employment;

2. preparation for life as active citizens in democratic societies;

3. personal development;

4. the development and maintenance of a broad and advanced knowledge base.

The purpose of referring to this list is that it reminds us that higher education has an important role to play in the other areas identified by the Council of Europe White Paper. How can we think of democratic governance among cultural diversity, or of democratic citizenship and participation, without thinking of competences? How can we think of spaces for intercultural dialogue without thinking of universities, as communities in themselves – dialogue on campus – and also as essential actors in broader society?

Democratic governance, citizenship and participation are partly questions of technical competence and partly of attitudes. Modern, complex societies cannot be governed, and politicians and voters cannot make sound decisions, unless decision makers as well as voters have a good understanding of a whole range of issues.

In modern societies, governance, citizenship and participation cannot disregard the need to include those with a different cultural background from the majority population. As we have seen, this is not uncontroversial in European political life, where citizenship is often taken to mean the name and the colour of the passport one carries and where democracy is thought of only in terms of voting. Of course voting is important, but democratic citizenship and participation refer to the participation and influence of members of a community on the lives and policies of their societies. Not least, it refers to the commitment of citizens to their own societies. No society can survive if its members are apathetic or if citizens treat their society only as a providers of services. That, incidentally, is one reason why it is so important to think of students as members of the academic community and not merely as clients.

---

4. Rec(2007)6 to Council of Europe member states on public responsibility for higher education and research.

Conclusion

I was particularly pleased by the participation in the Moscow conference of university rectors from Kazakhstan and Lebanon, and by the fact that the conference organised by the International Association of Universities was held in the latter country. These two countries represent parts of the world – Central Asia and the broader Mediterranean region with a strong Arab contribution – that are very important to Europe. We need to understand these regions, we need to appreciate their cultural background and we need to develop better co-operation with them. Higher education should be at the forefront of this co-operation. Not only is higher education essential to developing a deeper understanding of the need for mechanisms of intercultural dialogue. Higher education policies themselves offer an excellent topic for co-operation, one that will itself require an awareness of cultural differences.

As you know, the Council of Europe is strongly engaged in the Bologna Process. I firmly believe that the Bologna Process is an excellent basis for co-operation between Europe and other parts of the world, but I am also convinced that this co-operation can only be fruitful if it is approached from the point of view of intercultural dialogue. "Bologna policies" copied blindly are likely to fail, but "Bologna policies" adapted with due regard to the background of each region and country should have every possibility of success, and the Council of Europe is both a willing and – if I may be allowed to say so – competent partner in this endeavour.

I would also like to point to the Council of Europe's North-South Centre, in Lisbon, which has a particular mandate to work with non-European countries, not least those of the Mediterranean and the broader Arab world. Its brief, however, spans wider, and there is no reason why countries like Kazakhstan and Lebanon should not join the centre.

Part of the reason why the Council of Europe is a valuable partner in higher education policy is that we see higher education as an important part of society. As we have often said, in Bologna debates and elsewhere: structural reform is important, but only if it serves a purpose. Structures must be "structures with a mission". That purpose must be to develop societies that are fluent in intercultural dialogue, societies of a kind where we can live together as equals in dignity.

Some 10 years ago, the Council of Europe ran a pilot project on the university as a site of citizenship. Among other things, the project found that many academic staff – and probably also students – did not consider developing a culture of democracy as a task for higher education. Why do democracy when you can do chemistry? However, the two are intimately linked. Chemists are also citizens, and the citizenship mission of education does not stop at primary or secondary school. I suspect we may find many of the same attitudes to the role of higher education in promoting intercultural dialogue, and this is borne out by looking at the kind of issues on which the majority of university leaders engage. However, universities cannot engage in developing our future society unless they engage in developing intercultural dialogue. Universities cannot be universities unless their mission is to offer an education that is greater than the sum of their individual academic disciplines.

Let me end by quoting a key paragraph in the White Paper, because this paragraph illustrates my point very clearly. When it speaks about higher education, the White Paper says:

> Higher-education institutions play an important role in fostering intercultural dialogue, through their education programmes, as actors in broader society and as sites where intercultural dialogue is put into practice. As the Steering Committee on Higher Education and Research suggests, the university is ideally defined precisely by its universality – its commitment to open-mindedness and openness to the world, founded on enlightenment values. The university thus has great potential to engender "intercultural intellectuals" who can play an active role in the public sphere.

(Council of Europe: *Living Together as Equals in Dignity*, White Paper on Intercultural Dialogue, 2008: 31)

The role of higher education in fostering intercultural dialogue and understanding

Eva Egron-Polak

When the International Association of Universities and Notre Dame University Louaize embarked on the adventure of co-organising an international conference on the topic of fostering the culture of dialogue and understanding, there were certainly some obstacles and concerns to overcome, notably perceptions of insecurity and fear about coming to Lebanon among some and the recognised difficulty of treating such a complex topic. Yet, there was also much enthusiasm among the IAU board members to address precisely this topic and to meet at Notre Dame University in Lebanon to do so.

The IAU conference brought together nearly 200 participants from 37 countries. The two days of debate and discussion were very enriching and enjoyable. We regret deeply, though, that visa problems prevented some people from attending and participating in the dialogue. The wealth of ideas, comments, experiences and suggestions that were expressed cannot be summarised easily without the risk of reductionism. The conference topic invited us to listen and to hear each other. This is a precondition of, and an integral part of, dialogue and we did so intensely. But of course, each of us listens with our own ears, our own linguistic, religious, cultural, educational backgrounds and limitations, whether from Asia, Africa, Europe, Latin America or the Middle East, whether more or less versed and at ease in Arabic or French or English (the three languages of the conference).

Why would IAU hold a conference on this topic, why in Lebanon, why now?

Part of the enthusiasm of the IAU Board stems from the fact that by focusing on these issues, the IAU remains true to its initial *raison d'être*. It was founded so that universities could help humanity heal from the horror of the Second World War and, more importantly, to help prevent such wars and conflicts in the future by fostering co-operation and understanding among higher education institutions and thus among the peoples of the world. For this reason, intercultural dialogue among universities is always on our agenda.

The broader reason for convening a conference on this topic lay in our shared belief that without continued pursuit of dialogue as an approach to overcoming conflict at every level – global, international, regional and local, as well as among groups of individuals – the crisis that has been repeatedly mentioned during this conference becomes inevitable. In addition to a crisis of the current and dominant economic model, we face a crisis of values, an environmental crisis and a social crisis. Universities retain at least some, if not most, of the keys to avoiding following this negative path. Federico Mayor, President of the Culture of Peace Foundation, former Director-General of UNESCO, Co-Chair of the High Level Group United Nations Alliance of Civilizations and keynote speaker at the conference, reminded us of the urgent need to act since, despite the variety of very strong and consensual declarations and commitments voiced in many quarters, we are still calling for action, still questioning how to instil a culture of dialogue in universities and in society through the work of universities. We are still searching for ways to build bridges and breach gaps that are wider than ever.

In fact the urgency is growing and the complexity of the issues that threaten not just humanity but the planet itself is huge. Universities cannot solve all the problems of the world, yet universities have huge responsibilities and an obligation to speak the truth about the problems, searching and continually testing all possible solutions. As Juan Ramón de la Fuente, President of the IAU, and others stated, universities have a responsibility most of all to educate individuals who are locally rooted, well-informed global citizens able to make sound choices but also, I would add, who are able to recognise what they do not know and learn how to learn continually about the other – without prejudice, without preconceptions.

Finally, why meet in Lebanon, at Notre Dame University Louaize? We heard much about Lebanon as a laboratory, a model for creating conditions for living together in harmony, with a commitment to this at the highest level of the state. In a nation of four million people with 18 different religious groups living in very close proximity, this is both a challenge and a necessity. Notre Dame's commitment to serve as a microcosm for success in this effort shone throughout the presentations and justified our choice of meeting there.

What do we mean by a culture of dialogue and a dialogue among cultures?

The conference offered a rich discussion, highlighting many dimensions of the topic. We spoke about dialogue as a culture, as a way to behave, as a process – but also about dialogue between different cultures, or intercultural dialogue. In both cases, whether we see it as a process or as the substance, dialogue is a means to an end, not an end in itself. Instilling a culture of intercultural dialogue is the only means – peaceful, productive and lasting – to cross some of the boundaries and distances that separate us.

Key among these boundaries and distances are those based on religion or spirituality, ethnicity, tribal origins, language and race. In fact, depending on where we find ourselves, to examine intercultural dialogue colours the focus of the discussion. It may stress religious dialogue, as was the case in Lebanon, or race as is often the case in the United States, or the focus could be on the tensions between indigenous peoples or First Nations and more recent arrivals in countries like Australia and Canada or in parts of Latin America.

But there are other boundaries as well – those of academic disciplines that can stand in the way of dialogue, of collaboration, and which block the path to creative solutions and innovations which are needed to overcome old and persistent problems. Finally and importantly, there are boundaries and walls created by differences in power, whether that power is based on might and force or wealth, and these asymmetries must be also be recognised for what they are. They must be addressed with urgency and courage.

How?

The informative and thoughtful presentations at the IAU conference offered both broad-based directions and the more practical approaches that may need to be considered. Some called for universities to reassess in very fundamental ways their mission, their pedagogical approach, their research and curriculum in the pursuit and transmission of truth and knowledge, respectively. At the same time we also heard more pragmatic suggestions about how higher education institutions can prepare graduates who will build the Wisdom Society, as suggested a few years ago by a former IAU board member, Paulo Blasi.

We noted some of the basic building blocks that can serve as cornerstones or foundations for fostering dialogue:

- respecting the other's point of view even if we disagree and may think (s)he is wrong;
- recognising fully the contributions of all civilisations, all cultures, all religions and faiths;
- openness and sensitivity to the other, not fear of what we do not know but on the contrary curiosity about the unknown, not seeing the other as a threat but rather seeing difference as enriching;
- creating conditions of equality and dignity in dialogue and ensuring that we empower especially those who are most marginalised to take part in the dialogue.

The conference offered many other elements, too many to list here.

What next?

First and foremost, the answers to this question rest with all the conference participants and other IAU members. Indeed, if we wish to foster higher education that embraces dialogue as an integral part of its mission, we need action at the institutional, classroom level with stakeholders inside and outside the university.

But intercultural dialogue will remain a focus of study and attention in our work as part of the IAU's work on internationalisation, a major focus for the association. The IAU web pages on this topic, including most international declarations related to intercultural dialogue, continue to be updated regularly and the IAU remains open to receiving information about other resources that you may know about.

This publication, issued jointly with the Council of Europe and in co-operation with Notre Dame University as well as the Peoples' Friendship University of Russia, is also a direct outcome of the IAU conference as well as of the Council of Europe conference in Moscow in June 2009. It is also a logical follow-up to the Council's White Paper on Intercultural Dialogue, *Living Together as Equals in Dignity*.

Finally, the IAU 2010 international conference at Mykolas Romeris University in Vilnius, Lithuania, from 24 to 26 June 2010 should carry our reflections further. The theme of the conference, Ethics and Values in Higher Education in the Era of Globalisation, invites us to consider the ways in which we pursue not only the important economic role that universities fulfil today, but also the broader cultural and social mission of the university. Can we identify universal values and ethical codes that we all share in higher education? And what are some of the new threats that we face today in this regard? We must hope that we will one day look back on Vilnius as having been as rich, enjoyable and successful as the 2009 conference in Lebanon, where we learned so much.

II. Setting the scene: from dialogue on campus to dialogue in society

Intercultural dialogue on the university campus

Bernd Wächter

Introduction and context

The seminar Intercultural Dialogue on the University Campus was organised by the Department of Higher Education and History Teaching of the Council of Europe. It took place on the premises of the Council of Europe in Strasbourg, in the Palais de l'Europe, on 4 and 5 March 2008. The seminar was attended by about 50 delegates, as well as the speakers and Council of Europe staff. Delegates came from government departments (ministries of education) of signatory countries of the European Cultural Convention and higher education institutions, as well as European and international inter- and non-governmental organisations.

The March 2008 seminar took place in the context of an increased commitment to intercultural dialogue by the Council of Europe. Having already engaged in earlier projects on this theme, which falls within the Organisation's wider commitment to the promotion of democracy, human rights and the rule of law, the Council of Europe adopted and published a White Paper on intercultural dialogue entitled *Living Together as Equals in Dignity* (Council of Europe 2008). Other European organisations have likewise made intercultural dialogue a key policy objective, such as the European Union, which made 2008 the European Year of Intercultural Dialogue. Recent tensions in Europe and around the world bear witness to the urgent need for a dialogue of cultures and people.

There are at least two related roles that higher education institutions can and should play in promoting intercultural understanding. The first is direct and concerns the furthering of this dialogue on their own premises, within the institution. The second is indirect and concerns higher education's role in promoting intercultural dialogue in society generally, beyond the bounds of the institution. In line with its title, the seminar focused on the first of these issues – intercultural dialogue on campus, which is the focus of this article – but it also touched on aspects of outreach to society, which is the focus of the present book.

The approach to the theme was comprehensive, and speakers focused on both fundamental and overarching aspects, such as the link between intercultural dialogue and democracy, as well as specific examples of intercultural dialogue in practice, in universities in Europe.

This paper tries to capture the essence of the seminar, in its presentations and discussion, rather than attempting to recapitulate or otherwise deal in detail with individual contributions, which are readily available (Bergan and Restoueix 2009). It is divided into two sections: first, my conclusions as rapporteur – with observations on major issues at stake in the seminar – and then the recommendations of the seminar.

Conclusions as rapporteur

First conclusion: intercultural dialogue is very relevant

The first conclusion to be drawn is perhaps an obvious one, but it needs to be stressed nonetheless: intercultural dialogue is an issue of high relevance for Europe's higher education institutions. Indeed, there was palpable agreement at this seminar that it must become part of the mission of Europe's higher education institutions. And it must become a characteristic of their everyday life. There are various reasons for this.

– First of all, delegates put on record – with their active engagement and their meaningful and serious discussions over the two days of the seminar – that they attach importance to the issue. Delegates had different approaches to the theme, and thus emphasised different aspects of it, but this should not detract from the underlying consensus.

– Second, interculturally-motivated tensions are rising, in Europe as in the rest of the world. This is in no one's interest. The aim must be to ease tensions, to de-escalate conflicts. And, since intercultural problems often lie at the root of these conflicts, intercultural dialogue is needed to address the issue.

– Third, the Council of Europe, an organisation the delegates trust, has for some time now put an emphasis on this issue (for the reasons just given). As noted, it adopted the White Paper on Intercultural Dialogue in 2008 and its Steering Committee for Higher Education and Research adopted in 2006 a Statement on the Contribution of Higher Education to Intercultural Dialogue (CDESR 2006). The European Union has also underscored the importance of this issue, by making 2008 the European Year of Intercultural Dialogue.

– Fourth, and very substantially, there was a clear consensus among delegates that higher education has a broader mission than just imparting knowledge, skill and competence within a specific discipline and contributing to economic growth. As important as these objectives are, the European model of higher education has always pursued wider aims, fostering (for example) democracy, respect for human rights, the rule of law and international understanding. Intercultural dialogue is part of this European model.

Second conclusion: much needs to be done

The second conclusion follows straight from the first. It is that, despite the uncontested need for active intercultural dialogue on the campuses of Europe's universities and colleges, much work needs to be done still to make it a reality. Intercultural dialogue is far from common on our campuses; so far there has not been sufficient action. The fact that the seminar drew only a modest audience demonstrates that many people have not yet fully understood the significance of intercultural dialogue in European higher education. The presentations and discussions showed that as yet not many higher education institutions are strongly engaged in it. The examples of good practice presented at this seminar gained all the admiration they deserve; but they are the exception, not the rule.

Third conclusion: people need to be convinced

Therefore, and this is the third conclusion, it is necessary to make a very convincing case for the cause of intercultural dialogue on our campuses. Otherwise it will always remain a legitimate demand, but it will never become a distinguishing trait of our universities.

To make a very convincing case is also necessary because Europe's universities and colleges see the list of their tasks (or, at least, the expectations they are confronted with) extended almost by the month. Recent arrivals on the *cahier de charges* are lifelong learning, entrepreneurship and the creation of literacy in matters of information and communication technologies, to name but a few. There is a serious danger of overburdening the European university. In the competition between all the new arrivals, it is necessary to state very sound reasons for an engagement in intercultural dialogue. But, luckily, there are very good ones.

Fourth conclusion: every kind of intercultural dialogue is legitimate

The fourth conclusion is perhaps rather an observation. There was agreement among delegates that intercultural dialogue is multi-dimensional, and its different dimensions and aspects are of importance to different stakeholders, but they are all legitimate.

The conference approached its theme from many angles. Perhaps, therefore, it was marked less by heated controversy, but rather by a genuine and serious collective attempt to find a common basis of understanding, a joint point of reference. This endeavour has been successful in the realisation and acknowledgement that there is a large diversity of manifestations of intercultural dialogue – all of which are legitimate.

Fifth conclusion: challenges requiring intercultural dialogue

The fifth conclusion is that intercultural dialogue faces different challenges in different higher education institutions in different parts and countries of our continent. This only proves once again the well-known truth that Europe – and European higher education – is highly diverse.

The challenges to be tackled by intercultural dialogue are not the same in "the former Yugoslav Republic of Macedonia", in Spain and the Mediterranean region, in Russia, in Paris or in Frankfurt an der Oder on the German–Polish border.[5] The delegates learned impressively from the keynote speaker, Fatou Sarr, that key issues may look very different when viewed with African eyes.

Looking back at the presentations and discussions, when addressing these issues in diverse student populations, at least four challenges can be identified:

– ethnically, religiously and culturally heterogeneous student populations all from one country (as, for example, in "the former Yugoslav Republic of Macedonia");

---

5. Case studies were presented on all those different situations.

- minority student populations from inside the country (third- or fourth-generation immigrants, who have finally gained access to higher education);

- mobile foreign students, who have entered the country to study (for a short-term stay, for example, in the framework of exchange programmes, or for an entire degree course);

- multi-national – and possibly multi-ethnic and multi-religious – student bodies in which foreigners outnumber domestic students (Russian Peoples' Friendship University, London School of Economics and others).

No reductionist, one-size-fits-all approach can be applied to such diversity – even though, as will be seen later, some common principles can probably be applied.

Sixth conclusion: internationalisation is not clearly distinct

The sixth conclusion is that the relationship between internationalisation and intercultural dialogue requires further exploration.

Certainly there are close links between the two phenomena, as delegates easily agreed. But the exact relationship remained somewhat contested. On the one hand, there were those – presenters and participants – who seemed to equate the two. They thought that international mobility, mastery of languages and joint programmes (to name but some internationalisation activities) would alone "do the intercultural trick". On the other hand, there were those who considered internationalisation as a necessary precondition of the intercultural dialogue, but not as a sufficient one. They maintained that to be international was not yet to be intercultural.

I tend to agree with this latter point of view. Internationalisation creates the opportunity for intercultural encounters. But whether they actually come about is another matter – as often-quoted cases of isolated foreign students show – and even if encounters do come about, they can fail. What is implied by intercultural dialogue is a genuine encounter that "succeeds". For this, it is not enough that two people of different backgrounds find themselves in the same place at the same time.

Seventh conclusion: intercultural dialogue is lifelong

A seventh conclusion is this: higher education institutions are important actors in intercultural dialogue, but they are part of a chain of actors. Higher education's success in this area will be easier to achieve if intercultural matters play a strong role in earlier stages of education – in primary and secondary education, perhaps even pre-school education.

This is all the more so because delegates stressed that the success of intercultural dialogue hinges on general attitudes such as openness and a spirit of relating to others as equals, which are most easily fostered at an early age. Nor does the need for intercultural dialogue end with higher education. It is a process that continues, one that is *jamais acquis* – a lifelong task.

Eighth conclusion: the way to start

An eighth conclusion, or rather a set of conclusions, is the specific measures that need to be put in place to make intercultural dialogue a reality in European higher education.

Obviously, there was a very wide variety of proposals, ranging from the philosophical to the highly practical. It is not easy to do justice to such a diversity of approaches in a few sentences. But there were some points of strong consensus. Among them were:

- Intercultural dialogue should form an integral part of the mission statement of every higher education institution on the European continent.

- The minimum level of practical engagement would be that no student graduates from a higher education institution in Europe without a basic understanding of, and sensitivity to the needs of, intercultural communication; following Edo Poglia and his collaborators (Poglia et al. 2009), delegates referred to this minimum competence as "intercultural literacy".

- A set of generic learning outcomes and competences is needed to help define or describe this intercultural literacy; likewise, a publication with examples of good practice would help and would inspire higher education institutions to implement intercultural dialogue measures.

- The production of didactic material would be helpful for the same purpose (in the full knowledge that such material must not be prescriptive, but should be an offer to help).

Delegates also agreed that, in order to formulate a credible policy on intercultural dialogue, institutions would need to allocate adequate resources. They would also need to build an institutional culture of intercultural sensitivity, which would value the contribution that students of different national, cultural, ethnic and religious backgrounds made to the institution and which would seek to integrate them in campus life – in other words, to create a sense of belonging or the conditions that would allow them to feel "at home".

Discussions only briefly touched on the issues of the staff qualifications needed to implement a credible intercultural dialogue strategy. But there was an implicit agreement that professional development and training should be made available, and also that intercultural competence could play a role in staff recruitment.

Ninth conclusion: no drama, no crisis

A ninth conclusion was in the nature of a warning not to dramatise intercultural matters, in order not to jeopardise successful intercultural dialogue on campus. Delegates stressed that, actually, most intercultural encounters were successful. Failure to stress this expectation of a positive outcome could endanger successful attempts to deal with the really important cases of conflict, the major cases of the unresolved.

Tenth conclusion: intercultural dialogue must have a place in higher education

A tenth conclusion is this: intercultural dialogue needs to find a place as a policy priority in the post-2010 agenda for the European Higher Education Area. Everyone needs to recognise the wider role of higher education – not just the production and dissemination of knowledge and the advancement of economic objectives – or, to put it differently, what was earlier referred to as the European model of higher education.

Recommendations

Based on the above observations and conclusions, the participants in the seminar adopted the following eight recommendations.

Recommendation I: Intercultural dialogue is part of the public responsibility for higher education and research

Public authorities and university leaders should fully recognise the role of higher education in society and develop policies aimed at fulfilling its whole range of purposes, as outlined in the Committee of Ministers' Recommendation on public responsibility for higher education and research (Council of Europe 2007), a key part of which is offering equal opportunities for higher education to students of various cultural backgrounds.

Recommendation II: Intercultural dialogue is part of the mission of higher education

The leadership of higher education institutions should include intercultural dialogue as one of the aims of the university. They should consider including intercultural dialogue in the mission statement of the institution, and they should allocate adequate resources (both financial and staff) to implement intercultural dialogue. They should regard teaching and research that seek to foster intercultural dialogue on campus, as well as in society generally, as an integral part of the mission of higher education.

Recommendation III: Students and staff with different backgrounds need to be integrated and valued

The leadership of higher education institutions, and student unions and associations, should make it a priority to stimulate dialogue between students and staff from different backgrounds and encourage the participation of students in joint activities regardless of their background. Institutions, and their students and staff, should develop activities and policies that value the contribution students and staff of different linguistic, cultural, national and religious backgrounds can make to the institution, with activities and policies that seek to integrate them in its life.

Recommendation IV: Intercultural literacy should be a core aim of higher education

Public authorities and university leaders should see development of intercultural literacy as an important goal in the teaching and learning function of higher education, regardless of the discipline students specialise in. Credit systems should allow students to include interculturally relevant elements in their study programme, or regulations should be reviewed to ensure this.

Recommendation V: Intercultural training should be available

Higher education institutions should make available to students, and even more to staff, an adequate offer of training and professional development measures in the area of intercultural communication. Only with help of this sort will those willing to enter into intercultural dialogue actually be empowered to do so successfully.

Recommendation VI: A set of learning outcomes needs to be developed

The Council of Europe should explore the development of a set of learning outcomes and competences of particular relevance to intercultural dialogue; they would also help to define intercultural literacy. It should endeavour to collect, publish and share instructive examples of good practice in intercultural dialogue on campus. Likewise, the Council of Europe and other competent actors should develop didactical help materials for institutions.

Recommendation VII: Intercultural dialogue must be a part of the European Higher Education Area

While continuing with the necessary structural reforms, European governments should address and acknowledge, in the agenda for the European Higher Education Area (EHEA), the contribution of higher education to developing and maintaining the broader society, which needs to balance economic and environmental sustainability with social cohesion and democratic culture. Intercultural dialogue must be part of this extended agenda for the EHEA.

Recommendation VIII: Research to foster intercultural dialogue should be encouraged

Public authorities and universities should stimulate research designed to produce the new knowledge needed to foster intercultural dialogue and comprehension.

References

Bergan, Sjur and Jean-Philippe Restoueix (eds) (2009): *Intercultural dialogue on campus*, Higher Education Series No. 11, Strasbourg: Council of Europe Publishing.

CDESR [Steering Committee for Higher Education and Research of the Council of Europe] (2006): "Statement on the Contribution of Higher Education to Intercultural Dialogue", Strasbourg: Council of Europe.

Council of Europe (2007): Recommendation Rec(2007)6 by the Committee of Ministers to Council of Europe member states on public responsibility for higher education and research.

Council of Europe (2008): *White Paper on Intercultural Dialogue. Living Together as Equals in Dignity*, Strasbourg: Council of Europe.

Poglia, Edo, Manuel Mauri-Brusa and Tatiana Fumasoli (2009): "Intercultural dialogue in higher education in Europe", in Bergan and Restoueix (eds), *Intercultural dialogue on campus.*

Universities as actors of intercultural dialogue in wider society

Hilligje van 't Land

> It is difficult to imagine how a society can be fully democratic if it cannot conduct intercultural dialogue and it is equally difficult to imagine how intercultural dialogue can be conducted in societies that stray far from the ideals and practices of democracy. The competences needed for intercultural dialogue are therefore also largely those needed to develop and maintain a culture of democracy, and this culture cannot exist without education.
>
> (Battaini-Dragoni 2010)

> Higher-education institutions play an important role in fostering intercultural dialogue, through their education programmes, as actors in broader society and as sites where intercultural dialogue is put into practice. As the Steering Committee on Higher Education and Research suggests, the university is ideally defined precisely by its universality – its commitment to open-mindedness and openness to the world, founded on enlightenment values. The university thus has great potential to engender "intercultural intellectuals" who can play an active role in the public sphere.
>
> (Council of Europe 2008: 31)

There are two main roles for higher education to play in the promotion of intercultural learning and dialogue. The first is the furthering of the dialogue on campus; the second is the role of the institution in promoting intercultural learning and dialogue in wider society.

This article gives an analytical overview of the Council of Europe seminar held at the Peoples' Friendship University of Russia (PFUR) in Moscow on 2-3 June 2009. It presents views and recommendations expressed by various stakeholders involved in higher education policy and practice; it highlights the major dilemmas and challenges higher education institutions have to face today when developing strategies for intercultural dialogue; and it ends with some conclusions and recommendations adopted at the seminar.

The Council of Europe seminar in Moscow

Gabriella Battaini-Dragoni, Director General of Education, Culture and Heritage, Youth and Sport and Co-ordinator for Intercultural Dialogue, introduced the Council of Europe's views on the topic, and the principles and values underlying the Council of Europe's White Paper on Intercultural Dialogue (Council of Europe 2008).

The role governments can play was illustrated by Alf Rasmussen, senior adviser to the Norwegian Ministry of Education and Research, Department of Higher Education, who presented the Norwegian White Paper on internationalisation of education; he emphasised the importance of strengthening intercultural dialogue and of developing strong policies to facilitate and support such dialogue.

The role of university leaders in promoting intercultural learning and dialogue in universities was introduced by Lars Ekholm, who spoke on behalf of the European University Association (EUA) and presented the EUA's perspective. He was followed by four speakers describing actions undertaken to develop intercultural dialogue initiatives, with examples of policy development and challenges faced in Russia, Kazakhstan and Lebanon. The presentations were made by Professor Barasby S. Karamurzov, rector of the Kabardino-Balkarian State University and president of the Association of Russian Higher Education Institutions, Professor Bakhytzhan Zh. Abdraimov, rector of the L.N. Gumilyov Eurasian National University (ENU), Professor René Chamussy SJ, rector of the Saint-Joseph University of Beirut and Professor Vladimir M. Filippov, rector of PFUR.

The seminar was also open to students' voices. Olav Øye, member of the executive committee of the European Students' Union (ESU), introduced this aspect and was followed by students from five different countries. all studying at the PFUR, who gave their own presentations: Vladimir Chety, head of the PFUR Students Union; Ibrahim Naofav (Syria), president of the PFUR Association of Arab Universities; Miguel de la Cruz Salcedo (Peru), president of the PFUR Federation of Students from Latin America and the Caribbean; Dorothy Rotich (Kenya), a PhD student at the Faculty of Humanities in PFUR; and Chandra Saha Biplob (Bangladesh), president of the PFUR Association of Students from Asian Countries.

The role of university networks was debated as well. Joseph Mifsud, rector of the Euro Mediterranean University (EMUNI), and Marijke Wahlers, head of the international department of the German Rectors' Conference (HRK), presented their projects and policies, and made recommendations on the actions such networks could undertake.

Alain Mouchox, vice-chair of the Conference of International Non-Governmental Organisations of the Council of Europe, addressed the role INGOs do and can play. Finally, Ana Perona-Fjeldstad, executive director of the newly created European Wergeland Centre, explained this initiative and described the projects it will undertake. Germain Dondelinger, *premier conseiller de gouvernement*, Ministry of Culture, Higher Education and Research of Luxemburg, discussed the role public authorities are to play.

Sjur Bergan, head of the Department of Higher Education and History Teaching of the Council of Europe, chaired the concluding panel, which consisted of Professor Radu Damian, chair of the CDESR, Olav Øye (ESU), Professor Vladimir M. Filippov (rector, PFUR) and Professor Marina Larionova, vice-rector of the State University – High School of Economics. The discussion allowed for broader debate on the role that public authorities, higher education as a whole and students and staff in particular should play in promoting intercultural dialogue. Moreover, the value of, and the possibilities offered by, a European policy were discussed.

The 2008 White Paper

According to the White Paper published by the Council of Europe:

> Higher Education Institutions [are] to play an important role in fostering intercultural dialogue through their Education Programmes, as actors in broader society and as sites where intercultural dialogue is put into practice.

At the same time, the paper stresses that

> in order for this role to be taken up fully, it needs to be assisted by scholarly research on intercultural learning, to address the aspects of "learning to live together" and cultural diversity in all teaching aspects (Council of Europe 2008: 31).

The White Paper lists seven cornerstones of any political culture valuing diversity: [the values of] democracy; human rights and fundamental freedoms; the rule of law; pluralism; tolerance; non-discrimination; mutual respect. It also identifies five policy approaches to the promotion of intercultural dialogue:

- The development of democratic governance of cultural diversity through
  - a political culture valuing diversity,
  - human rights and fundamental freedoms.
  - equality of opportunity leading to equal enjoyment of rights;
- The fostering of democratic citizenship and participation;
- The promotion of learning and teaching of intercultural competences –
  - key competence areas: democratic citizenship, language, history;
  - levels of education: primary and secondary education; higher education and research; non-formal and informal learning;
  - actors: teachers, professors, administrative/support staff and the leadership of universities, other higher education institutions and education institutions at all levels;
- The creation of adequate spaces for intercultural dialogue;
- Policies and practices that ensure intercultural dialogue in international relations.

Building on the White Paper

> Universities cannot be universities unless their mission and the education they provide are greater than the sum of its individual academic disciplines. (Gabriella Battaini-Dragoni)

Building on these principles, speakers reiterated the fact that universities are communities in themselves and that diversity on campus is a reality that needs to be fully seized and valued. Yet, at the same time, universities are key actors in broader society. Both core academic activities, education and research, need to take this up. Facilitating students' access to the job market is one of the aims of higher education; providing them with adequate competences and qualifications to enable them to become well-informed and critical citizens, aiming to live together as equals in dignity on campus and certainly outside it, locally as well as globally, is another essential goal. Hence, to better take part in the development of our future societies, universities need to foster intercultural dialogue, and they need to ensure that citizenship education is embedded in the very mission of teaching and learning. Students need to be prepared for sustainable employment, for life as active citizens in democratic societies, for personal development and for the development and maintenance of a broad and advanced knowledge base (Council of Europe 2007).

Intercultural competences should be a key element in citizenship and human rights education; those are to provide the learners with a broad world view, or what the Council of Europe calls 'multiperspectivity' (Council of Europe 2001), one that allows them to grasp the complexity of the society they live in. Citizenship education is not only a right but an obligation and, as one of the outcomes, the competences acquired should help foster and maintain a culture of democracy.

In order to take intercultural dialogue and citizenship education on board, universities and their staff are expected to "design and implement curricula and study programmes at all levels of education, including teacher training and adult education programmes" (Council of Europe 2008: 43). Foreign language education for all is one area to be developed further. It not only fosters better communication but also provides appropriate tools for a better understanding of diverse entry points to realities. History teaching is likewise important. It also provides keys to a better understanding of the views of others. Alternative and probably new teaching methods may need to be developed, along with new teaching and learning programmes that would provide space for such disciplines to be taken up across the faculties and the disciplinary divides.

The Council of Europe has called for the principles of intercultural dialogue to be translated at the level of higher education. The basic assumption underlying that call is that:

> The risks of non-dialogue need to be fully appreciated. Not to engage in dialogue makes it easy to develop a stereotypical perception of the other, build up a climate of mutual suspicion, tension and anxiety, use minorities as scapegoats, and generally foster intolerance and discrimination. The breakdown of dialogue within and between societies can provide, in certain cases, a climate conducive to the emergence, and the exploitation by some, of extremism and indeed terrorism. Intercultural dialogue, including on the international plane, is indispensable between neighbours. ... Only dialogue allows people to live in unity in diversity. (Council of Europe 2008: 16)

As such, and in Europe in particular, the debate on integrating intercultural learning and dialogue into curricula should form part of the discussion on higher education reform stimulated by the Bologna Process. This structural reform is important, but it becomes significant only if it serves a purpose. The new European higher education structures should be 'structures with a mission'. Their purposes and missions should include ways to develop the kind of society in which people can live together as equals in dignity and in which all citizens are fluent in intercultural dialogue.

Intercultural dialogue as an integral part of internationalisation

The need for the principles of intercultural dialogue to be further integrated into higher education governance and further promoted by government policies was well illustrated by the adoption in Norway of a White Paper on internationalisation of education (Kunnskapsdepartementet 2008). The paper stipulates that intercultural dialogue is to be seen as an integral component of the overall process of internationalisation of higher education. Norway's White Paper was drafted to help education institutions and other stakeholders make strategic choices as to what skills or competences students need to act and interact better in a globalised world. The issue of quality – quality in education, in mobility, in teaching and research – is at the heart of the Norwegian initiative. The ultimate aim is to help learners overcome intercultural barriers, to foster more openness and foster better understanding of oneself and the other(s), at home and abroad.

To internationalise higher education, governments are called on to help develop and promote:

- joint degrees and study programmes;
- transfer of training and improvements – Tuning-like projects[6] – across national borders;
- pilot projects in short-cycle professional studies;
- closer co-operation between education and research in order to show that research is possible and desirable;
- research on effects, best practices, problems and drivers within internationalisation of higher education to better understand what is at stake;
- develop high-quality opportunities at policy level to study abroad and facilitate mobility through financing.

How can university leaders promote intercultural dialogue?

Considering that students take their essential values with them into their professional careers and their future lives, universities are to be held responsible for teaching and promoting the basic values needed for democratic citizenship. We should not conceive of students in higher education as clients in a knowledge market; they are citizens who take part in the life of the community they live in and the life of society at large. They need to be equipped with – and they themselves need to develop – norms and values associated with democracy, international understanding, human rights, acceptance of all people irrespective of social background, awareness of their own limitations and readiness to incorporate the unknown.

The translation from words and concepts into policy and practice is not a straightforward exercise. No single model can be applied to all institutions in all socio-political contexts. Some universities are very much internationalised, so intercultural

---

6. Tuning educational structures in Europe; see http://tuning.unideusto.org/tuningeu/.

dialogue can lean on programmes and policies already available. Where internationalisation is not yet developed, mechanisms need to be put in place to introduce intercultural learning and dialogue. This requires specific policy measures and support. Speakers advocated sharing good practice at leadership level.

The prevalent socio-political context in some countries makes the introduction of intercultural dialogue principles a must, but also problematic. Lebanon was and is interesting in that respect; it may serve as a case study to be developed and analysed further. Tensions in the country and region were presented as unavoidable, in view of past and present circumstances. Intercultural dialogue being inextricably linked to issues of inter-religious dialogue, and the socio-political context of the region being what it is, it unfortunately often leads to violence, it jeopardises dialogue and it is even a threat to social stability. Speakers stressed that dialogue cannot always be the solution to conflict, but it is nonetheless a stepping stone to creating better conditions for a possible dialogue. Initiatives based on the assumption that dialogue can only succeed if based on fraternity and respect for each other's differences were presented as being successful and leading to concrete and important results. Again, speakers recommended developing an electronic database to enable easy access to, and sharing of, information on such initiatives.

The initiatives showed the importance of providing adequate 'spaces' for dialogue. Whatever their form, such spaces are there to help counter violence or simply enable us to open up to others, to better understand the world we live in. This came up in the presentations given by the students and again in the presentations of initiatives undertaken by university networks.

In order for initiatives to succeed and have a real impact throughout, higher education leadership needs to get actively involved; policy and action at the governance level are essential to promote intercultural dialogue perspectives and actions at all levels in the institutions. Speakers placed special emphasis on the need to also develop research on cultural and historical backgrounds. Solid and, as far as possible, objective knowledge of one's own culture and history – and the ability to look at them with some distance – are the best basis for good dialogue.

A plea was made to reinforce education of ethnic cultures, national traditions and cultures, and languages. At the same time, no culture is static; on the contrary, they evolve constantly and research on such evolution and its mechanisms is also required. Education should take that into consideration and emphasise the importance of a multiperspectival approach to culture, history and related aspects of the socio-political and cultural environment in which one lives and grows.

What about the students themselves?

Speakers urged the active participation of students in the continuing reform of higher education, to ensure better inclusion of intercultural dialogue and learning in policy and practice.

Study-abroad policies were to be promoted further, but institutional policies were also to be developed to improve dialogue and exchange between foreign and local students, between the culture of the foreign students and the local culture. Too often, on-campus meetings aimed at integrating foreign students better into university life are mostly meant only for foreign students or attended mainly (if not only) by foreign students. Enhancing dialogue with local students and others on and off campus is a real challenge. Better integration mechanisms are needed.

Student organisations do participate in the process through publications, concerted actions and short- and long-term national, regional and international projects. Speakers called for a global student union, along with intergovernmental support for the creation of such a structure.

The roles that associations and networks can play

Associations and networks can, should and often do play an active role in promoting intercultural dialogue and understanding. Clearly, they are mainly concerned with issues relevant to their members; networks, associations and similar bodies need to show that promoting intercultural dialogue is one such issue. It is relevant at institutional, national and international levels.

Thematic groups, regional networks or alliances, and international disciplinary initiatives can all lead to intercultural dialogue and thus help to improve understanding between individuals from diverse backgrounds. The impact can be significant, so action plans for intercultural dialogue should be promoted at all levels in such organisations and among their members. Networks, associations and similar organisations can also facilitate the creation of centres of expertise and stimulate inter-university, inter-regional or international co-operation projects.

(I)NGOs have a similar role to play. Lessons from the past hardly seem to be retained and history keeps on repeating itself, so speakers asked for continuous support for the development of intercultural dialogue mechanisms. (I)NGOs involved in education develop significant national, regional, international partnerships. Intercultural dialogue is promoted continuously at all levels of education, including in lifelong learning.

The European Wergeland Centre[7] aims to help build bridges between people and cultures, and between initiatives. It is meant to help universities, other institutions and education stakeholders move from principles to policy, from policy to practice, and it offers a valuable channel for co-operation. Access to quality information and networking can move the agenda forward.

---

7. See www.theewc.org/.

The role of public authorities

Last but not least, public authorities should get more involved, especially strategically. They should create and support spaces in which civil society can play a role and where intercultural dialogue can take place.

For strategies to be more successful – or, rather, for them to be implemented more fully – policy development and concerted actions need to be framed legally. In the European Union, certain legal frameworks are available. The EU places great emphasis on social cohesion; it supports the cultural diversity approach and aims to provide legal or political recognition of defined minority cultures and identities. The least binding dialogue approach is the one promoting artistic events and special media programmes. These can help create a specific environment that fosters civic responsibility, and help establish an ambience suited to intercultural dialogue. They should:

– stimulate internationalisation and the conditions needed for constructive intercultural dialogue;

– guarantee academic freedom;

– create conditions for equitable access and success;

– create conditions for a better understanding of cultural diversity.

Dilemmas and barriers

If the promotion and support of intercultural dialogue and understanding are must-do activities and if all stakeholders are in principle convinced, why then is intercultural dialogue not a priority today? What negative factors prevent higher education from getting involved fully? How can these factors be countered?

The major dilemmas and challenges higher education has to face today are those of striving for excellence, competition, accountability, serious financial constraints and efficiency. Higher education leaders, administrators, teachers, researchers and students know all too well the ramifications and implications of these concepts.

Reforms that are being implemented, especially in Europe in the context of the Bologna Process, make heavy demands on administrators, teachers and researchers, who are all to become more and more multi-tasked and efficient – perhaps with a somewhat narrow concept of efficiency as simply getting things done, without checking whether the things done are perceived as legitimate – with the result that priorities must constantly be re-evaluated and adjusted, students see their study plans and time constrained and little space is left for improvisation.

The commercialisation of higher education and its market-oriented implications also stand in the way of better integration of intercultural learning and dialogue principles in higher education. Financial constraints are such that leaders look for efficiency at all levels; little or no space is available for innovation that is not directly accountable, or at least 'visible'. Intercultural dialogue and understanding is not a discipline; administratively, it is not directly visible or accountable. Since it requests interdisciplinary collaboration and action, and thus requires time, can it be integrated into existing core curricula or will it be relegated to extracurricular activities? What mechanisms need to be developed to ensure active and committed participation by all?

How in such a context can higher education leaders be convinced of the importance of intercultural dialogue being supported and translated in practice at all levels of the institution? And, if leaders are convinced, how can they then convince their administrators and academic staff of the importance of integrating intercultural dialogue policy and practice into their work?

The impact of market-oriented forces and logic on higher education is not a new phenomenon, but the focus has shifted considerably. Market forces have had and do have positive impacts on higher education but, unfortunately, today they have a tendency to overrule all other concerns, such as the social responsibility of higher education. Market forces need to be counterbalanced by values of relevance for the society as a whole as well as a coherent vision of the kind of societies in which we would like to live and the role of higher education in shaping this society.

What next?

Taking all the above into account, the seminar concluded that all higher education stakeholders and partners need to safeguard and stimulate human and ethical approaches to teaching and learning. The seminar made the following recommendations.

First, intercultural competences should form an integral part of higher education learning outcomes. Students need to be literate in the complexity of the societies they live in and capable of addressing the increasingly interrelated issues at stake locally and globally. Universities should be models of the state of the art in this area; in particular, university leadership should get on board, around the globe, and turn policy into action at all levels within their institutions.

Second, universities and similar institutions need to share and disseminate information and best practices nationally, internationally and globally. Frameworks for implementing the principles of intercultural learning and dialogue should be developed, and norms and values adopted, to ensure proper intercultural teaching and learning, and to favour dialogue. Tensions and conflicts are apparently – unfortunately – unavoidable but they need to be addressed, and higher education can help provide tools. Intercultural dialogue can also be a conflict-prevention mechanism.

Third, to further foster intercultural dialogue, access to higher education for all is of great importance; where needed, regional university systems should be strengthened so that individuals can gain access to higher education and benefit from it.

Last but not least, the seminar delegates reaffirmed a strong need for mutual and joint activities to counter stereotypical views of cultures of the other – in other words, to better guarantee high-quality internationalisation and co-operation.

References

Battaini-Dragoni, Gabriella (2010): "Intercultural dialogue and higher education: a Council of Europe view", in the present volume.

Council of Europe (2001): Recommendation Rec(2001)15 of the Committee of Ministers to member states on history teaching in twenty-first-century Europe.

Council of Europe (2007): Recommendation Rec(2007)6 by the Committee of Ministers to member states on the public responsibility for higher education and research.

Council of Europe (2008): *Living together as equals in dignity*, White Paper on Intercultural Dialogue, Strasbourg: Council of Europe.

Kunnskapsdepartementet (2008): St. meld. nr. 14 (2008-2009) Internasjonalisering av utdanning [Report to Parliament No. 14 (2008-2009): Internationalisation of education].

III. Higher education as an actor of intercultural dialogue

Higher education "as" free dialogue: pedagogy in a global age

Edward J. Alam

Many will argue that higher education has a major role to play today in fostering a culture of dialogue and understanding. But unless higher education itself is transformed into a culture of dialogue, I am afraid it has little chance of playing such a role. Thus, in the title, I put the emphasis on "as". Such transformation is a daunting task because, though it is fashionable to talk about the importance of interdisciplinary and intercultural dialogue, the reality is, in all but a few institutions of higher education around the globe and especially in the West, that specialisation and departmentalisation – both disciplinary and cultural – continue to intensify. Specialisation is so intense today that even people in the same discipline sometimes cannot converse.

Specialisation and the whole

Where does that leave interdisciplinary conversation? This tendency to specialise is in some ways perhaps inevitable, and in some ways advantageous, but the challenge is to achieve accuracy and efficiency in the particular branches of knowledge, without giving up the search for the whole – or, dare we say, without searching and re-searching for "holiness". By "holiness" I do not mean some petrified, static notion of religious piety that uncritically dismisses all of Enlightenment thought or irrationally condemns all forms of secularity as a sign of a disintegrating and corrupt civilisation. Not at all! This is what Jürgen Habermas calls the "pathos of religion". Genuine holiness, rather, involves the search for the whole – the whole truth about the whole person living in the whole cosmos. Of course, this search is unending and calls for research again and again. And it must involve, as I have indicated, the whole person, not just reason, since we learned in the twentieth century that pure instrumental, reductive reason has its own dangerous "pathos". And finally it must involve a search for the whole truth in the context of the search for singular and endlessly varied specific truths. It was not by accident that the great centres of learning in ancient and medieval times were called universities – a study of the universe in a universe of studies.

Now the challenge to hold the singular in just the right tension with the universal is as old as philosophy itself, as we see in the tension between Platonic and Aristotelian metaphysics – a tension that has pedagogical reverberations down through the ages to the present. But, despite this tension, both approaches concur on a central point: the need for unifying science, what in the Middle Ages was called a "Queen of the Sciences". Of course, it is impossible to return to such a conception, nor is it desirable given the genuine (though, I would argue, much exaggerated) progress

63

that has come from specialisation as it grew out of the eighteenth-century German Enlightenment, but the point is that without a central, unifying science, or what might be called a highest science, unity in the curriculum is impossible. And without a unity and wholeness in the curriculum that facilitates genuine dialogue among members of the faculty from the same disciplines, there can never be the kind of interdisciplinary and intercultural dialogue that is so urgent in our global age.

I have stated above that the move to specialisation has shown its advantages and that in some ways the philosophical shift which anchors this move was, perhaps, inevitable. I say "in some ways" and "perhaps" because, viewed from another angle, the shift was not inevitable at all.

As far as the West is concerned, Francis Bacon, the father of modern science, could have chosen an altogether different path to take in his interpretation of Aristotelian logic and epistemology. Likewise, René Descartes, the father of modern philosophy, could have approached Aristotelian metaphysics quite differently. The obvious rejoinder here is "Well, if Bacon and Descartes had not taken these new directions, others surely would have". But this is highly disputable and nearly impossible to defend. At any rate, the point here is that the shift from a more robust to a more restricted and myopic approach to knowledge – a shift with its foundations in 16th-century England and 17th-century France, one which reduced philosophy primarily to epistemology, thereby radically changing the very definition of knowledge prevalent in ancient and medieval times, a shift towards seeking knowledge in order to "master nature" in Bacon's terms – was not simply inevitable. Thought develops in certain ways because of thinkers who make choices that are not determined from the outset. If this were not the case, meetings like those convened by the Council of Europe or by the International Association of Universities would be pointless, because what the scholars at such meetings are trying to do is to move higher education in a certain direction – in a direction of genuine intercultural and interdisciplinary dialogue. We could very well have chosen a different direction.

I would like to turn briefly then to ways of cultivating a cosmic vision, but without ignoring or downplaying just how important specialisation and modern scientific method have been and are.

Again, this modern quandary is an old metaphysical problem that will never go away, and it never should go away, because it is not a problem to be solved, but a mystery to be explored and lived, the mystery, that is, of seeing, and holding in the right tension, what the great medieval philosopher, scientist and statesman, Nicholas of Cusa, called the different and dynamic levels of unity – the mystery of the whole in the parts and the parts in the whole, which, for our present purposes, applies not only to the various colleges (departments, faculties) making up the university, but also to the various nations or cultures that constitute our global world.

Today, the success of interdisciplinary education depends directly on the success of intercultural education, and vice versa. It is crucial to see this. And there are more and more academics and politicians and religious leaders who do see it. Professor

64

Mayor Zaragoza's excellent keynote address at the IAU International Conference 2009, a revised version of which appears in the present volume, underlines the tremendous progress that has been made in this regard: the worldwide attention to dialogue in 1998, and then to peace in 1999; to culture in 2000 and to cultural diversity in 2001; and since then the many clear, high-level statements on the importance of inter-religious and intercultural dialogue, which has led to so many joint statements about universal values from so many diverse cultures and religions. And in October 2009 our President of Lebanon called upon the United Nations to designate Lebanon as a centre for intercultural and inter-religious dialogue. But, as Professor Mayor Zaragoza rightly said, seeing it, though a crucial first step, is not enough. It must be achieved; it is time for action. And the university must play a key role in this regard.

Now the fact that so many people from so many different parts of the world, and from so many different academic disciplines, have come to Lebanon and gathered at Notre Dame University Louaize on the occasion of the IAU conference to discuss this theme is a notable action, and is an achievement which must be acknowledged, but once again, how do we proceed from here? What do we do when we return to our own countries, our own departments, our own disciplines and specialisations? There is no one answer here, no ultra-rigorous, super-scientific method for achieving things as profound as unity in knowledge and community among nations, for such unity and community must encompass diversity and individuality. But the following general prescription has guided the work of the Council for Research in Values and Philosophy,[8] which I represent and which has been promoting intercultural dialogue in higher education across the globe for the last 30 years. The written fruits of this council are freely available in the 220 volumes from all corners of the world that are published on the council's website.

Research and reason

The first guiding principle in the work of this research council, as the name indicates, is research. But it is research into values and philosophy, which, we contend, is the most fundamental kind of research – perhaps a strange claim, given the way the scientific method has come to usurp the meaning of research – a method that still tends towards a reductive and restrictive epistemology, despite the epistemic breakthroughs in 20th-century physics. And this is not to mention the practical side of the reductionist impetus at the heart of so much of this one-sided research – another point alluded to by Professor Mayor Zaragoza. I am speaking, of course, about the obscene amount of money made available for so-called free research being conducted today in the best universities in the world, research that is driven simply by the production of more and more sophisticated weapons of mass and indiscriminate murder, weapons that we here in Lebanon unfortunately know all too well. Research in the natural sciences must be set free from the slavery of this

---

8. For information on the history and activity of this organisation, see www.crvp.org.

corrupt and brutal power, for if the universities cannot free themselves from the interests of unbridled market forces, so much of which is connected to the weapons industry, then there is little hope that the university can fulfil its timeless mission of free research into the things that matter most: values, culture, philosophy, religion.

In any case, it is clear to me that the very same science responsible for an essential change in our understanding of man and the world can never provide the meta-physical foundations necessary for genuine intercultural dialogue. If dialogue does not eventually lead to the search and re-search for what is ontologically good, and true, and beautiful, and is not engaged in the ethical activity of discovering why one ought to do the good, or search for truth, or desire the beautiful, then it is not genuine dialogue. Needless to say, the method necessary for such research cannot ignore the achievements of modernity and late modernity, but it seems wise, following the groundbreaking work of the great phenomenological tradition in Western philosophy, from Edmund Husserl to Hans Georg Gadamer via Martin Heidegger, to admit that the road we have been following, the road of instrumental reason and utilitarian ethics, the road of "mastering nature" has gone as far as it can go; to pursue it further will lead to total destruction.

One great success that phenomenology has already had, by going back to the original point of departure, is the way it has cultivated a more robust and unified sense of reason in natural law theory. One encouraging result has been a new expression of human rights that distances itself from the deistic and rationalistic presupposi-tions operative in earlier rights documents. This new expression, embodied in the Universal Declaration, is "incomprehensible without the presupposition that the human being *qua* human being, is the subject of rights and that the human being bears within itself values and norms that must be discovered – but not invented" (Ratzinger and Habermas 2006: 71).

When we lose sight of this insight, we also lose sight of the fact that human beings have rights only because they have duties, and that both rights and duties are rooted in a unified individual human nature which is ordered to participate progressively in greater and greater dimensions of unity in families, communities, cultures and religions. Upon such foundations, it is possible to conduct intercultural dialogue, the aim of which must be to cultivate a global culture – not one in which diversity disappears, but one rather in which diversity and individuality are not perceived as threats, but as unique, complementary and irreplaceable living cells of the one global body. It sounds idealistic because it is, and too often falls prey to the temptation of ideology – even the ideology of dialogue itself runs this risk.

Dialogue is exchange

In fact, not a few have written about the "dialogue industry" – turning the call to dialogue into a multi-million-dollar industry, just another cog in the market forces of unbridled capitalism. But dialogue cannot be for its own sake; the exchange of ideas across academic disciplines and across cultures must, as the word indicates, lead to change or it is not a genuine exchange at all. And dialogue cannot be made compulsory through some kind of broad curriculum shift imposed from the top down – even in the name of an important and meaningful concept such as dialogue.

No. Dialogue must be chosen freely, and it must spring from the deepest resources present in the cultural and religious heritages of the people involved. The very concept of a United Nations presupposes this kind of dialogue, and it was a remarkable achievement of the twentieth century when this concept took flesh after the horrendous years of war. But, as Pope Benedict has forcefully stated in his most recent encyclical *Caritas in Veritate*, it is imperative that this organisation now be reformed:

> In the face of the unrelenting growth of global interdependence, there is a strongly felt need, even in the midst of a global recession, for a reform of the United Nations Organization, and likewise of economic institutions and international finance, so that the concept of the family of nations can acquire real teeth. One also senses the urgent need to find innovative ways of implementing the principle of the "responsibility to protect" and of giving poorer nations an effective voice in shared decision-making. This seems necessary in order to arrive at a political, juridical and economic order which can increase and give direction to international co-operation for the development of all peoples in solidarity. To manage the global economy; to revive economies hit by the crisis; to avoid any deterioration of the present crisis and the greater imbalances that would result; to bring about integral and timely disarmament, food security and peace; to guarantee the protection of the environment and to regulate migration: for all this, there is urgent need of a true world political authority, as my predecessor Blessed John XXIII indicated some years ago. Such an authority would need to be regulated by law, to observe consistently the principles of subsidiarity and solidarity, to seek to establish the common good and to make a commitment to securing authentic integral human development inspired by the values of charity in truth. (Pope Benedict XVI 2009, paras 146-147)

For higher education to be transformed "into" a culture of dialogue and understanding, it too must be inspired first and foremost by these same values of charity in truth.

References

Pope Benedict XVI (2009): *Caritas In Veritate*, Encyclical Letter, Rome: Vatican Press.

Ratzinger, Joseph and Jürgen Habermas (2006): *Dialectics of Secularization: On Reason and Religion*, San Francisco: Ignatius Press.

Developing attitudes to intercultural dialogue: the role of higher education

Sjur Bergan

Introduction

For dialogue to be possible there must be two parties, but two parties do not guarantee dialogue. If one party does all the talking, as in a classic auditorium lecture or a televised speech, there may be tens, hundreds or thousands of participants, but communication is one-way. Monologue has its rightful place in many situations. If a fire breaks out, shouting "get out" is more justified than engaging in a dialogue about the potential harm of overly high temperatures. One-way communication can also bring forth positive or negative reactions, which perhaps cannot be expressed immediately but may give rise to intense communication later. Few who heard President Obama's acceptance speech at the Nobel Peace Prize ceremony (Obama 2009) will have been unmoved; the speech may have given rise to numerous conversations and it will certainly be studied in classrooms and seminars in many countries.

Dialogue, then, requires the ability of two or more participants to speak and to listen in real time. Both acts are equally important: someone who leaves time for his or her interlocutors to speak, but who spends this time preparing the next set of arguments rather than listening to those of the interlocutors will not contribute to dialogue. In this case, we will have serial monologues rather than dialogue.

Intercultural dialogue requires several participants from different cultural backgrounds. For a large part of human history, most people would have had problems finding interlocutors with whom to hone their skills in intercultural dialogue and many would even have been unaware that other cultures existed. This does not mean that interaction between cultures is a modern phenomenon, however. Cultures have interacted for as long as human beings became numerous enough, or lived closely enough together, to come across beings of a similar nature but raised in different circumstances, learning different languages, different customs and different sets of behaviour and values. Cultures learned from each other and adapted values, beliefs and words that at first seemed foreign to fit their own frames of reference.

What is modern is not the phenomenon of dialogue across cultures but the extent to which most members of society are faced with the phenomenon. It is this urgency that led the Council of Europe to draft a White Paper on Intercultural Dialogue, which is significantly called *Living Together as Equals in Dignity*. The White Paper defines intercultural dialogue as:

> a process that comprises an open and respectful exchange of views between individuals and groups with different ethnic, cultural, religious and linguistic backgrounds and

heritage, on the basis of mutual understanding and respect. It requires the freedom and ability to express oneself, as well as the willingness and capacity to listen to the views of others. Intercultural dialogue contributes to political, social, cultural and economic integration and the cohesion of culturally diverse societies. It fosters equality, human dignity and a sense of common purpose. It aims to develop a deeper understanding of diverse worldviews and practices, to increase co-operation and participation (or the freedom to make choices), to allow personal growth and transformation, and to promote tolerance and respect for the other. (Council of Europe 2008: section 3.1)

Frames of mind

For intercultural dialogue to take place, then, not only must the potential interlocutors have the physical or technological means to communicate; they must also have a frame of mind that will make dialogue possible. On this score, many individuals and many cultures have a long history of closed minds. Europe is not alone in this, but it offers ample examples and since my own background is European, these are the ones that most easily come to mind.

For a long time, the Middle Ages were referred to as the Dark Ages because, since we knew less about this period than about the glories of ancient Greece and Rome, it was supposed that people of the Middle Ages had contributed little to cultural development. Even as our knowledge and understanding of this period of our history has improved and our understanding of culture has deepened so that we no longer look for a single "gold standard" from the distant past, the expression has somehow seemed to stick. Ignorance is also betrayed by our persistent belief that the history of the Americas began with the arrival of the first Europeans to settle permanently. Even if attitudes and awareness are changing in this respect, the belief is sufficiently persistent to have guaranteed the success of a book on the Americas before Columbus[9] (Mann 2006).

Language reveals our frames of mind. English is not alone in making an etymological connection between what is "strange" and the "stranger", cf. French *étrange* and *étranger* or Spanish *extraño* and *extranjero*. In Europe's often-heated debate on immigration and identity, some political movements try to make a point of distinguishing between foreigners who are closer to them in culture and those who are less close and consequently are presumed to be more "strange". For this, several Germanic languages have coined precise terms, exemplified by the German *Fernkulturellen*, literally "those who are culturally distant".

Education is about changing attitudes and helping develop our frames of mind. In an age in which contact with individuals with very different cultural backgrounds is not an option but an everyday reality, education cannot remain indifferent to this basic fact of human existence. Even if the majority of people live in or close to their place of origin and even if many will continue to work mainly in local or national contexts, they will at various times in their private and professional lives

---

9. A name that is itself a Latinised form of the original Italian Colombo and the Spanish Colón.

come into contact with people of different backgrounds. One important task for our schools and universities is to prepare our citizens for these encounters, to recognise cultural diversity as an intrinsic value and an opportunity for cultural enrichment rather than as a danger. Historically, it is not the cultures that have learned from others that have perished but those that have tried to isolate themselves or that have stubbornly stuck to their own ways even in an unfamiliar environment, as the Norse colonies in Greenland did (Diamond 2006).

The ideals of higher education

Few endeavours should be better suited to promoting an understanding of the need for, and value of, intercultural dialogue than higher education; and few endeavours should be better suited to developing and transmitting the competences needed. The origins of universities are international and, even if most early universities were concentrated in south and central Europe, their students came from much further afield. It may be objected that, even if medieval students and teachers varied in their national origins, they shared an academic language and culture. This is undoubtedly true, but it is equally true that this was the native culture of few of them and the native language of none.

The medieval academic community displayed exactly the kind of mix – of what its members had in common, and what was particular to each or some of its members – that characterises our broader society today. After all, intercultural dialogue requires not only open minds but also a common language, and increasingly this dialogue is carried out in a language that is native to few or even none of the interlocutors. The spread of the most frequently used language of international communication, English, is often compared to the extended use of Latin in the Middle Ages, but the comparison is halting for at least two reasons. Firstly, by the Middle Ages no native speakers of Latin remained, whereas now the different varieties of English have several hundred million native speakers. Secondly, the use of Latin was restricted to a social and intellectual elite in Europe. Even if a working knowledge of English is far from universal, it is not restricted to a single segment of the population or to a single continent.

Higher education is committed to assessing ideas not on the basis of their origin but on the basis of their intrinsic merit. Like the Ten Commandments, this commitment is often honoured in the breaching of it, but it nevertheless represents an ideal against which our actual performance – our openness of mind – is measured. It is an ideal that sets a powerful standard for intercultural dialogue, which cannot take place unless each participant admits the possibility of good ideas originating with others from very different backgrounds. If one enters into verbal exchange with the purpose of demonstrating the superiority of one's own views and refuting the views of others, the result may be entertaining but it hardly qualifies as dialogue – at most it is what French refers to as *un dialogue de sourds*: a dialogue of the deaf.

Linked to this focus on intrinsic merit is another basic characteristic of higher education and research, namely the assumption that progress is made by challenging received ideas. Had it not been, we would still have sought to explain mental illness as a lack of balance among four basic body fluids and the changing night sky as the stellar constellations moving around Earth, the fixed point at the centre of the universe. Yet it takes courage to challenge received wisdom, even at universities. Research aims to develop new knowledge and European higher education underlines the link between teaching and research but, at times, university teachers have been obliged to teach in accordance with established dogma whereas they expressed very different ideas in their published works (de Ridder-Symoens 2007).

The history as well as the ideology of higher education should therefore grant it a particularly important place in furthering intercultural dialogue, and we would seem to be justified in expecting higher education institutions and graduates to be particularly open-minded and fluent in intercultural dialogue. Alas, this cannot be taken for granted. The horizon of many staff and students is restricted to the limits of their own discipline and they often see little reason to engage in broader issues (Plantan 2004). It is not difficult to think of academics who have done much to further dialogue and democratic culture, standing up for democracy at great personal risk – for example, the Weisse Rose, the student group around Hans and Sophie Scholl; the theologians Dietrich Bonhoeffer (Protestant) and Fr Alfred Delp SJ (Catholic) in Nazi Germany (Gotto and Repgen 1990); Portuguese students under Salazar, especially from 1960 onwards; Chilean students under the Pinochet regime; Greek students under the regime of the colonels; Academician Andrei Sakharov in the Soviet Union; the Alternative Academic Education Network under the Milošević regime and many more. The list could be much, much longer.

Unfortunately, it is also easy to think of counter-examples of academics who have led or assisted oppressive and dictatorial regimes closed to dialogue and looking askance at the concept that valid ideas may originate outside the regime's culture or ideology. This list includes many right-wing German academics and students in the 1930s (Hammerstein 1991); the leaders of the Salazar regime, who had their roots at the University of Coimbra (Torgal 1999); the "Chicago boys" – the economists from the University of Chicago and the Universidad Católica de Chile, who played an important role in the Pinochet regime (Huneeus 2001); academically trained judges in the DDR (German Democratic Republic) and other Communist states (Mählert 1999); the leaders of far too many universities and academies of science who served the same regimes; the teachers and students at the University of Ayacucho who founded the Peruvian left-wing terrorist movement Sendero Luminoso and those involved with European left-wing terrorist groups like the Rote Arméefraktion (Baader-Meinhof) in Germany or the Brigate Rosse in Italy. Alas, this list, too, could be made much longer.

The image of the ivory tower is, I believe, a considerable exaggeration. Had it been exact, it is difficult to believe that universities would have survived for so many centuries. Yet, we often talk about the "society surrounding higher education" and forget that this is not an ocean surrounding an island. It is the very society of which higher education is a part. The examples mentioned also show that we cannot take for granted that the ideals underlying higher education describe actual practice. Higher education needs to disengage sufficiently from everyday issues to be able to consider the fundamental questions of our societies and take a longer-term view, but it does need to engage with these fundamental issues as well. Even a perfunctory look at modern societies would make it difficult to argue that developing our ability to conduct intercultural dialogue is not among them.

The purposes of higher education

Not least, higher education must engage in a thorough reflection on its purposes in a modern, complex society. While Europe has been successful in reforming its higher education structures and to a considerable extent also its practices through the Bologna Process, we have been less successful in considering the purposes for which we reform our structures (Bergan 2009).

An outsider following the public debate on higher education in Europe could easily be led to believe it has one purpose and one purpose only: to prepare learners for a productive life as future economic actors, mostly as employees, though entrepreneurship is increasingly on the higher education as well as the political agenda. This is a reductionist view of education, not because preparation for employment is not an important purpose but because it is not the only important purpose. We do not need to look far to see why preparation for employment matters and, if a reminder were needed, autumn 2008 served it with the most serious financial crisis in decades. At the same time, the financial crisis reminded us that the competences needed for a prosperous economy span considerably wider than those usually associated with business studies. Had the main economic actors, most of them graduates, had a somewhat sounder and more holistic view of their activities and their obligations to broader society, and had they had a better education in the true sense of the word, the economic crisis might have been less serious.

Without downplaying the obvious role of higher education in preparing for the labour market, then, we need to take a more coherent view of its multiple purposes. While the details of these may be debated, we suggest that higher education has four broad purposes (Bergan 2005; Council of Europe 2007):

– preparation for the labour market;

– preparation for life as active citizens in democratic societies;

– personal development;

– development and maintenance of a broad, advanced knowledge base.

These purposes are equally important and they are not mutually exclusive. Rather, they should reinforce each other: the qualities and competences that make learners well suited for employment, such as analytical ability, communication skills and proficiency in foreign languages, may also help make them active citizens in democratic societies and further their personal development.

A major challenge in European policies is to explicitly recognise the multiple purposes of higher education, not least the fact that the education of the whole person is not something that can safely be concluded at the latest by the end of secondary education. In this sense, European higher education leaders and policy makers have much to learn from the US concept of liberal education, which takes a much broader view of what is "useful" (AAC&U 2007; Zernike 2009). That leads us to consider the purposes of higher education from a slightly different angle: what kinds of competences should higher education put before its learners?

Competences for intercultural dialogue

The issue of competences permeates the discussion of what higher education could and should contribute to modern societies. Although its contribution cannot be reduced to the development of competences in learners, this aspect is particularly important for the purpose of this article, which addresses the issue from three angles: competences for intercultural dialogue, competences for dialogue and, more generally, higher education competences, focusing in particular on the distinction between generic and subject-specific competences.

One way of seeing education is as a process of developing a set of competences in individuals. This is admittedly a somewhat reductionist view of education, but it may nevertheless be useful to adopt it temporarily. It immediately leads to the question of what we mean by competences. The classic definition of learning outcomes contains three elements (Bergan 2007):

- knowledge;
- understanding;
- ability to act.

This is at variance with the most traditional view of education, which emphasises its role in developing and transmitting knowledge. Most likely, this would also be the view of education expressed most frequently if we were to question the proverbial "man in the street".

Of course knowledge is important, and encyclopaedic knowledge is often admired, but knowledge alone is insufficient. To revert to the example of language learning, it is not easy for someone with a different linguistic background to master the intricacies of the case declensions of Slavic languages like Russian or Serbian, or Baltic languages like Lithuanian. Learning the different declensions according to gender and class of noun and adjective requires patience and persistence. It is, however, only useful if one also comes to understand when the different forms should be used and what connotations the cases convey – for instance, that the accusative may convey a sense of movement and the locative a fixed position, that the accusative may signal a direct object and the dative an indirect one. Nevertheless, operational language learning has been accomplished only when knowledge of the declensions and understanding of their function and connotations have been supplemented by the ability to use them correctly in practice.

Competence, then, is made up of knowledge, understanding and an ability to act, and this author has increasingly come to ask whether the definition should not include a fourth element: attitude. This is hardly a revolutionary thought, since a traditional aim of education has been to socialise young people into the societies of which they form a part by developing identification with that society's values, as exemplified by Norwegian education legislation, which says:

> The pupils and apprentices shall develop knowledge, skills and attitudes allowing them to master their lives and in order to participate in work and community. They shall be allowed to develop the joy of creativity, engagement and the need to investigate.

> The pupils and apprentices shall learn to think critically and to act ethically and to be conscious of the environment. They shall share in responsibility and have the right of participation.[10]

At the same time, the traditional goal of instilling these values in a way that leaves them unquestioned cannot be an educational goal in today's world. That would prevent dialogue, since we would all then limit our discussions with those from other backgrounds to defending the position of our own societies. These may be deeply held values, but they may equally well be unquestioned habits. Our definition of competences should include attitudes, and one of the attitudes it should develop is the willingness to question and reassess one's own values and habits. The goal is not to throw all the values of one's own culture and society overboard but rather to reassess them critically as our societies evolve. This will ultimately strengthen our fundamental values and also help us find ways in which these values may be made a living reality in evolving societies.

This view of competences must mean that education is about much more than developing "knowledge of facts". Again, Europe will find much of interest in the concept of liberal education. As defined by the Association of American Colleges and Universities, it is

> an approach to learning that empowers individuals and prepares them to deal with complexity, diversity, and change. It provides students with broad knowledge of the wider world (e.g., science, culture, and society) as well as in-depth study in a specific area of interest. A liberal education helps students develop a sense of social responsibility, as well as strong and transferable intellectual and practical skills such as communication, analytical and problem-solving skills, and a demonstrated ability to apply knowledge and skills in real-world settings.[11]

The ability to deal with complexity, diversity and change is required in almost every nook and cranny of the workplace, but it is equally required when we act as citizens in democratic societies and when we interact with people from other societies and backgrounds – as neighbours or as colleagues, as casual visitors or as friends.

---

10. See www.stortinget.no/no/Saker-og-publikasjoner/Vedtak/Beslutninger/Odelstinget/2008-2009/beso-200809-042/ (accessed on 27 December 2009), author's translation.
11. See www.aacu.org/leap/What_is_liberal_education.cfm (accessed on 27 December 2009).

Education at all levels, including higher education, must have a strong responsibility for developing the competences that allow learners to participate in all aspects of the life of their society as well as internationally and, again, it would be difficult to argue that these competences should not be defined with a view to intercultural dialogue. Education must be seen as more than the sum of the knowledge an individual will gain in the course of a programme of study, in the same way that universities must be more than the sum of their individual academic disciplines.

A practice of dialogue

Higher education, then, must seek to convey competences that make their students and graduates fit and willing to engage in intercultural dialogue. Before turning to consider the kind of competences needed, it is important to underline that these competences cannot be developed through classic study programmes alone. Intercultural dialogue must also be practised on campus and beyond. One can no more learn dialogue by listening to lectures than one can learn how to swim without getting into the water.

Many higher education institutions aspire to attract foreign students and many already have a high number of students from outside the country where they are located. A large foreign student population as well as a large body of national students from various cultural backgrounds should provide an excellent opportunity to put the principles of intercultural dialogue into practice on campus, yet many institutions do not seem to seize the opportunity. In many cases, staff and students focus on their own academic discipline and do not consider the broader goals of higher education to be their concerns. Undoubtedly, what a previous project found to be widespread rejection among staff and students of a role of the university as a site of democratic citizenship (Plantan 2004) is equally true for the role of higher education institutions as sites of intercultural dialogue. It is also a measure of what remains to be done that many institutions seem to consider this an issue to be left to the personal choice of staff and students. Few institutions seem to have a policy of creating a climate of intercultural dialogue on campus, and often foreign students spend their spare time with other students from the same linguistic and cultural background instead of developing friendships with students from the host country and other countries.

There are nonetheless examples of good practice. The policies that Queen's University Belfast instituted to make members of both major communities in Northern Ireland feel welcome on campus (Plantan 2004) can also be adapted to making foreign and minority students and staff an integrated part of the local academic community. A number of European universities have developed institutional policies to value the cultures and specificities of foreign and minority students while also making them well acquainted with the language and culture of the host institution (Bergan and Restoueix 2009).

A practice of intercultural dialogue on campus must take as its point of departure the fact that higher education is a learning process and not just a matter of teaching. It must see the institution as a holistic learning environment that spans disciplines and extends beyond the lecture hall and library. It must provide space and opportunities for students and staff from different backgrounds and different disciplines to interact with and learn from each other. It must encourage extracurricular activities that offer foreign and minority students opportunities to share their own culture with fellow students and staff as well as to get acquainted with the culture(s) of the host country. These opportunities must extend beyond folklore to explore fundamental values and cultural patterns and they must be open to respectful debate based on the basic principles of intercultural dialogue as outlined in the Council of Europe White Paper.

Higher education competences

If we go back to the "man in the street" and ask what kind of competences higher education should develop, chances are that the answer would emphasise knowledge of specific disciplines, like physics, history or law. This is, of course, an important aspect of higher education: we do expect a history graduate to be knowledgeable about history, if we go to a medical doctor, we expect him or her to have a solid understanding of medicine and we would not be happy with a dentist whose competence was limited to pulling teeth.

We call these subject-specific competences; they designate what higher education graduates know, understand and are able to do in a specific discipline. Subject-specific competences are complemented by generic or transversal competences, which describe what every higher education graduate may be expected to acquire (Bergan 2009: 45-67). They include analytical ability, communication skills, the ability to work individually as well as a part of a team and the ability to make decisions on the basis of incomplete evidence and under pressure of time.

The list of possible generic competences is quite long, but the project TUNING Educational Structures in Europe (González and Wagenaar 2005), which brought the distinction between subject-specific and generic competences fully into European higher education debate, points to three main categories. Instrumental competences are those that serve as instruments in applying subject-specific competences or in putting one's whole range of competences to use, such as the ability to communicate, to use technical aids (such as information technology), organise ourselves or make decisions. For the latter, think of a competence that is too often lacking: the ability to bring a discussion to a structured conclusion. Interpersonal competences enable us to relate to others and to function in a social environment, whether that environment is our own or that of another culture. They include what we are able to do as individuals, such as expressing our own ideas clearly as well as understanding the ideas of others (provided they are in their turn expressed understandably), as well as what we are able to do together with others, such as developing a project as a member of a team. System-specific competences enable us to understand how elements fit into a whole – a system – and to understand how changes in individual elements may change the system.

77

I have devoted more space to describing generic than subject-specific competences, not because they are more important but because they are less easy to grasp intuitively. An education that provided only one set of competences without the other would be incomplete. It may be true that the academic world provides examples of those who focus only on subject-specific competences – the attitudes to activities that fall outside the academic discipline, as described in the survey by Plantan referred to above, reinforce this impression. On the other hand, both the "new public management" and parts of the business community overemphasise generic at the expense of subject-specific competences, as demonstrated by the belief that once someone has been recruited to a company or an organisation, the person is qualified for most jobs within the organisation at a given level. German has a fitting term for those who possess mainly subject-specific competences: *Fachidiot*, literally "subject idiot". On the other hand, English may have the best term for those who believe one can get along in life with only generic competences: management consultant.

In defining the competences it wishes to give its graduates, higher education needs to find a reasonable balance between subject-specific and generic competences; it must avoid the Scylla of *Fachidioten* and the Charybdis of management consultants. Finding the proper balance requires continual reflection. I believe our higher education institutions are excellent at training highly competent subject specialists with a detailed understanding of specific academic fields. I am less sure we are equally good at educating intellectuals, by which I mean graduates with a good general culture and the ability to put their own academic discipline into a broader context, able to assess advantages and disadvantages in terms of their own discipline, the effects on broader societal goals and in a longer-term perspective, and also able to take account of knowledge and understanding from several academic fields. Nevertheless, it is essential that our higher education institutions provide us with intellectuals as well as subject specialists. Higher education graduates need to be both, but it is essential that our broader society is able to value intellectuals. As the Canadian philosopher John Ralston Saul puts it:

> Of course, separating out elements in a complicated world is a valid intellectual activity. It must be done. But the capacity to see how the elements fit together is a completely different form of intelligence and is of equal if not greater importance. (Saul 2009: 37)

I would add that higher education must aim to enable its graduates to combine these two kinds of intelligence. The survival of our societies will depend on the ability to understand the elements and then put them together in a coherent whole. How else will we be able to meet the challenges of climate change and the need not only to live peacefully but to co-operate and interact constructively with our neighbours?

Another essential competence that higher education should convey is awareness of the limits of our knowledge and understanding. It is this awareness that drives research since, if we were omniscient, there would be no reason to explore further.

On the other hand, if we believe we know and understand everything, there is no reason to enter into dialogue with others in order to benefit from their wisdom. In this case, our purpose in talking to others would be limited to conveying our wisdom to them, and then we would engage in monologue rather than dialogue. As Ambrose Bierce reminds us in his usual laconic style, education is "that which discloses to the wise and disguises from the foolish their lack of understanding" (Bierce 1983: 105).

Competences for dialogue

The competences needed for dialogue are a mix of the subject-specific and the generic. Language proficiency is an obvious competence, since – as we have already mentioned – dialogue is impossible without a common language. It is equally important to be aware of the potential pitfalls of a common language, especially one that is spoken in several varieties, like English or Spanish, or is frequently used by non-native speakers who may transfer expressions and habits from their native languages to the languages used for international communication. To take a banal example, a Dutch, German or Scandinavian who asks you to come at "half ten" will expect you at 9.30 whereas a Scot or Irish person using the same expression will intend you to come at 10.30. An awareness of potential linguistic and cultural pitfalls in intercultural communication is important for all higher education graduates.

Beyond the ability to communicate, knowledge of foreign languages also serves to make us aware that ideas can be expressed in several different ways and that translations can sometimes be misleading. Translations are of course indispensable since nobody can know all languages, but there is a grain of truth in the Italian expression *traduttore – traditore*: translator – traitor. Germanic languages use varieties of "I am right" or "I have right" (*jeg har rett*), whereas Romance languages prefer to say that "I have reason" (*tengo razón* or *j'ai raison*). Several Slavic languages have masculine and feminine forms not only of common nouns but also of proper names, including family names, and Lithuanian – a Baltic rather than a Slavic language – even has separate forms denoting married or unmarried women. These forms arise from an age when divorce was unthinkable, but modern society challenges this linguistic convention and also the one that distinguishes unmarried from married for feminine forms only. The importance of distinguishing gender in Indo-European languages contrasts with Turkic languages, where grammatical gender is unknown for nouns and adjectives, and even for personal pronouns. The point is not that certain choices are better than others, so that a language that marks gender is more or less sophisticated than one that does not, but rather that getting acquainted with a language that makes choices different from the ones we have come to take for granted helps us see issues from different angles and question some of our own basic assumptions.

The Association of American Colleges and Universities provides an interesting summary not only of what the competences required for a "global world" may be but also of how the concepts have evolved, under the headline "remapping liberal education" (AAC&U 2007: 18):

	Liberal Education in the 20th Century	Liberal Education in the 21st Century
What	• an elite curriculum • nonvocational • an option for the fortunate	• a necessity for all students • essential for success in a global economy and for informed citizenship
Where	• liberal arts colleges or colleges of arts and sciences in larger institutions	• all schools, community colleges, colleges, and universities; across all fields of study (recommended)
How	• through studies in arts and sciences fields ("the major") and/or through general education in the initial years of college	• through studies across the entire educational continuum: school through college (recommended)

One of the key competences that higher education should provide may be summarised as multiperspectivity. This concept was developed by the Council of Europe in its programme on history teaching (Council of Europe 2001; Stradling 2001) but its validity is not restricted to history. All higher education graduates need the ability to analyse issues from different points of view. In history teaching, the point that no country or culture has developed in isolation from its neighbours and that others – neighbours or those further away – may legitimately hold dissenting views of the history of one's own country has been accepted in principle. Accepting this in practice sometimes proves difficult when the principle is applied to the more painful parts of history, of which no country is entirely devoid. It is much easier to flag one's heroes than one's villains. To take an example from this author's country of origin, it is much easier for a Norwegian to refer to Fridtjof Nansen, who was not only a natural scientist and Arctic explorer but also a diplomat and prominent in efforts by the League of Nations to help refugees in the aftermath of the First World War, than to Vidkun Quisling, one of Nansen's assistants in the League of Nations efforts but who then went on to become the archetypical traitor in the Second World War by collaborating with the Nazi occupation, to the extent that his name has become a common noun for 'traitor' in several languages.[12] That Norwegians are after all relatively open in discussing Quisling is possibly due to the fact that he is seen as representing an alien regime with little local support rather than as a home-grown phenomenon. Had he been a civil war leader in a divided nation, open discussion would be much more painful.

---

12. One resistance joke during the Second World War had Quisling arriving to visit Hitler and announcing himself to the guards by saying "I am Quisling", to which the guard replies: "Yes, I know, but what is your name?"

What is true for history is equally true for other areas of education and research. Literature, arts, social conditions and habits, values and religious views have benefited from external influences over the centuries, and it is difficult to think of a single thriving culture that has not received strong impulses from outside. It is equally difficult to think of a thriving culture that has not to some extent been selective about what it has adopted from the outside and that has not adapted outside impulses to its own circumstances. As has been said about the 17th century, during which European interaction with other parts of the world changed:

> With second contacts, the dynamic of encounter changes. Interaction becomes more sustained and likelier to be repeated. The effects they produce, however, are not simple to predict or understand. At times they induce a thorough transformation of everyday practices, an effect that Cuban writer Fernando Ortiz has called "transculturation". At other times they provoke resistance, violence, and a loss of identity. In the seventeenth century, most contacts generated effects that fall between these two extremes: selective adjustment, made through a process of mutual influence. Rather than complete trans-formation or deadly conflict, there was negotiation and borrowing; rather than triumph and loss, give and take; rather than the transformation of cultures, their interaction. It was a time when people had to adjust how they acted and thought in order to negotiate the cultural differences they encountered, to deflect unanticipated threats and respond cautiously to equally unexpected opportunities. (Brook 2009: 21)

Intercultural dialogue requires the ability to look at issues from several angles and to understand the reasons that may lead others to conclusions and values very different from our own. Understanding, however, does not necessarily mean acceptance, and intercultural dialogue is not a prescription for moral relativism.

The US journalist and author Sandra Mackey, who is intimately familiar with the Arab world, claims:

> "Understanding" is perhaps the most used and abused word in the realm of human relationships. Nevertheless, comprehending the experiences, values, psychological anchors, broken moorings, soaring pride, and debilitating fears of the "other" is where accommodation begins. (Mackey 2008: 255)

Saying that others may be right is not the same as saying all views are equally valid. There are such things as good and evil, and examples of both can be found in all cultures. Some values are absolute, and the Council of Europe points in particular to those enshrined in the European Convention on Human Rights. Competences for intercultural dialogue must therefore also include a thorough consideration of values. In this context, it may be useful to point out that, though the forms and manifestations of democracy evolve, its basic value remains. As underlined by the Council of Europe's Steering Committee on Higher Education and Research:

> Intercultural dialogue must be founded on a firm and well reflected set of values as well as on a willingness to consider the values of others and to reassess one's own convic-tions in the light of new and convincing evidence. Dialogue presupposes openness of mind in all partners, including the capacity to look at their own values and frame of reference with critical distance. These are also essential values and characteristics of higher education.

European higher education is based on the conviction that each human being has intrinsic value as an individual, and also that each human being is inherently responsible for the development and well being of other human beings, of human society as a whole and of the environment on which we depend for our survival.

The CDESR is committed to the Council of Europe's key values human rights, democracy and the rule of law. In this context, the CDESR sees the main contribution of higher education – as well as the main contribution of other areas of education – as helping develop, maintain and transmit to new generations the democratic culture which is indispensable to making democratic institutions and democratic laws work and to make democratic societies sustainable. (CDESR 2006)

Commitment to intercultural dialogue should start at home, but it should not end there. We should express concern when European countries attempt to ban minarets but we should also express concern when non-European countries ban churches or synagogues. We should protest when any society obliges its members to profess certain beliefs as well as when it prevents them from doing so.

The rationale for education

As someone who has spent decades in education, first as a student and then as a policy maker, I will be among the last persons to deny the intrinsic merit of education. Yet intrinsic merit is insufficient justification in an age where competition for public attention and public funding is fierce. Education is important because it provides our societies with the competences we need to survive and because it provides individuals with the competences they need to thrive.

Education is important because it opens minds, because it develops awareness of values as well as of different approaches to life, because it teaches us not to take things for granted or accept them at face value and because it teaches us the importance of time: what may be beneficial in the short run may be disastrous in the long run. Higher education, in particular, must develop knowledge, understanding, attitudes and the ability to act, all at the same time. Higher education must educate the whole person – and in our age and time, this cannot be done without opening the horizon of each individual to the world that lies beyond our immediate neighbourhood.

We still have some way to go before our higher education institutions fulfil this role and we may have even further to go before our political decision makers and our societies at large accept this as the true role of education. As John Ralston Saul says:

I find our education is increasingly one aimed at training loyal employees, even though the state and the corporations are increasingly disloyal. What we should be doing is quite different. It turns on our ability to rethink our education and our public expectations so that we create a non-employee, non-loyal space for citizenship. After all, a citizen is by definition loyal to the state because it belongs to her or him. That is what frees the citizen to be boisterous, outspoken, cantankerous and, all in all, by corporatist standards, disloyal. This is the key to the success of our democracy. (Saul 2009: 318)

Higher education must aim to develop the competences that will help make Earth – not just our own country – the kind of place in which we would like our children and grandchildren to live (Tironi 2005). It must engage in the debate on what the kind of society we would like to live in should look like and how we can make it a reality. We need societies that are sustainable environmentally and politically, socially and ethically, economically and culturally. Higher education must provide a workable and inspiring vision of the contribution of higher education to a society based on democracy, human rights and the rule of law, and proficient in intercultural dialogue; a society coherent enough to be strong, and diverse enough to be interesting; a society unafraid to engage with the broader world. Neither our curiosity nor our responsibility stops at our national borders, and even if we were tempted to withdraw and leave the rest of the world to others, we would not live long in the illusion that what happens elsewhere is not important to us.

Ultimately, higher education must inspire and prepare us to do well, but also to do good. We cannot do that unless we are able and willing to engage in intercultural dialogue.

References

AAC&U [Association of American Colleges and Universities] (2007): *College Learning for the New Global Century*, Washington, DC: AAC&U.

Bergan, Sjur (2005): "Higher education as a 'public good and a public responsibility': what does it mean?" in Luc Weber and Sjur Bergan (eds), *The Public Responsibility for Higher Education and Research*, Higher Education Series No. 2, Strasbourg: Council of Europe, pp. 13-28.

Bergan, Sjur (2007): *Qualifications. Introduction to a Concept*, Higher Education Series No. 6, Strasbourg: Council of Europe.

Bergan, Sjur (2009): Introductory statement at the ministerial meeting of the Bologna Process, Leuven/Louvain-la-Neuve, 28-29 April 2009, available at www.ond.vlaanderen.be/hogeronderwijs/bologna/conference/documents/CoE_address_Leuven_280409.pdf, accessed on 26 December 2009.

Bergan, Sjur and Jean-Philippe Restoueix (eds) (2009): *Intercultural Dialogue on Campus*, Higher Education Series No. 11, Strasbourg: Council of Europe.

Bierce, Ambrose (1983 [1911]): *The Enlarged Devil's Dictionary*, ed. E.J. Hopkins, London: Penguin American Library.

Brook, Timothy (2009): *Vermeer's Hat. The Seventeenth Century and the Dawn of the Global World*, London: Profile Books.

CDESR [Council of Europe's Steering Committee on Higher Education and Research] (2006): Statement on the Contribution of Higher Education to Intercultural Dialogue.

Council of Europe (2001) Recommendation Rec(2001)15 of the Committee of Ministers to member states on history teaching in twenty-first century Europe.

Council of Europe (2007): Recommendation Rec(2007)6 by the Committee of Ministers to member states on the public responsibility for higher education and research.

Council of Europe (2008): *Living Together as Equals in Dignity*, White Paper on Intercultural Dialogue, Strasbourg: Council of Europe.

Diamond, Jared (2006): *Collapse. How Societies Choose to Fail or Survive*, London: Penguin.

González, Julia and Robert Wagenaar (eds) (2005): *TUNING Educational Structures in Europe. Universities' Contribution to the Bologna Process. Final Report of Pilot Project Phase 2*, Bilbao and Groningen: Publicaciones de la Universidad de Deusto.

Gotto, Klaus and Konrad Repgen (eds) (1990): *Die Katholiken und das Dritte Reich*, Mainz: Matthias-Grünewald-Verlag.

Hammerstein, Notker (1991): "Universities and democratisation: an historical perspective. The case of Germany", paper written for the Council of Europe conference on Universities and Democratisation, Warsaw, 29-31 January 1992, reference DECS-HE 91/97.

Huneeus, Carlos (2001): *El régimen de Pinochet*, Santiago de Chile: Editorial Sudamericana.

Mackey, S. (2008): *Mirror of the Arab World. Lebanon in Conflict*, New York: W.W. Norton.

Mählert, Ulrich (1999): *Kleine Geschichte der DDR*, München: Verlag C.H. Beck.

Mann, Charles C. (2006): *1491. The Americas Before Columbus*, London: Granta Books.

Obama, Barack (2009): Speech in acceptance of the Nobel Peace Prize, available at www.nytimes.com/2009/12/11/world/europe/11prexy.text.html (accessed on 26 December 2009).

Plantan, Frank (2004): "The university as site of citizenship", in Sjur Bergan (ed.), *The University as Res Publica*, Strasbourg: Council of Europe, pp. 83-128.

Ridder-Symoens, Hilde de (2007): "The intellectual heritage of ancient universities in Europe", in Nuria Sanz and Sjur Bergan (eds), *The Heritage of European Universities*, 2nd edn, Higher Education Series No. 7, Strasbourg: Council of Europe.

Saul, John Ralston (2009): *A Fair Country. Telling Truths about Canada*, Toronto, Ontario: Penguin Canada.

Stradling, Robert (2001): *Teaching 20th-century European History*, Strasbourg: Council of Europe.

Tironi, Eugenio (2005): *El sueño chileno. Comunidad, familia y nación en el Bicentenario*, Santiago de Chile: Taurus.

Torgal, Luis Reis (1999): *A Universidade e o Estado Novo*, Coimbra: Livreria Minerva Editorial.

Zernike, Kate; "Making college 'relevant'", online version of the *New York Times*, published 29 December 2009, www.nytimes.com/2010/01/03/education/edlife/03careerism-t.html?pagewanted=1&em (accessed 4 January 2010).

Intercultural competence in higher education and intercultural dialogue

Darla K. Deardorff

Framework and definition

Intercultural competence is an oft-discussed term in the field of international education and beyond, but rarely understood or defined. This term is currently a hot topic within higher education in the United States and other countries, with questions being asked about how post-secondary institutions can help students develop intercultural competence. If educators are to be successful in helping students become more interculturally competent, it is important to explore definitions and frameworks of intercultural competence, some of which have been debated and discussed for several decades (i.e. Baxter Magolda 2000; Bennett 1993; Byram 1997; Chen and Starosta 1996; Collier 1989; Dinges 1983; Gudykunst 1994; Gundling 2003; Hammer et al. 1978; Hampden-Turner and Trompenaars 2000; Hanvey 1976; Hofstede 1997; Hoopes 1979; Koester and Olebe 1989; Magala 2005; Miyahara 1992; Paige 1993; Pedersen 1994; Ruben 1976; Spitzberg 1989; Triandis 1994; Yum 1994; Zhong 1998; see Spitzberg and Changnon, 2009, for a more thorough discussion). These frameworks and definitions can be used to guide higher education efforts to help students not only get along better with those from other cultures, but work together on the pressing global challenges that confront humankind in the 21st century.

A national study in the United States (Deardorff 2006, 2009) provides such a research-based framework, discussed further in this article. The consensus among leading intercultural experts in this study was that intercultural competence may be defined as "effective and appropriate behaviour and communication in intercultural situations". The elements they agreed on were categorised into attitudes, knowledge, skills and internal or external outcomes; each is explored briefly below. We can place these five elements in a visual framework, which can be applied in various programmes and contexts to guide and assess intercultural competence development.

Attitudes

Based on this study, key attitudes emerged, those of respect, openness, curiosity and discovery. Openness, curiosity and discovery imply willingness to risk and to move beyond one's comfort zone. In communicating respect to others, it is important to demonstrate that others are valued. This begins through showing interest in others – in their families and their cultures – and in simply listening attentively. These attitudes are foundational to the further development of knowledge and skills needed for intercultural competence, as well as crucial for successful intercultural dialogue.

One way to move others towards these requisite attitudes is by challenging assumptions. (Later in this article, we will explore a tool that can do just that.)

Knowledge

In the United States, there is some debate about the "global knowledge" needed by today's college graduates. What knowledge is needed for intercultural competence? Intercultural experts agreed on the following: cultural self-awareness (meaning the ways in which one's culture has influenced one's identity and worldview), culture-specific knowledge,[13] deep cultural knowledge (including understanding other world views) and sociolinguistic awareness. All the intercultural scholars agreed on the importance of understanding the world from others' perspectives.

Skills

The skills that emerged from this study were ones that addressed the acquisition and processing of knowledge: observation, listening, evaluating, analysing, interpreting and relating. This agrees with an observation by the former president of Harvard University that institutions need to teach students to "think interculturally" (Bok 2006).

Internal outcomes

The attitudes, knowledge and skills ideally lead to an internal outcome that consists of flexibility, adaptability, an ethnorelative perspective and empathy. These occur within the individual as a result of the acquired attitudes, knowledge and skills necessary for intercultural competence. Ultimately, empathy plays a crucial role in reaching the desired external outcomes – with empathy focusing more on "the platinum role" of doing to others what they wish to have done to them. Once empathy is developed, individuals are able to see from others' perspectives and to respond to them according to the way in which the other person desires to be treated. Individuals may reach these internal outcomes with varying degrees of success.

External outcomes

The summation of the attitudes, knowledge and skills, and the internal outcomes, is demonstrated through the behaviour and communication of the individual. How effective and appropriate is this person in intercultural interactions? This behaviour and communication become the visible external outcomes of intercultural competence. This then becomes the agreed definition of the intercultural scholars, that intercultural competence is effective and appropriate behaviour and communication in intercultural situations. However, it is important to understand that this definition is predicated on the elements highlighted in this essay. It is also important to understand the implications of "effective" and "appropriate" behaviour and communication. Effectiveness

---

13. There are many definitions of the word "culture." Here, "culture" is defined as values, beliefs and norms held by a group of people. Culture shapes how individuals communicate and behave, that is, how they interact with others.

can be determined by the interlocutor but the appropriateness can only be determined by the other person – with appropriateness being directly related to cultural sensitivity and the adherence to cultural norms of that person.

These five overall elements can be visualised through the model of intercultural competence shown in Figure 1, thereby providing a framework to further guide efforts in developing intercultural competence in our students and in promoting successful intercultural dialogue.

Figure 1: Process model of intercultural competence (© Dr Darla K. Deardorff)

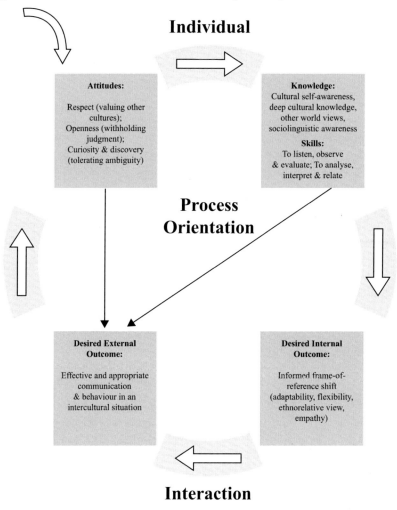

Source: Deardorff 2006, 2009
Note: Begin with attitudes; move from individual level (attitudes) to interaction level (outcomes)
Degree of intercultural competence depends on acquired degree of attitudes, knowledge/comprehension and skills

The intercultural competence framework

This framework illustrates that it is possible for an individual to have the requisite attitudes and be minimally effective and appropriate in behaviour and/or communication, even without further knowledge or skills. Adding the necessary knowledge and skills may ensure that an individual is more effective and appropriate in his or her intercultural interactions. With added flexibility, adaptability and empathy, one can be even more effective and appropriate in intercultural interactions, thus demonstrating degrees (or levels) of intercultural competence.

This framework also illustrates that intercultural competence is a process – a lifelong process – and there is no one point at which an individual becomes completely interculturally competent. Thus, it is important to pay as much attention to developing it – how one acquires the necessary knowledge, skills, and attitudes – as to intercultural competence itself.

It is interesting to note that intercultural scholars in the United States could not agree on the role of language in intercultural competence development, noting that language alone does not ensure one's competence in a culture. Thus, language is a necessary but not sufficient skill for intercultural competence. Language, however, can be a notable vehicle through which to understand others' worldviews.

Unfortunately, intercultural competence does not just happen for most people; it must be intentionally addressed and developed (Kohls 1996; Storti 1997). Addressing intercultural competence development at post-secondary level – for both domestic and international students – is essential in graduating global-ready students. Having a framework of intercultural competence such as the one discussed in this article can help guide efforts to ensure a more comprehensive, integrated approach – within post-secondary education and beyond.

A key limitation of this model is that it represents a US-centred perspective of intercultural competence, given that most of the scholars involved in the study were from the United States. However, since the only element agreed upon by all the scholars in the study was the importance of being able to see from multiple cultural perspectives, the next question must be: What are other cultural perspectives on intercultural competence?

In reviewing literature from other countries and other parts of the world on various cultural perspectives on intercultural competence (Bordas 2007; Chen and An 2009; Imahori and Lanigan 1989; Kim 2002; Manian and Naidu 2009; Mato 2009; Medina and Sinnigen 2009; Miike 2003; Moosmueller and Schoenhuth 2009; Nwosu 2009; Nydell 2005; Taylor and Nwosu 2001; Ting-Toomey 2009; Zaharna 2009; see also Deardorff 2010, a report written for UNESCO, *A comparative analysis and global perspective of regional studies on intercultural competence*), several overarching themes emerge. Those include the importance of relationship in intercultural competence, the necessity of considering historical, social and economic contexts (especially in immigrant societies and those with a history of colonialism), the crucial role that identity plays in intercultural competence and the need for cultural humility, which consists of both a strong sense of cultural self-awareness and recognition of multiple viewpoints, coupled with respect for and truly valuing others from diverse backgrounds.

Starting point of intercultural competence – attitudes

As noted, attitudes of openness, respect and curiosity are essential to the further development of intercultural competence. In order to change existing attitudes that may hinder its development, the assumptions underlying attitudes must be challenged. One of the key skills that emerged from this study was the importance of observation, coupled with the skills of analysis and evaluation. A tool that addresses these essential elements of intercultural competence is called the OSEE Tool (see Figure 2), which not only allows students to challenge their assumptions but also moves them to explore other perspectives, through observation and analysis. Based on the scientific method, this tool has been used in cross-cultural training programmes and courses, as well as in pre-departure programmes.

Figure 2: The OSEE Tool

O – Observe what is happening
S – State objectively what is happening
E – Explore different explanations for what is happening
E – Evaluate which explanation is the most likely one
(Deardorff and Deardorff 2000)

OSEE starts with the basics of observation – and listening – of really being aware of what is occurring in intercultural situations. As noted in the intercultural competence model discussed in this article, this is an essential skill and a key starting point. Careful cultural observations require both patience and reflection. In observing and listening in intercultural situations, it is important not only to be aware of one's physical surroundings but to pay attention to people's verbal and nonverbal communication during the interactions.

The next step is to state as objectively as possible what is happening – this is much more difficult than it sounds and there are a variety of activities that can be used to help students practise the development of objective statements, including viewing brief film clips and writing about them. Objective statements should be free from judgment or cultural assumptions, and based entirely on what was actually observed during the interaction.

Once objective statements have been made, the next step is to explore different explanations for what could be happening, which addresses the need to see from others' perspectives. It also allows one to begin to move beyond initial assumptions that may have inadvertently been made. Different explanations could include personal and cultural explanations of what is happening, the latter of which necessitates the need to know culture-specific information, another aspect of the intercultural competence model.

The last step – that of evaluation – may be the most difficult since it is often challenging to know which explanation(s) would be the most likely one(s) for the situation that is occurring. For example, if someone is not making eye contact, the different explanations from a US perspective for this could include that the person is bored, that the person is trying to hide something or lie, that the person is blind, that the person comes from another culture in which direct eye contact is considered rude and so on. There are a number of ways to evaluate the likely explanation(s), including collecting further information through conversations with the person involved or with others, through actual research or through further observation. When these steps are followed, one is able to view behaviours more objectively, thus challenging initial assumptions.

Implications of intercultural competence framework

What are the implications of this intercultural competence framework for educators? Since intercultural competence is not a naturally occurring phenomenon, educators must be intentional about addressing this at post-secondary institutions, through curricular and co-curricular efforts. One key element of intercultural competence to address in courses is that of other worldviews. This means ensuring that multiple perspectives are addressed in courses (from the sciences to the humanities), including through lectures, courses, texts and so on. Another implication for educators is making sure instructors themselves understand the concept of intercultural competence and incorporate interculturally competent practices into their teaching. This becomes especially important in increasingly diverse classrooms, brought about by such external forces as the Bologna Process.

What does it mean to be an interculturally competent instructor? (See the appendix to this article for a set of reflection questions, based on the Deardorff model, that can be used by instructors for self-reflection; see also Clayton 2003; Brown and Kysilka 2002). This question also has implications for how post-secondary institutions are preparing primary and secondary teachers – are these teachers being adequately prepared to teach students from diverse backgrounds? Are intercultural competence concepts infused throughout the teacher education curriculum? Are courses offered specifically on culturally responsive teaching? It is imperative that institutions of higher education ensure the careful and thorough preparation of teachers within an intercultural context (Heyl and McCarthy 2003; Cushner and Mahon 2009).

In utilising such a framework, these intentional efforts can be included in a more comprehensive, integrated approach to intercultural competence development instead of a random, ad hoc approach that currently occurs at many post-secondary institutions. It is also important that assessment of such efforts occurs – both to improve what is being done to develop intercultural competence among students and also to provide meaningful feedback to students themselves that could aid them in developing their own intercultural competence. Intercultural competence assessment is complex but possible, and absolutely essential in moving higher education towards a greater understanding of intercultural competence development. Such assessment needs to involve a multi-method, multi-perspective approach, given the complexity of the nature of intercultural competence. (For more on assessing intercultural competence, see Deardorff 2009.)

Conclusion

Reflection is an important part of intercultural competence development. In reflecting upon the intercultural competence framework discussed in this article, several questions arise. First, since the model presented here is primarily a US-based view of intercultural competence, what does intercultural competence "look like" from other cultural perspectives? How interculturally competent are educators themselves and what can be done to develop their competence further? How can the process of intercultural competence development be integrated into courses and programmes? How will assessment of intercultural competence be addressed at post-secondary institutions as an essential learning outcome?

Reflecting on these questions will lead ultimately to the necessity of building stronger relationships with those from other cultural backgrounds. For it is in the deepening of relationships that understanding is achieved (Wheatley 2002). Seeking to understand each other better and to interact more successfully – and peacefully – with each other are essential as we address pressing human needs together. Our very survival as humans depends on this. In the words of Nobel Peace Laureate Martin Luther King Jr, "We must learn to live together as brothers or perish together as fools." Higher education plays an important role in helping us learn to live together in the 21st century through the development of intercultural competence.

Appendix: Interculturally competent teaching – a reflection guide[14]

Attitudes

– How truly open am I to those from different cultural, socio-economic, and religious backgrounds?

– Do I make quick assumptions about a student? Do I pre-judge students or situations or do I withhold judgment while I explore the multifacets of the situation?

– Do I measure a student's behaviour based on my own culturally-conditioned expectations or do I try to understand a student's behaviour based on his or her own culturally-conditioned background?

– Do I value those from different backgrounds? How do I demonstrate that I value others, even when I may disagree with their beliefs and opinions?

14. Reflection questions based on the Deardorff Intercultural Competence models, 2006, 2009.

93

- Am I eager to learn about different cultures and specifically, am I eager to learn about my students' backgrounds and experiences? Do I make an effort to learn more?

Knowledge

- Can I describe my own cultural conditioning? For example, what cultural values affect how I behave and communicate with others? What are some of my core beliefs and how have they been culturally influenced?
- How would I describe my worldview?
- How would I describe some of my students' worldviews? How might these differ from the ways in which I see the world?
- How much do I know about my students' cultural backgrounds? What information am I missing and how can I get that information?
- How can I incorporate my students' worldviews into my course materials?
- What worldviews are demonstrated through the course materials I currently use? How can I enhance those materials so that other worldviews are represented?

Skills

- How much do I really listen to my students?
- Do I engage in active observation in my classroom, paying attention to subtle nuances and dynamics among my students? In my interactions with my students?
- Do I engage in active reflection of my teaching practice and of my interactions with those from different cultural backgrounds? Do I seek to understand not only why something occurred but what lessons I learned from the situation?
- Do I know how to evaluate interactions and situations through an intercultural lens, seeking to understand underlying cultural explanations for what occurred?

Internal outcomes (adaptability, flexibility, etc.)

- Do I know how students want to be treated or do I assume they want to be treated by my cultural standards?
- Am I able to adapt my behaviour and communication style to accommodate students from different culturally-conditioned communication styles?
- Am I able to be flexible in responding to students' learning needs, seeking to understand those needs from their cultural perspectives?
- Can I easily view knowledge, cultural artefacts or a situation or issue from multiple perspectives?

External outcomes (communication, behaviour)

- How culturally appropriate have I been in my interactions with my students? In my teaching? How would my students answer this question?

- Was I able to meet my goals in an appropriate and effective manner?
- What could I do differently in the future to be more appropriate and effective in my communication and behaviour, both in interpersonal interactions and in my teaching?

General reflection questions

In reflecting on how teachers can help development students' intercultural competence, the following questions arise:

- How can teachers specifically incorporate students' cultural perspectives into the course?
- How can teachers allow space for students to reflect on their own intercultural competence development?
- What role can teachers play in mentoring students in this development?
- What role can others in the broader community play in developing students' intercultural competence?
- What role can technology play in students' development of knowledge and skills in relating to those from different backgrounds?
- How can teachers help students demonstrate respect (in culturally appropriate ways) and openness to other ways of viewing the world?
- How can students work together effectively and appropriately in small groups during the course?
- How can teachers move beyond "objective culture" in the classroom to pushing students to learn more about "subjective culture," which affects the ways students actually interact with others?
- How can teachers help students develop an "intercultural lens" through which to view the world?

References

Baxter Magolda, M.B. (ed.) (2000): *Teaching to promote intellectual and personal maturity: Incorporating students' worldviews and identities into the learning process*. San Francisco: Jossey-Bass.

Bennett, M.J. (1993): "Towards ethnorelativism: a developmental model of intercultural sensitivity", in R.M. Paige (ed.), *Education for the intercultural experience*, 2nd edn. Yarmouth, ME: Intercultural Press, pp. 21-71.

Bok, D. (2006): *Our underachieving colleges: A candid look at how much students learn and why they should be learning more*. Princeton, NJ: Princeton University Press.

Bordas, J. (2007*): Salsa, soul and spirit: Leadership for a multicultural age*. San Francisco: Berrett-Koehler.

Brown, S. and Kysilka, M. (2002): *Applying multicultural and global concepts in the classroom and beyond.* Boston: Allyn & Bacon.

Byram, M. (1997): *Teaching and assessing intercultural communicative competence.* Clevedon, UK: Multilingual Matters.

Chen, G.M. and An, R. (2009): "A Chinese model of intercultural leadership competence", in D.K. Deardorff (ed.), *The SAGE Handbook of Intercultural Competence*, Thousand Oaks, CA: Sage.

Chen, G.M., and Starosta, W.J. (1996): "Intercultural communication competence: a synthesis". *Communication Yearbook 19*, London: Routledge, pp. 353-383.

Clayton, J. (2003): *One classroom, many worlds: Teaching and learning in the cross-cultural classroom.* Portsmouth, NH: Heinemann.

Collier, M.J. (1989): "Cultural and intercultural communication competence: current approaches and directions for future research", *International Journal of Intercultural Relations*, Vol. 13, pp. 287-302.

Cushner, K. (2009): "The role of study abroad in preparing globally responsible teachers", in R. Lewin (ed.), *The handbook of practice and research in study abroad.* New York: Routledge.

Cushner, K. and Mahon, J. (2009): "Developing the intercultural competence of educators and their students: creating blueprints", in D.K. Deardorff (ed.), *The SAGE Handbook of Intercultural Competence*, Thousand Oaks, CA: Sage.

Deardorff, D.K. (2006) "The identification and assessment of intercultural competence as a student outcome of internationalization at institutions of higher education in the United States". *Journal of Studies in International Education*, Fall 2006, pp. 241-266.

Deardorff, D.K. (2008): "Intercultural competence: a definition, model and implications for education abroad", in V. Savicki (ed.), *Developing Intercultural Competence and Transformation: Theory, Research, and Application in International Education.* Sterling, VA: Stylus.

Deardorff, D.K. (ed.) (2009): *The SAGE Handbook of Intercultural Competence.* Thousand Oaks, CA: Sage.

Deardorff, D.K. (2010): *A comparative analysis and global perspective of regional studies on intercultural competence.* Paris: UNESCO.

Deardorff, D.K. and Deardorff, D.L. (2000): *OSEE Tool.* Presentation at North Carolina State University, Raleigh, NC.

Dinges, N. (1983): "Intercultural competence", in D. Landis and R.W. Brislin (eds), *Handbook of intercultural training, volume 1: Issues in theory and design*, New York: Pergamon Press, pp. 176-202.

96

Gudykunst, W.B. (1994): *Bridging differences: Effective intergroup communication*, 2nd edn, London: Sage.

Gundling, E. (2003): *Working GlobeSmart: 12 people skills for doing business across borders*, Palo Alto, CA: Davies-Black.

Hadley, A.O. (2001): *Teaching language in context*, 3rd edn, Boston, MA: Heinle & Heinle.

Hammer, M.R., Gudykunst, W.B., and Wiseman, R.L. (1978): "Dimensions of inter-cultural effectiveness: an exploratory study". *International Journal of Intercultural Relations*, Vol. 2, pp. 382-393.

Hampden-Turner, C.M., and Trompenaars, F. (2000): *Building cross-cultural competence: How to create wealth from conflicting values*, New Haven, CT: Yale University Press.

Hanvey, R.G. (1976): *An attainable global perspective*. New York: Global Perspectives in Education.

Heyl, J. and McCarthy, J. (2003): "International education and teacher preparation in the U.S.," paper presented at Global Challenges and U.S. Higher Education: National Needs and Policy Implications, Duke University, Durham, NC, 24 January 2003.

Hofstede, G. (1997): *Cultures and organizations: Software of the mind*. New York: McGraw-Hill.

Hoopes, D.S. (1979): "Intercultural communication concepts and the psychology of intercultural experience", in M. Pusch (ed.), *Multicultural education: A cross-cultural training approach*, Yarmouth, ME: Intercultural Press, pp. 9-38.

Imahori, T.T., and Lanigan, M. (1989): "Relational model of intercultural commu-nication competence", *International Journal of Intercultural Relations*, Vol. 13, pp. 269-286.

Kim, M.-S. (2002): *Non-Western perspectives on human communication: Implications for theory and practice*, Thousand Oaks, CA: Sage.

Koester, J., and Olebe, M. (1989): "The behavioral assessment scale for intercul-tural communication effectives", *International Journal of Intercultural Relations*, Vol. 12, pp. 233-246.

Kohls, L.R. (1996): *Survival kit for overseas living*, 3rd edn, Yarmouth, ME: Intercultural Press.

Magala, S. (2005): *Cross-cultural competence*, London: Routledge.

Manian, R. and Naidu, S. (2009): "India: A cross-cultural overview of intercul-tural competence", in D.K. Deardorff (ed.), *The SAGE Handbook of Intercultural Competence*, Thousand Oaks, CA: Sage.

Mato, D. (2009): "Contextos, conceptualizaciones y usos de la idea de interculturalidad", in Aguilar, Miguel et al., *Pensar lo contemporáneo*, Barcelona-México: Rubi-Anthropos.

Medina-López-Portillo, A. and Sinnigen, J. (2009): "Interculturality versus intercultural competencies in Latin America", in D.K. Deardorff (ed.), *The SAGE Handbook of Intercultural Competence*, Thousand Oaks, CA: Sage.

Miike, Y. (2003): "Beyond Eurocentrism in the intercultural field: searching for an Asiacentric paradigm", in W. Starosta and G.-M. Chen (eds), *Ferment in the intercultural field: Axiology/value/praxis*, Thousand Oaks, CA: Sage, pp. 243-276.

Miyahara, A. (1992): "Cross-cultural views on interpersonal communication competence: a preliminary study proposal", *Human Communication Studies (Journal of the Communication Association of Japan)*, Vol. 20, pp. 129-143.

Moosmueller, A. and Schoenhuth, M. (2009): "Intercultural competence in German discourse", in D.K. Deardorff (ed.), *The SAGE Handbook of Intercultural Competence*, Thousand Oaks, CA: Sage.

Nwosu, P.U. (2009): "Search for coexistence: the Okonko ethos", *Benue Valley Journal of Humanities*, Benue State University, Makurdi.

Nydell, M.K. (2005): *Understanding Arabs: A guide for Westerners*. Yarmouth, ME: Intercultural Press.

Paige, R.M. (ed.) (1993): *Education for the intercultural experience*. Yarmouth, ME: Intercultural Press.

Pedersen, P. (1994): *A handbook for developing multicultural awareness*, 2nd edn, Alexandria, VA: American Counseling Association.

Ruben, B.D. (1976): "Assessing communication competence for intercultural communication adaptation", *Group and Organization Studies*, Vol. 1, No. 3, pp. 334-354.

Spitzberg, B.H. (1989): "Issues in the development of a theory of interpersonal competence in the intercultural context", *International Journal of Intercultural Relations*, Vol. 13, No. 3, pp. 241-268.

Spitzberg, B.and Changnon, G. (2009): "Conceptualizing intercultural competence", in D.K. Deardorff (ed.), *The SAGE Handbook of Intercultural Competence*. Thousand Oaks, CA: Sage.

Storti, C. (1997): *Culture matters: The Peace Corps cross-cultural workbook*. Washington, DC: Peace Corps Information Collection and Exchange.

Taylor, D. and Nwosu, P. (2001): "Afrocentric empiricism: A model for communication research in Africa", in V. Milhourse, M. Asante, and P. Nwosu (eds), *Transcultural realities: Interdisciplinary perspectives on cross-cultural relations*, Thousand Oaks, CA: Sage, pp. 299-311.

Ting-Toomey, S. (2009): "Intercultural conflict competence as a facet of intercultural competence development: multiple conceptual approaches", in D.K. Deardorff (ed.), *The SAGE Handbook of Intercultural Competence*, Thousand Oaks, CA: Sage.

Triandis, H. (1994): *Culture and social behavior.* New York: McGraw-Hill.

Wheatley, M. (2002): *Turning to each other: Simple conversations to restore hope to the future.* San Francisco: Berrett-Koehler.

Yum, J.O. (1994): "The impact of Confucianism on interpersonal relationships and communication patterns in East Asia", in L.A. Samovar and R.E. Porter (eds), *Intercultural communication: A reader*, Belmont, CA: Wadsworth, pp. 75-86.

Zaharna, R. (2009): "An associative approach to intercultural communication competence in the Arab world", in D.K. Deardorff (ed.), *The SAGE Handbook of Intercultural Competence*, Thousand Oaks, CA: Sage.

Zhong, M. (1998): "Perceived intercultural communication competence in cross-cultural interactions between Chinese and Americans", *Critical Studies*, Vol. 12, pp. 161-179.

Students and intercultural dialogue: more than just talk

Olav Øye and Andrea Blättler

For university leadership and staff, internationalisation has been seen as a way to enrich academic debates, encourage diversity in the student population or simply to make more money. Although the European Students' Union (ESU) strongly rejects the idea of international students being part of a scheme merely to increase institutional income, we support student mobility which has an academic purpose and which expands the cultural horizons of students.

The main aim of this article is to present a student's view of intercultural dialogue at higher education institutions and to consider how intercultural dialogue differs from student and staff mobility. At the end of the article, we discuss how both political and non-political organisations allow students to engage in discussions on theory as well as substance and how this contributes heavily to intercultural dialogue in the everyday life of the institution.

While not forgetting that the "average student" is an increasingly irrelevant concept in terms of age, we can look at higher education as a space where young people meet other young people with a significantly different cultural background. While societies in general are becoming more and more diverse, and many children already grow up in a multicultural environment, higher education is still an arena where many people for the first time get the experience of interacting with individuals of other cultural backgrounds.

Students take their perceptions with them when they go home and talk to their families and their social circle in general, just as much as in discussions with their friends and other people they meet at university. The behaviour and attitudes we learn during our studies are the ones that we are likely to keep throughout our professional and private lives. It is for this reason that higher education institutions have a strong responsibility to function as a place where students learn how to interact with other students, regardless of origin, age or socio-economic background. In the academic quest, one of the most important matters is how to ask questions and how to strive to answer them – higher education institutions must thus be a place where dialogue is not just a possibility but rather a requirement.

Campus life

Conversation starters

For most students, intercultural dialogue often means occasional chats with one or more of the international students of their university or college. Talk might revolve around practicalities to begin with, and the initial chats are probably rather superficial. If the students meet more often, they are likely to engage in discussions about curricula, the professor's way of teaching, their programme's impact on themselves and its importance in society as a whole. When discussions start moving from trivialities to matters that require more understanding and reflection, it is easier to see the added value of internationalisation. Students (and teachers too) start seeing their own views and reality from a different perspective, acquire a skill that is increasingly needed by world citizens and, through international interaction, begin to grasp the concept of globalisation.

In 2010, it is easier than ever to write an e-mail or a Facebook message or make a Skype call to a friend or colleague in close or faraway corners of the world. While these are very good channels for keeping in touch, a good experience with face-to-face intercultural discussions on campus often lays the foundation for continuing discussions and meetings later in life.

Mobility as a tool to enhance intercultural dialogue?

Student mobility increases intercultural dialogue, even if the impact varies greatly from place to place. ESU has successfully pushed for a benchmark of 20% mobile students in the European Higher Education Area by 2020, and the target has been adopted by the Bologna Process (Bologna Process 2009). If this target is reached, there is hope that it will at least lay the basis for vivid intercultural dialogue on campus. Naturally however, this Bologna effort for more interculturalism in higher education institutions is limited. On the one hand, the main aim is clearly more mobility within Europe. On the other hand, ESU believes it is vital that support for mobility is guaranteed in order not to create movement only among European students with high socio-economic background. And last but certainly not least, the fact that a significant number of students crosses a border does not per se bring intercultural dialogue into an institution.

It is rather difficult to measure the exact benefits of more student exchanges. It is nevertheless a fair assumption that more and better arenas for intercultural meetings breed more dialogue. But this cannot be taken for granted, no matter what the percentage of foreign students on campus.

One of the discussions at the Council of Europe seminar in March 2008, on intercultural dialogue on the university campus, concerned whether student or staff mobility and language learning more or less by themselves create intercultural dialogue. The general rapporteur of that event argued convincingly that this in itself is not sufficient (Wächter 2009).

Language and integration

Before they leave home, students going abroad should have the opportunity of taking language courses. But they should also be made aware of what it means to be part of the student society and the wider society they are entering. Language courses should include this information or be complemented by separate courses on the cultural and historical situation of the country or region they are studying in.

English is widely used as an academic *lingua franca*, but international students should also be helped to attend modules taught in the predominant language of their host country and have the opportunity to take a language course in the language(s) used by local people. This not only enables students to engage in basic conversation and follow the modules in this language as well as possible; it also nurtures curiosity, opens possibilities of understanding other written and spoken communication inside and outside their studies, on and off campus, and stimulates real intercultural dialogue in student society. This benefits both mobile and local students.

It is important that language courses are provided before and at the beginning of a stay abroad, but language tuition should be available throughout the study period abroad and it should be seen as an essential element of this experience. In order to avoid barriers to mobility and in order to promote successful integration, language tuition in all periods of study must be free of charge.

Dialogue within one's own group and with the rest of campus and society

When students are enabled to study abroad for a semester or for a whole degree, higher education institutions need to make sure that the visiting students are able to meet not just other international students, or even students from their own country. The role of international students on campus is connected to the contribution of student mobility to intercultural dialogue in the wider society. This is particularly important because the social composition of mobile students today is mostly representative of students with relatively high socio-economic backgrounds. If international students only meet other international students, they will not get a hands-on experience of the discussions that take place in the actual local community they are living in.

We often see that international students are far from fully integrated even into the student life on campus. Foreign students often end up in dormitories that are separated from the local students. Better integration of foreign students into campus society and the wider society is a prerequisite for more intercultural dialogue.

Intercultural dialogue and integration in general requires active strategies. As a basic example, in the University College of Oslo's strategic plan for 2008-2011, one of the main aims is to, "through systematic and targeted work, increase the number of students and staff with a minority background" (Høgskolen i Oslo 2008). To some higher education institutions this aim might seem obvious, or it might even be a natural part of everyday campus and academic life. But it is sometimes forgotten than intercultural dialogue does not only mean exchanges between countries, but also within one country, region or other community.

Students as actors

While we are thinking of multiculturalism, we may note that the campus where students study is not only a space where people with different cultural backgrounds meet. Students are also actors in the academic community. They are building democratic structures with the capacity to represent whole student communities. Through such organisations, students engage in debates within the governance bodies of higher education institutions, bringing the voice of all students into academic and public dialogue. It is vital that these student bodies are supported by the rest of the academic community and included at every level of higher education decision-making.

However, student organisations naturally can only represent the diversity of a society insofar as the national or regional situation allows equal access for all to higher education. The goal should always be that higher education communities mirror the society as a whole. The London Communiqué (Bologna Process 2007) takes this up as one of the goals of the Bologna Process. The fundamental human right to education must be enforced and, in order to achieve this, the social dimension of higher education has to be respected by governments as well as by academia.

A sure bet for intercultural dialogue: international student organisations

Space for discussion

The Council of Europe's White Paper on Intercultural Dialogue stipulates that "Developing a political culture supportive of cultural pluralism is a demanding task" (Council of Europe 2008). The White Paper also notes that this political culture must entail "an education system which generates capacities for critical thinking and innovation, and spaces in which people are allowed to participate and to express themselves" (*ibidem*, Article 79). Some of these spaces can be found within student organisations.

When people start disagreeing, they are forced to look at themselves from a different perspective. If something is at stake, they are also forced to compromise. This is one of the reasons why student organisations are key to improving significant inter-cultural dialogue in higher education, both at an individual and at a structural level.

The European Students' Union believes that students should not merely be viewed as future employees, but also as active citizens. ESU believes that higher education has a responsibility to prepare students for life as active citizens in democratic societies. This was also one of the views of the Council of Europe's forum on Converging Competences: Diversity, Higher Education and Sustainable Democracy, which took place in October 2008. The global societal and democratic responsibility of higher education institutions on the one hand and the public responsibility for higher education on the part of governments on the other hand also formed one of the themes at the annual conference of the International Association of Universities in November 2009.

Political dispute and intercultural dialogue

Student bodies meet each other regularly across national and regional borders. The European Students' Union is an umbrella organisation, bringing together 45 national students' unions from 37 countries (as of April 2010).

ESU tries to build bridges between students and student organisations in Europe. It organises at least four major events each year, where students from across Europe meet and discuss the situations in their own countries and in Europe as a whole. Two of those events include the meeting of the ESU general assemblies, which last for three days. They are intense experiences of European diversity, with student representatives from about 35 countries aiming to reach a consensus on policy as well as the organisational direction for the European Students' Union in the near and more distant future. Other events are large seminars where topical issues in higher education are discussed, like the social dimension, mobility, the Bologna Process or student finance. Some of ESU's co-operation partners, such as the Erasmus Student Network, the International Federation of Medical Students' Associations and the school student organisation OBESSU,[15] also contribute to intercultural dialogue through their ordinary activities like conferences, training and internal discussions on political, cultural or educational issues.

In January 2009, ESU brought together students from all over the world to debate current and future challenges for students. The meeting was sponsored and supported by UNESCO and Education International, and had as its main aim to jointly prepare a set of statements and recommendations for the UNESCO World Conference on Higher Education in July the same year. ESU also organised a meeting after the World Conference, to explore the possibilities of firmer co-operation among the regional student platforms of the world.

One of the surprises at these meetings was how few difficulties the organisations faced when trying to reach consensus. Though the situations in Ghana, Nepal and Australia were very different, we encountered few problems when discussing and agreeing on major topics and priorities. The reason might be that the level of abstraction was rather high, and that the outcome of the discussions could be said to be not very controversial. But the agreement was remarkably clear on policy issues such as student participation in university decision-making, the right to free education and a strong position against the introduction of tuition fees, as well as the right to not be discriminated against on race, religion, sexuality or other non-academic criteria. The meeting in January 2010 was the third of its kind within 12 months. This meeting was also the one where participants were able to agree on the most concrete measures and plans for future dialogue and co-operation, which outline what the regional student organisations of the world deem to be priorities in higher education today (Global Student Statement 2010; Global Student Declaration 2010).

---

15. Organising Bureau of European School Student Unions.

Barriers

Interculturalism – in a format of dialogue leading to mutual understanding – is in general challenging. From the experience of the European Students' Union we can witness that language differences constitute the most obvious obstacle to dialogue, let alone to firm and long-term co-operation. However, if it comes to work for a joint cause or in support of fellow students when their rights are neglected, it can easily be seen that such barriers can be overcome. For example, few European student representatives speak Persian (Farsi). Nevertheless, the most visible student rights focus of ESU between July 2009 and April 2010 (the time of writing) was support for the Iranian student movement and in particular the organisation Office for Strengthening Unity (Persian: *Daftar-e Tahkim-e Vahdat*). In April 2010, ESU nominated the Iranian activist and student leader Bahareh Hedayat, imprisoned at the time of writing, for the Student Peace Prize. Hedayat had been imprisoned for sending a video greeting to ESU and OBESSU, "talking to foreign media", "insulting the Supreme Leader" and similar charges. While European and Persian history and culture might take different stands on several issues, the fundamental right to free speech is something that European students share with student activists across the world.

Being a European organisation representing students from 37 countries with very diverse languages (Finnish, Georgian, Hebrew, Portuguese, Serbian and Ukrainian to name a few), ESU engages hundreds of students in short- and long-term dialogue every year. The intensity of debates and a step-by-step greater understanding of students' common and different challenges create friendship bonds that last longer than a short career as a bachelor, master or PhD student.

When students (and professors and other higher education staff) meet people from other countries at international meetings or conferences, they have to consider abandoning their national whims. For example, quite a few student union representatives from northern and western Europe need to accept – or at least come to terms with – the fact that it is not a universal European value to be punctual. This might be a smile-inducing example to some readers, but lack of basic cultural knowledge can hinder good debates on the real issues. Otherwise we risk finding we can only talk to those who think and behave like ourselves.

Other obstacles to international student NGO work

What can be done to improve this student NGO work? Funding is most often the main obstacle to the logistics of international co-operation. The Council of Europe already does a very important job of funding projects involving international student and youth NGOs. Some of the latest Council of Europe-funded examples from ESU are a student union development handbook (European Students' Union 2008), which allows the various students' unions of Europe to compare similar and less-similar organisations and practices with their own; a conference in February 2009 on student empowerment and co-operation on all levels of student participation; and a study session in July 2009 to empower students from diverse countries in

Europe to become stronger actors in national and institutional debates on the quality of higher education.

Student unions are dependent on funds for day-to-day and year-to-year activities, and a substantial part of their budgets often relies on varying amounts of project funds. More stable funding, from universities or other sources, would mean more possibilities for proactive work rather than the sometimes re-active approach that organisations need to take because they are dependent on project funding and on individual applications in order to get basic funding that allows students to travel and meet.

If a student organisation tries to establish short- or long-term dialogue with students from another cultural background, this should be encouraged in any way possible. Sometimes it might mean helping to find translators or other practicalities; at other times it might mean funding travel and accommodation for visiting students or higher education institutions' own students.

Conclusion

Higher education institutions are already a breeding ground for the start-up of big and small variations of intercultural dialogue. But the potential is far from being exploited to its full extent. Universities and colleges, leadership, staff and students and the rest of society can help each other improve the dialogue. But it does mean that we need to find time to sit down and talk about it between the speeches that brag about how many nationalities can be found on campus. We need to establish an understanding of higher education institutions as actors enabling, promoting and maintaining intercultural learning and dialogue. Graduates need to be capable of critical thinking as well as controversial questioning and empathetic listening, in order to cope with the increasing complexity of our more and more specialised and at the same time globally connected society. As such, the higher education institution developing into a space that empowers its students and teachers to engage in discussion and dialogue must become the rule. The short-term gain of severely increased pressure to perform is bringing about the much higher risk of a passive and mute academic society, incapable of facing the challenges of our time as open and responsible citizens as well as creative workers and researchers.

References

Bologna Process (2007): "Towards the European Higher Education Area: responding to challenges in a globalised world", London Communiqué.

Bologna Process (2009): "The Bologna Process 2020 – The European Higher Education Area in the new decade", Communiqué of the Conference of European Ministers.

Council of Europe (2008): *Living Together as Equals in Dignity*, White Paper on Intercultural Dialogue, Strasbourg: Council of Europe.

European Students' Union (2008): *The Student Union Development Handbook:* Brussels: European Students' Union.

Global Student Declaration (January 2010): www.esu-online.org/documents/statements/2010_Global_Student_Declaration.pdf (accessed on 22 April 2010).

Global Student Statement to the UNESCO World Conference on Higher Education +10: www.esu-online.org/index.php/documents/statements/566-world-conference-on-higher-education-wche10-global-student-statement (accessed on 22 April 2010).

Høgskolen i Oslo (2008): "Strategiplan for HiO og JBI 2008-2011" ['Strategic plan for Oslo University College and the Unit for Journalism, Library and Inforamtion Studies']; www.hio.no/Enheter/Avdeling-for-journalistikk-bibliotek-og-informasjonsfag/Om-JBI/Strategi-planer/Strategiplan-for-HiO-og-JBI-2008-2011 (accessed on 22 April 2010).

Wächter, Bernd (2009): "Intercultural dialogue on the university campus", in Sjur Bergan and Jean-Philippe Restoueix (eds), *Intercultural dialogue on campus*, Higher Education Series No. 11, Strasbourg: Council of Europe, pp. 133-139.

The role of public authorities in promoting intercultural dialogue

Germain Dondelinger

Definition

In May 2008 the Committee of Ministers of the Council of Europe adopted the White Paper on Intercultural Dialogue. However, intercultural dialogue had already gained new weight on the Council of Europe's agenda by 2005. Indeed that year the 3rd Summit of Heads of State and Government identified intercultural dialogue (including its religious dimension) as a means of ensuring European integration, cohesion of society and reconciliation.

In this context it is worth recalling the definition the Council of Europe provides in its White Paper. Intercultural dialogue is an "open and respectful exchange of views between individuals, groups with different ethnic, cultural, religious and linguistic backgrounds and heritage on the basis of mutual understanding and respect. It operates at all levels – within societies, between the societies of Europe and between Europe and the wider world" (Council of Europe 2008: 10-11). Under this remit, intercultural dialogue is not conducted for the sake of intercultural dialogue. It links up with the welfare of society. It means talking and listening to each others' perspectives, experiences and needs as well as responding to them. It entails co-operating for the purpose of keeping our societies intact, ensuring their growth and their peace.

Intercultural dialogue is thus not a showcase for different cultures or a mere celebration of difference. The focus is on respectful exchange and interaction between individuals or groups of individuals. This is corroborated by a survey conducted for the European Union in 2007, the main findings of which are shown in Table 1.

Table 1: Intercultural dialogue in Europe – what does this mean to people? (EU27)

Communication among different communities	23%
Co-operation, exchange, transnational mobility	13%
Living together, knowing and understanding different cultures	11%
Cultural events and access to culture	10%
Co-existence and cultural diversity	9%
Shared European culture	8%
Dealing with linguistic diversity	5%
Tolerance, equal rights	4%
Education, exchange of information and ideas	3%
Dialogue in the sphere of politics and economics	3%
Immigration/minorities	3%
Preserving traditions	1%
Other opinions	8%

Source: European Institute for Comparative Cultural Research 2007: 13.

Trigger issues

The background to the Council of Europe's renewed initiative on intercultural dialogue is to be found in the changing nature of our societies. Against the backdrop of migration, globalisation, international and domestic security issues and increasingly multicultural societies, the development of intercultural competences and the promotion of intercultural dialogue are fundamental. Intercultural dialogue contributes to a number of strategic priorities, such as respecting and promoting cultural diversity and favouring the commitment to solidarity, social justice and reinforced cohesion. It is therefore an integral part of the *res publica* and it is articulated in various diversity policies.

Borrowing from the work by Tony Bennett for the Council of Europe (Bennett 2001), it is possible to identify four contexts in which such cultural diversity needs to be articulated:

1. the civic contexts that bear upon the cultural rights and entitlements awarded to different cultural streams in the population;
2. the social contexts or objectives that these policies are connected to;
3. the administrative contexts that determine how cultural communities are dealt with or given agency;
4. the economic contexts, most notably the cultural industries sector.

Intercultural dialogue is grounded in cultural diversity and it is thus related to the protection and promotion of diversity. Intercultural dialogue is a positive concept, but it can only take place if a person is not only acknowledged but is also guaranteed freedom, safety, equality, dignity. This is the reason why the Council of Europe White Paper definition of intercultural dialogue places it within the framework of human rights, since it implies specific individual and group rights.

Legal frameworks

However, this does not put intercultural dialogue into a legal category that would normally be regulated by national or international law. The only international document specifically addressing intercultural dialogue is the Council of Europe *Declaration on Intercultural Dialogue and Conflict Prevention*, adopted in Opatija, Croatia on 22 October 2003 by the European ministers responsible for cultural affairs. Though not binding like a ratified convention, such a declaration carries a kind of moral authority influencing the development of national laws and practices.

The anchoring of intercultural dialogue in human rights, and especially in the universal nature of human rights, may lead to tension. The affirmation of cultural differences may seem to negate the very possibility of finding common ground on which to base these rights. Another important issue is the distinction between individual and collective rights. In the past, some countries emphasised the collective elements of human rights, seeing in them a chance for their members to assert their own individual rights. However, collectivism with strict borders can contribute to

110

parallel societies that fail to take account of multiple identities or second- or third-generation immigrants.

Ultimately the conceptual link between cultural diversity and intercultural dialogue entails that individual rights prevail over collective rights in intercultural dialogue contexts. International legal instruments act as a protection for individuals belonging to minority groups and secure the foundation for intercultural dialogue to take place and to promote or enforce human rights. Within the EU framework, provisions for individual rights are laid down in the EU Charter of Fundamental Rights (European Union 2000a), some articles of which are of particular importance to intercultural dialogue, especially those addressing:

- equality (non-discrimination and cultural, religious and linguistic diversity);
- freedoms (e.g. freedom of expression, of thought, conscience and religion);
- citizens' rights (e.g. freedom of movement and residence, to vote).

Furthermore, within this same EU context, directives implement principles of equality. The most important ones are the Racial Equality Directive (European Union 2000b) and the Employment Equality Directive (European Union 2000c). The latter implements the principle of equal treatment in employment and training irrespective of religion, belief, age, disability and sexual orientation. It includes identical provisions to the Racial Equality Directive on definitions of discrimination, rights of legal redress and the sharing of the burden of proof.

Societal issues

When intercultural dialogue is linked to and takes place within diverse, heterogeneous societies, it is necessary to reflect upon the normative and structural conditions of dialogue. Traugott Schoefthaler (in ERICarts 2008) distinguishes two ways of approaching cultural differences and similarities. On the one hand, a substantive approach insists on deeply rooted cultural differences between Europe and other parts of the world; on the other hand, a commitment approach focuses on the implementation of universal values like supporting democracy, integration and social development. Intercultural dialogue is then burdened not only by the kind of reservations, stereotypes and historical experiences out of which mutual mistrust often grows, but also by normative demands such as commonly agreed procedures for intercultural dialogue. Moreover, these normative demands and social reality may diverge. This means that intercultural dialogue and the way it is conducted between groups also depends on the overall national social policy.

It is also useful to distinguish between two approaches to internal minority–majority relations: policies that aim to bring about greater social cohesion and strategies that aim to promote diversity and dialogue.

Within the European Union the social cohesion approach prevails, which aims at a more unified society. A socially cohesive society rests on political stability, internal security, economic growth and equal opportunities for all individuals and groups, regardless of their origin, to participate in both the work environment and social spheres. The social cohesion approach relies on developing a national identity and the use of a main national language. In this context, intercultural dialogue-related programmes aim at supporting the socio-cultural integration of groups or individuals with a migrant background. However, it should be noticed that with reference to refugees and asylum seekers, or social fringe groups, priority is placed on improving socio-economic conditions rather than on intercultural dialogue. If social inclusion – that is, realistic opportunities for young people from migrant families to integrate into the labour market and society at large – is missing, intercultural dialogue is not considered an appropriate solution to address such conflicts.

The cultural diversity approach rests on the legal or political recognition of defined minority cultures and identities that co-exist within nation states. It is characterised by affirmative or positive action for cultural diversity and equality, such as quota regulations, strong legal action against racist or hate crimes, empowering or protecting marginalised groups. This approach may also include rights-based strategies officially recognising minority groups, such as passing a law which defines the scope of special rights for the Roma community.

Finally, the dialogue approach emphasises intercultural encounters through artistic events, special media programmes and so forth.

Generally speaking, integration is the main goal of both the social cohesion and diversity approaches and most often there is a mix of approaches according to the sector concerned. The approach could be cohesion-led in the field of education or internal security and diversity-led in the field of culture. However, we need to distinguish between a "cultural" perspective and other policy fields like housing, the labour market or social welfare. Arts cannot solve social conflicts. Success or failure of open dialogue is determined by where people live and communicate, in other words at the local level of society. Children's success at school, adolescents finding a job, the appearance of the public space in the city environment, building a new place of worship are issues that are uppermost in citizens' minds, and intercultural dialogue evolves around these.

Actors

As has been stated, intercultural dialogue is strongly related to other policy areas; it is becoming part of an emerging governance of diversity/integration policies. This entails that in addition to the international level, public bodies and civil society actors become increasingly involved.

At the national level, ministries responsible for the integration of minorities, ministries with specific portfolios like youth, culture and education, and ministries for foreign affairs contribute to creating opportunities for intercultural dialogue. They are supported by semi-public organisations or quango agencies such as human rights committees and youth or education boards, as well as by regional and local authorities.

However, it is the non-governmental civil society actors that play a leading role in promoting intercultural dialogue. Local NGOs – be they local neighbourhood groups, church organisations and charities, arts, youth or sports clubs, or national professional organisations – provide important services and organise numerous intercultural dialogue events. Their scope ranges from providing documentation for initiatives aimed at better understanding to protection of minorities' rights. They provide opportunities for direct encounters between professionals, independent spaces for confrontation and dialogue, and they often do so trans-nationally.

Therefore, the role of public authorities is twofold. Government ministries create a framework for implementing policies in various fields that also foster intercultural dialogue. For example, such policies can aim at integrating aspects of cultural diversity and issues of human rights into local urban planning and development. But above all, public policies must create a space within which civil society can act out intercultural dialogue. In return, civil society actors often play an unofficial monitoring role besides carrying out work of a more activist nature.

A selected sector: education

The preceding articles have referred to the links between intercultural dialogue and various policy fields. Among those, education features prominently. This sector faces its own challenges. The various assessments by the OECD,[16] measuring how far pupils near the end of compulsory education have acquired the knowledge and skills needed for full participation in society, show that in most European countries the proportion of migrant students in secondary schools who reach this level is below average, and is even smaller at university level. Yet, education has a primary role to play when it comes to equipping pupils and students with the skills they need to deal with cultural differences. These are skills in intercultural communication and conflict solving, understanding the workings of a multicultural society, and analysing one's own cultural values, standards and assumptions. According to the International Association of Universities,

> in an increasingly global and independent world, where encountering cultural difference can scarcely be avoided, the ability to enter into a tolerant and respectful dialogue is a vital skill for nations, communities and individuals. Disciplines, teaching methods, student skills and knowledge itself can be strengthened through an intercultural dialogue approach.[17]

In education, intercultural dialogue tends to be organised around civic education and intercultural education. The former focuses on developing knowledge and skills that enable individuals to participate in diverse societies and, where necessary, to resolve conflict, whereas the latter often includes the linguistic integration of immigrants.

---

16. Material from the OECD's Programme for International Student Assessment (PISA) studies, notably for 2000, 2003 and 2006, is available at www.pisa.oecd.org/pages/0,34 17,en_32252351_32235731_1_1_1_1_1,00.html.
17. See www.iau-aiu.net/id/index.html (accessed on 11 December 2009).

However, intercultural dialogue can only be fostered if the whole organisational structure of education caters for the needs of intercultural dialogue. This is best done if the school is conceived of as a community promoting the pupils' well-being. Therefore, public authorities need to develop strategies in the following domains:

- Provision: segregated schools and kindergartens ought to be avoided and the participation of parents, mentors and friends should be encouraged.

- Staff: the composition of the professional staff should be such that it reflects the diversity of the population; both initial and in-service training should stimulate the professional development of teachers that are competent in multicultural environments; the training of trainers should equip them with intercultural literacy.

- Curriculum: at the content level, the intercultural perspective should be included in educational and science textbooks, special resources for teachers should be produced and a deeper and more differentiated knowledge of major world religions ought to be developed.

- Language provision: Multilingualism needs to be viewed as an asset, since communication in one's mother tongue and communication in foreign languages are two key elements in intercultural dialogue, though this may imply that migrants have to acquire competence in three or four languages, so successful completion may be an issue; at least, supplementary classes ought to be organised to improve students' native language capacity.

More specifically, for intercultural dialogue to take place in higher education, public authorities may need to ensure they are

- guaranteeing academic freedom;

- creating a framework for the internationalisation of universities by attracting an international student body and international staff, which entails revisiting immigration, recruitment and employment conditions;

- creating conditions for equitable access and completion through outreach policies that are an integral part of the financing of the institutions;

- creating conditions for a better understanding of cultural diversity through the defining and financing of research programmes, and by acknowledging and favouring interdisciplinary approaches;

- evaluating the intercultural policy of the institution via the quality assurance mechanisms.

Conclusion

In general, the main role of public authorities is to create and sustain an environment of legal certainty with full implementation of binding international anti-discrimination standards, based on the concept of human rights as individual rights. It is an environment that recognises multiple as well as specific cultural identities. In terms of actors concerned, civic responsibility is fostered and there is thus reliance on the participation of civil society organisations.

Finally, intercultural dialogue should be seen as a means of coming to terms with different world views, traditions and lifestyles through empathy, non-violence and creativity. However, it should be acknowledged that the concept of "identity" – on which intercultural dialogue hinges – is not a static concept. The main idea should be to free the "dialogue" from its conceptual bipolarity, in which people are not from the outset perceived merely as representatives of some predefined cultures and religions, but instead have the opportunity to challenge and change existing cultural patterns as well as to cross historical boundaries.

References

Bennett, T. (2001): *Cultural policy and cultural diversity: mapping the policy domain*, Cultural Policy Note 7, Strasbourg: Council of Europe.

Council of Europe (2003): *Declaration on Intercultural Dialogue and Conflict Prevention* (the Opatija Declaration), Strasbourg: Council of Europe.

Council of Europe (2008): *Living Together as Equals in Dignity*, White Paper on Intercultural Dialogue, Strasbourg: Council of Europe.

ERICarts [European Institute for Comparative Cultural Research] (2008): *Sharing Diversity: National Approaches to Intercultural Dialogue in Europe*. Study for the European Commission (Report, March 2008), Bonn: ERICarts.

European Union (2000a): Charter of Fundamental Rights of the European Union ((2000/C 364/01).

European Union (2000b): Council Directive 2000/43/EC of 29 June 2000 implementing the principle of equal treatment between persons irrespective of racial or ethnic origin.

European Union (2000c): Council Directive 2000/78/EC of 27 November 2000 establishing a general framework for equal treatment in employment and occupation.

A broad approach: beyond training professionals to educating responsible citizens

Yazmín Cruz and Cristina Escrigas

Context

In this global era, preparation to become a global citizen who will interact with society through the exercise of a profession requires a comprehensive vision of reality. It also implies the need for certain abilities and values: a deep understanding of human being and life; sustainability, as a collective social process to be learned; common recognition of, understanding of and respect for different cultures; inter-cultural relationship and support of diversity; the ability to deal with an exponential expansion of technology, without losing the human capacity to put it to common human service; and the ability to set aside fear in order to confidently co-operate in peace building at any level of activity. This article reflects on the role of higher education in contributing to positive social transformation by preparing responsible citizens, taking into account the challenge of intercultural understanding.

GUNI

The Global University Network for Innovation (GUNI) was created in 1999 by UNESCO, the United Nations University (UNU) and the Universitat Politècnica de Catalunya (UPC). It was founded to follow up the main decisions taken at the 1998 UNESCO World Conference on Higher Education and to facilitate their implementation. Since then, GUNI has extended to include UNESCO chairs, higher education institutions, research centres and networks involved in innovation and the social commitment of higher education.

GUNI's mission is to contribute to strengthening the role of higher education in society, by reforming and innovating higher education policies across the world according to the principles of public service, relevance and social responsibility. Therefore, GUNI promotes the exchange of resources, ideas and innovative experiences to facilitate the role of higher education in bringing about social transformation through institutional change. It encourages co-operation between higher education institutions and society, and contributes to reducing differences between developed and developing countries in the field of higher education.

This is a important moment for universities to reappraise their purposes, functions and practices through critical engagement in dialogue and discourse with the citizenry on the problematic issues of our societies. In that sense, GUNI works from a global perspective to promote and exchange emergent ideas that could inspire and motivate higher education actors, especially policy makers, and institutions to overcome the inertia of the current model beyond the paradigm of the "ivory tower" or the "market-oriented university" and reorient higher education so as to better be able to respond to society's challenges.

A different world

There is evidence that the changes in the fields of thinking, science, economics, and society – such as the revolution in information and communication technology – have created a very different world map in comparison to fifty years ago. Today we are able to document the interrelationship of environmental, social, economic and human problems. We can also document the unsustainability of an economic model in which the poverty of some co-exists with the wealth of others, who seem unaware of the limits of those who lack everything. Society has a global map of the world's problems and this view allows us to explore solutions and even to bring about a paradigm shift for reconstructing societies in answer to these challenges, and building a better world for future generations.

Therefore, recovering the human capacity to evaluate, compare, choose, decide and act is more crucial now than ever before. According to Freire (2001), the idea of change presupposes that this is possible, but it is essential to understand the reality that is the starting point as well as the vision we are working towards. This implies a process of change and transition between the past, where we find our identity; the present, which defines our needs; and the future, towards which we direct our aspirations and efforts.

We live in interconnected worlds – not a single one – and as a global society we are faced with two main kinds of conflict: one in the relationship between humans, their co-existence, and the other in the relationship between humans and nature. Thus, we cannot understand our present situation adequately without taking into account all its dimensions: environmental, social, economic and cultural. Even more, we cannot neglect the multi-faceted nature of our present, which is best seen as a dynamic relationship rather than a new kind of reality.

Actually, one of our main concerns is promoting harmonious intercultural co-existence by means of specific solutions aiming to remedy the negative consequences of multiculturalism in different societies and to make diversity a source of enrichment rather than conflict (Bennani 2008). Some critics argue that multiculturalism leads directly to restrictions in the rights and freedoms for certain groups. There is an extensive literature which analyses the concept and its limitations and proposes one more step that is already reflected in the concept of interculturality.

The diversity of civilisations and cultures is a basic feature of human society and a driving force of human progress. As Marga (2008) defines it, diversity refers to life-styles, technological acquisitions, concepts, value representations, behaviours and institutions, explanations, interpretations, value rankings and traditions. Civilisations and cultures reflect the great wealth and heritage of humankind; their nature is to overlap, interact and evolve in relation to one another. There is no hierarchy among cultures; all cultures have contributed equally to the evolution of humanity.

Change and the contribution of higher education

Education is key to change. It should inspire, provoke and motivate the free and active participation of individuals in their reality and equip them with tools that enable them to construct a new approach to issues in their physical and temporal environment. It supports a process of self-discovery and learning, fosters personal development, and helps people find their role in society, as well as in strengthening communities and stimulating social progress.

One of the key aims of higher education is to foster all-round personal development and educate citizens who are responsible, informed and committed to working for a better future. Achieving these objectives requires a profound transformation of higher education to create a system that is capable of anticipating the needs of society and individuals. Unfortunately, as Tajin (2007) mentions, rather than universities changing the world, it is economic globalisation that has been effective in dominating the policy agenda of higher education institutions in their effort to position themselves favourably and gain an edge in the global market.

A new world, however, calls for a new kind of university, one that creatively redefines its missions and functions, that reinvents itself if necessary so it can continue to serve as a space for reflection and creativity, and that provides the tools needed for social analysis, critical thinking and sustainability.

Social changes have shaped higher education institutions (HEIs), and this is reflected in their pursuit of social relevance and their capacity to respond to external demands. The need to be relevant underlies the multiple relationships between universities and their environment and is a decisive factor that reflects the alignment between the aims of HEIs and social expectations. The vision and mission for higher education need to be clearly reoriented towards societal challenges, to reinvent an innovative and socially committed response that anticipates and adds value to the process of social transformation. It is very important for HEIs to become, consciously and intentionally, analysts of the profound changes that are happening and of possible initiatives in shaping, anticipating, intervening in and guiding these changes towards another possible world.

There is evidence that something is changing: for example, the Alliance of Civilizations provides an excellent political framework for higher education to move forward in helping to reduce cross-cultural tensions and to build bridges between communities. The final report of the High Level Group of the Alliance of Civilizations[18] highlights the fact that education systems today face the challenge of preparing young people for an interdependent world that is unsettling to individual and collective identities. Education about one's own history fosters

---

18. See www.unaoc.org/repository/HLG _Report.pdf (accessed on 28 May 2010).

community and solidarity, but it must be balanced by knowledge of global issues and an understanding and appreciation of other societies and cultures and how they influence each other.

If we understand that cosmopolitanism implies interaction and cultural encounters, as well as socio-cognitive development, the university should be an agent of cosmopolitanism by playing a leading role in shaping the social and cultural horizons of the knowledge society. In that sense, the university is one of the few institutions in society that is specifically related to the development of collective learning processes. If knowledge is increasingly inseparable from citizenship and democracy, universities have a central role to play in linking the concepts of knowledge and citizenship.

Although there is no doubt that higher education plays a fundamental role in trans-forming society, the contribution of higher education and research to intercultural co-existence is still largely absent from the agendas of institutional authorities. It is also absent from higher education policies and practices in different parts of the world, because it is considered a political issue, rather than a strategic matter for academic debate and research (Bennani 2008). Indeed, teaching is not just the transfer of knowledge; there is always an educational context of the structures, methodologies and assumptions underlying the curricula. Higher education has much to do in fostering intercultural dialogue in society by mobilising the values of understanding and respect for difference, harmony and peace. Higher education can equip graduates with the attitudes, knowledge and abilities required to undertake this process of co-existence. It can also develop and provide knowledge for the basis of living together.

The Second Forum of the Alliance of Civilizations, held in Istanbul in 2009, clearly indicated some of the priorities that would guide its work in the run-up to the Rio Forum of the Alliance in 2010. One of these priorities is to make education and youth two of the top areas of action for the alliance. Its report also emphasises that education is one of the most effective tools in shaping shared narratives across potential divides. Education plays a critical role in promoting peaceful co-existence in multicultural societies. To achieve this goal, we need to rethink education in its broadest sense – education for human rights; education for citizenship and respect for others; education for intercultural understanding and dialogue; education in media literacy; education about religions and beliefs; and education about world history. All these are indispensable strategies if we want to make the world a better and safer place to live together in mutual respect.

How intercultural dialogue and understanding are understood in and by higher education

Cultural understanding means more than describing or knowing a culture: it means the ability to place ourselves, even if only hypothetically, in the role of somebody who has embraced that culture (Dallmayr and McCarthy 1997). Thus, the first challenge is to change the strange monocultural way of evaluating peoples, cultures and knowledge (Muñoz 2008). This approach is at odds with the plurality and diversity of the world.

Besides, intercultural communication is not limited to the transmission of information from one culture to another, or to simply living together in an information universe (Ting-Toomey 1999). It means, first and foremost, a motivating interaction in order to find solutions to common problems (Samovar and Poster 2004). Therefore, dialogue should be considered not as an end in itself but as a strategy for guaranteeing the required intercultural co-existence both within and beyond national borders and internationally. Such dialogue should be based on enrichment through difference, not merely on tolerance of others.

Actually, people of different backgrounds can hardly find places to mix, learn from each other, understand their divergences or discover their commonalities. As a social institution, the university could develop a vision of a diverse and tolerant environment, featuring a pluralistic and cosmopolitan community and promoting respect for a diversity that includes age, ethnicity, gender, disability, nationality, religious belief, political ideology, economic background and national/geographic origin (Tajin 2007). Higher education can play a decisive and fundamental role in terms of the teaching content, values and skills it incorporates.

Higher education institutions need to adapt their functions to this reality, taking into consideration the fact that new generations will be operating within this context. It is important that HEIs think differently about the social context of students, not only in terms of similar or different experiences of domestic and international students but also in terms of how societies are becoming more interconnected and interdependent (Stuart 2008). HEIs should enable their students to gain a critical consciousness of the world they inhabit. This should help them to better anticipate, articulate and animate alternative processes that can lead to widespread human and social development, as opposed to uneven, temporary surges in economic growth. There are different approaches that can be applied to achieve this objective and one of them is the redesigning of curricula.

Curriculum design

Curricula offer us a great possibility for supporting most of the challenges faced by HEIs and their emerging roles as key actors in a globalised world. The challenge is to integrate new areas of knowledge and practice within curricula transversally, taking into account the contextualisation of knowledge. The new generations should learn to think together, building consensus through participatory methodologies. At the curriculum level, GUNI has suggested the need to promote education in shared values; education for national and global citizenship and cosmopolitanism, and (even more) education for dialogue that enables students to act as global citizens, recognise the rights of others and work towards improved conditions for others in their local context as well as at the national and global levels.

These changes involve a deep transformation of the curriculum; we need to understand more fully the kinds of learning that our future citizens will require. In addition to an ongoing requirement for technical skills in a broad range of areas, a key learning need seems to be the ability to make connections across a wide array of knowledge in the face of increasingly diverse problems and challenges – and to do this in a way that places equal value on the nature and quality of our relationships with the world at large (Taylor 2008b). In doing this, more emphasis should be placed on including the following aspects of the curriculum: learning to think in terms of networks, valuing the plurality of ways of being and thinking, creating epistemological bridges between cultures to facilitate dialogue and the joint solution of common problems; using knowledge and opportunity to adapt to and function in unfamiliar contexts.

Although curriculum innovation rarely seems to address issues of intercultural dialogue and understanding explicitly, in recent years some of these aspects have begun to be included. As an example, some higher education institutions offer educational programmes on peace building and studies about conflict and war. In addition, there have been courageous attempts at developing curricula in conflict-affected societies in order to address conflict and peace quite explicitly in a range of ways. But as Marga (2008) remarks, if we accept that universities train people in 'competences' – meaning the knowledge and general and technical skills required for superior performance – university programmes should be starting to include the formation of global and intercultural competences.

We need to differentiate between 'intrapersonal competences', 'interpersonal competences' and 'intercultural competences'. Anyone who acquires 'intercultural leadership competences' is able to perform specific tasks: to clarify his/her own notion of culture, which has to be well formed; to apply it; to understand his/her cultural background; to analyse and evaluate intercultural situations; to negotiate and motivate participants in these situations; to take decisions in a multicultural environment; to form intercultural teams; to exert intercultural leadership (Marga 2008). Obviously, these all require communication, teamwork, critical thinking and innovation; in other words, universities must train students to examine, test and articulate visions.

Beyond training professionals: the need to educate responsible citizens

As we said at the beginning, any professional career implies the need for certain abilities and values – understanding of human life, sustainability as a social process, recognition of and respect for other cultures, dealing with new technology without losing humanity, and the ability to confidently co-operate in peace building – and any profession interacts with some of these factors, if not with all. In addition, we need to break the hegemony of the singular mindset that seems to be advancing rapidly in globalised society. We must therefore accept the complexity of reality and interdependence of all knowledge in a real interdisciplinary approach to education.

In recent years, higher education institutions have come under a lot of pressure to meet social and societal needs. This has been explicitly linked to training individuals with specialised knowledge, focused on a specific profession, to contribute to economic growth under parameters of increasing competitiveness. Research too is increasingly oriented towards satisfying the demand and needs of those who can pay for it. Delanty (2008) emphasises that one of the most important social and cultural challenges to universities is to find a new idea of the university for the 21st century, to express an alternative to the current corporate global culture and its market rationality, without universities being exclusively state agents. This involves a change of paradigm from a system that emphasises the individual and competitiveness to one that emphasises the social and collective, as shown in Table 1.

Table 1: From individual and competitive to social and co-operative

from individual and competitive	*to social and co-operative*
Focused on content	Focused on content, abilities and values
Focused on training productive professionals	Focused on training citizen–professionals
Oriented to labour-market needs	Oriented to the needs of society as a whole
Social use based on individual status and enrichment, and economic growth	Social use based on contributing to the collective good, to society building and to human and social development

Source: Escrigas (2008).

Higher education is responsible for training professionals who will attain positions of the greatest responsibility. We can choose merely to train professionals or we can educate citizens who will carry out a profession. Identifying individual and collective responsibility in professional decision-making within new global ethical paradigms will be a concern for the near future. Decisions in all areas of activity and all professions can be made using an approach that focuses on the common good. We are not sufficiently aware of the collective implications of our behaviour and our individual decisions.

Higher education institutions have reached a critical moment in their long evolution as producers and disseminators of knowledge and they are also facing global challenges. These include the rapid development of science and technology, demands related to the creation of knowledge societies and the growing competition between increasingly multicultural and interdependent societies that are dominated by market forces. Such challenges require the world's educational systems to adopt new roles and adapt their missions.

The ten proposals from GUNI

The role of higher education in the world is essential, as it has been in the past and will be in future societies. Once this premise has been accepted and shared – which has occurred globally in the past decade – the relevant question then is: what education and for what purposes? This debate is completely new and the answers not at all obvious. Contributing to this debate, GUNI presented to the UNESCO 2009 World Conference ten proposals for transforming the role of higher education in society to make it more proactive and committed:

1. Open up to society. Proactive engagement in dialogue with citizens.
    Create a true knowledge-based society through engagement with society as a whole. Provide a plurality of expert advice in dealing with the problematic issues of the day.

2. Incorporate sustainability transversally into teaching, research and institutional action.
    Shift paradigms from individual competitiveness, economic profitability and a short-term focus to the collective, with human and social benefits and sustainable in the long term.

3. Become cosmopolitan centres of global culture. Build bridges between different cultures and sources of knowledge.
    Knowledge is no longer produced and consumed exclusively within universities. Instead, their task is to connect different kinds of knowledge, linking knowledge and citizenship.

4. Renew thought for society.
    Break the conformity of thought by proactively and constructively criticising the world of ideas. Transform the established paradigms and beliefs in society, economics and politics, in the way we organise our community and how this is reflected in our education systems.

5. Go beyond educating professionals to educating citizens in ethical awareness and civic commitment.
    Know how to contribute to the common good through professional practice. Educate for "glocality", democracy, citizenship, intercultural relations, peace building and a deep understanding of life's dynamics.

6. Introduce complexity, uncertainty and transdisciplinarity into the curriculum and in research.
    Move towards a holistic vision of reality. Link different areas of knowledge in order to understand complex issues and help solve the great challenges locally and globally.

7. Analyse the ethical, social and environmental implications of the advance of knowledge.
    Increase the resources invested in analysing the impact of science and technology, and augment the capacity to absorb their expansion, in all aspects of human life.

8. Democratise access to knowledge.
   Remove barriers in an effort to give open access to expert knowledge, making it as useful as it can be. Move towards the idea of socially relevant knowledge as human heritage.

9. Network for "glocality". Co-operation and co-creation of knowledge.
   Local needs require local proposals in global frameworks, and global challenges require global solutions that are locally acceptable. However, global solutions can come from local experience and vice versa.

10. Link research to local needs and to the global development agenda.
    This entails the combination of research, decision-making and development to inform decisions that affect large segments of the population. Explore how to link scientific research and political decision-making related to collective well-being.

Conclusions

An open, proactive reconsideration of the role of higher education in society is an obligation of public commitment and social responsibility. Consequently, we need to avoid succumbing to the weight of inertia and not determine the social role of higher education on the basis of a partial analysis of past needs or present complexity.

If we value socially relevant knowledge, and if "relevant" means appropriate to the context, then what is appropriate to the current context? How can we link the needs of different levels of the context in which all higher education institutions and systems are immersed simultaneously? How can we work so that co-operation between institutions leads to higher education systems that are relevant to their societies or communities? How can we link systems and institutions so that higher education is accessible and relevant worldwide?

GUNI has proposed and analysed a reciprocal course of action: to go from an education at the service of the economic world – now facing a major crisis – to an education that drives sustainability – a challenge that is more urgent than ever. At the same time, students need to be educated to anticipate human, social and economic needs, while giving greater priority to relevance, co-operation and the social value of knowledge than to competition and competitiveness.

These emerging proposals could provide a range of useful alternatives for designing institutional missions – and local, national and regional systems, with their corresponding associations and links at a global scale – in order to ensure fundamental human rights.

Bibliography

Bennani, A. (2008): "The contribution of higher education to multicultural existence: present and future challenges", in GUNI, *Higher Education: New Challenges and Emerging Roles for Human and Social Development*, Basingstoke, UK: Palgrave Macmillan.

Cruz López, Yazmín (2009): *La acreditación como mecanismo para la garantía de la calidad del compromiso social de las universidades*. Doctoral thesis. UNESCO Chair on Sustainability. Universitat Politècnica de Catalunya.

Dallmayr, Fred R., and Thomas A. McCarthy (eds) (1997): *Understanding and Social Inquiry*, Notre Dame, IN: University of Notre Dame Press.

Delanty, G. (2008): "The university and cosmopolitan citizenship", in GUNI, *Higher Education: New Challenges and Emerging Roles for Human and Social Development*, Basingstoke, UK: Palgrave Macmillan.

Escrigas, C. (2008): "Foreword", in GUNI (2008), *Higher Education: New Challenges and Emerging Roles for Human and Social Development*, Basingstoke, UK: Palgrave Macmillan.

Freire, Paulo (2001): *Pedagogía de la indignación*, Madrid: Ediciones Morata.

GUNI [Global University Network for Innovation] (2008) *Higher Education: New Challenges and Emerging Roles for Human and Social Development*, Higher Education in the World No. 3, Basingstoke, UK: Palgrave Macmillan.

Marga, A. (2008): "Multiculturalism, interculturality and leadership", in GUNI (2008), *Higher Education: New Challenges and Emerging Roles for Human and Social Development*, Basingstoke, UK: Palgrave Macmillan.

Muñoz, M. (2008): "Higher education challenges emerging from the interchange between science and ancestral knowledge in Central and South America", in GUNI (2008), *Higher Education: New Challenges and Emerging Roles for Human and Social Development*, Basingstoke, UK: Palgrave Macmillan.

Samovar, Larry A.R. and Richard E. Poster (2004): *Communication between Cultures*, Stamford, CT: Thomson Wadsworth.

Sheridan, Eileen (2005): *International Leadership Competencies for U.S. Leaders in the Era of Globalization*, Dissertation, University of Phoenix.

Stuart, M. (2008): "The concept of global citizenship in higher education", in GUNI (2008), *Higher Education: New Challenges and Emerging Roles for Human and Social Development*, Basingstoke, UK: Palgrave Macmillan.

Tajin, M. (2007): "Globalization and higher education: issues and concerns of cultural diversity". Paper presented at the workshop on Intercultural leadership and changes during the UNU/ UNESCO Conference Pathways towards a Shared

Future: Changing Roles of Higher Education in a Globalized World, 29-30 August 2007, Tokyo.

Taylor, P. (2008a): "Introduction", in GUNI (2008), *Higher Education: New Challenges and Emerging Roles for Human and Social Development*, Basingstoke, UK: Palgrave Macmillan.

Taylor, P. (2008b): "Higher education curricula for human and social development", in GUNI (2008), *Higher Education: New Challenges and Emerging Roles for Human and Social Development*, Basingstoke, UK: Palgrave Macmillan.

Ting-Toomey, Steela (1999): *Communicating Across Cultures*, New York/London: The Guilford Press.

Wiseman, J. (1998): *The global nation: Australia's response to globalization.* Melbourne: Cambridge University Press.

Xercavins, J. (2008): "Higher education and its institutions and the civilizational paradigm crisis: reflections from the perspective of a forum of international civil society organizations", in GUNI (2008), *Higher Education: New Challenges and Emerging Roles for Human and Social Development*, Basingstoke, UK: Palgrave Macmillan.

IV. Higher education for intercultural dialogue: examples of practice

The university as an actor of intercultural dialogue: an example from north Caucasus

Barasby S. Karamurzov

How can university leadership promote intercultural dialogue in broader society? To think about such topics in modern Russia means to think politically. The country is still in a situation where pivotal, strategic decisions are needed in major areas of its life. Such decisions involve the ability to:

1. take into account the immense variety of socio-cultural environments in which institutions of higher education are functioning;

2. understand clearly the outcomes of the preceding period of "post-Soviet transition";

3. identify adequately the basic social and cultural processes that are determining factors for the future.

In this article I aim to state my principal position on the role of the university in promoting intercultural dialogue beyond its own campus, conceptualising that role by reference to my experience of the social functions a regional university centre must fulfil in the specific situation of the north Caucasus.

North Caucasus is a plural region in various respects – linguistic, ethnic and religious. Here, side by side on a comparatively small area there live peoples who also differ in their economies, ways of life, traditions and customs. Such diversity has existed since time immemorial and is still preserved.

Under such conditions it was inevitable that the peoples of the Caucasus formed the concepts of "one's own" and "someone else's", "another's" and of course "others'". The idea of one's own was seen at different levels: "one's own family", "one's own kinship, neighbours, settlement (village), people". The priority of "one's own" is vividly demonstrated by Caucasian folklore. The preference given to "one's own" developed a somewhat alert attitude to "someone else's". The peoples of the Caucasus think that no one can be happy except in their motherland, even in the very place of their birth; this is where they are bound to settle and live the rest of their days.

But there is commonality of basic values and normative structures in the indigenous cultures of the north Caucasus, whereas all of them are marked by "otherness" in reference to Russia's cultural mainstream. So, mutual ability (or inability) to maintain intercultural dialogue may be seen as a constant issue for local communities, as well as for greater Russian society and the regional policies of the state. Not of lesser importance is the inner duality of the socio-cultural systems of the peoples of north Caucasus, which are structured around indigenous elements and borrowings from other civilisations, reflecting historical tradition and values of modernity.

Towards the end of the Soviet period, local societies began to show characteristics that allowed them to participate fruitfully in Russia's transition to democracy and a market economy. But the transition is vulnerable to any factor that can activate the powerful elements of traditionalism, which then also weaken the social and political governability of the region. In practice, democratisation and economic reform in Russia have suffered from many such activating factors.

In the north Caucasus, the major social and political upheavals at the end of the 20th century had very specific preliminary results: the crisis and destruction of the Soviet system, the laisser-faire economic reforms and Russia's transition to democracy were all shaped to a large extent by the dominant socio-cultural factors.

Firstly, the initiative and the major impulses for the political and economic changes proceeded from the socio-political and cultural/ideological "centre" of Russian society, whereas what happened in the north Caucasus may be seen as a reaction – and adaptation by – local ethno-social communities to the radical changes in the "surrounding" socio-political environment. These regional developments in turn later became part of the general process of change in Russia as a whole. Evidently, the local responses to modernising initiatives depended on the mode of their specific refraction in various socio-cultural contexts. In these conditions not only social groups and political units, but ethno-cultural communities also have become actors in the political process.

Secondly, mass political mobilisation in the region mainly concentrated around symbols and slogans, aimed at preserving ethnic or national identity, and reviving national languages and cultures, indigenous traditions and customs. These problems have become the focal points for national political movements and have since been incorporated into the activity of governmental structures. As a result, the vital mechanisms of ethno-cultural reproduction have acquired legal and institutional recognition.

Thirdly, the crisis of statehood, disruptions of the social order, violation of normal functioning of the social mechanisms at all its levels – all of this objectively conditioned a compensatory and stabilising counter-reaction by local societies in the form of partial restoration of regulative functions of a number of traditional social institutions. This brought about the actualisation of corresponding patterns of identity, mental structures, values, norms and modes of social behaviour. And this was in parallel to the purposeful politics of cultural revivalism.

One must say that the north Caucasus at the end of the 20th century faced the challenge of archaisation rather than opportunities of modernisation. Extreme and even violent expressions of these processes – the growth of ethnic nationalism, separatism, interethnic conflict, increasing influence of Islamic fundamentalism and terrorism – have long been actively discussed by experts, the political elite and mass media. It has now become obvious that some "conjunctural" aspects of the post-Soviet transition in the north Caucasus acquired a "structural" content upon which the prospects of regional development essentially depend.

If compared with Russia's average economic indicators, the region is characterised by structural "backwardness". This factor will, for a long time, significantly limit the ability of the regional community to solve its main social and economic problems without external assistance. This gives rise to destabilising factors and negative social phenomena – marginalisation and criminalisation of a certain part of society, and the growing influence of religious radicalism and nationalism on youth. It is worth emphasising that this takes place not in a stagnant patriarchal society, but in an awakened society which got rid of rural isolation. So, it is impossible to merely localise these phenomena and isolate the rest of the population from them.

All previous experience of reform shows that culture in society performs basic rather than superstructural functions. It is the values and norms that dominate a society's culture that actually determine individual behaviour and social practices. It is obvious that the cultural space of Russia tends towards fragmentation and disintegration. Society as a whole and young generations especially are, on the one hand, being influenced by mass culture devoid of national content or symbols. On the other hand, they are influenced by the traditional, indigenous cultural forms now being revived. These may be characterised by ethnic and religious exceptionalism.

Some experts consider that if the prevalent trends that are now transforming the demographic, socio-economic and cultural mapping of north Caucasus continue, the result by the middle of the 21st century will be the overall restoration of the region's demographic structure of the early 20th century. Further divergence of the two cultural strata – one Russian and Orthodox Christian, the other Caucasian and predominantly Muslim – is predicted.

So, current cultural processes acquire some ambivalence: they can serve either as a dynamic factor that enhances intercultural dialogue or as a source of xenophobia and national and religious intolerance. However, this must not give rise to the question of what to do with the ethnic diversification of the region, but instead to the question of how to fruitfully create a culture of intercultural dialogue and polylogue, which will help to prevent ethnic conflicts.

The tensions created in the dual structures of social and spiritual life of the north Caucasus during the transitional period of 1990s have not yet abated. They cannot be removed by any single action in the legal, administrative or political sphere. At the same time, the intensity and multiplicity of economic, political and cultural interactions with the surrounding world must naturally lead to variability and unpredictability in regional development.

In such conditions, the opportunities to realise any rational strategy will depend on an adequate knowledge of the structure of identities, variable patterns of value orientation and social action among younger generations. Hence comes the specific role of the education system in regional development. Education remains, as a matter of fact, the only social institution which has a long-term and universal effect on youth. Its efforts ought to be directed towards forming general conditions that will enable the rising generations to organically adopt the norms and values of the society and simultaneously be open to positive innovations.

The crises and conflicts of the last decade of the 20th century cannot be explained by the mere multiplicity of ethnic and confessional groups encountering each other in this area. It is rather caused by the fact that all of them, and the region as a whole, have reached some culminating point in time, from which all the complexities of their past, contradictions of their present and uncertainties of their future are most obviously seen. Ultimately, such destructive phenomena as separatism or religious fundamentalism can be overcome only by further modernisation of the local communities, with the simultaneous preservation of their cultural and historical identity. Evidently, this cannot be achieved by education only. A purposeful and sustainable policy of regional modernisation, with the system of education playing the key role in it, is needed.

Current tensions and conflicts should pose before us not the question of "What to do with ethnic diversity?" but rather the question of "How to build a culture of peace in interethnic relations?" This is one of the most reliable means to prevent ethnic conflicts and to foster the development of mutual tolerance and positive co-operation of peoples in the multicultural environment of the north Caucasus. The movement towards a peaceful democratic order and securing human rights in this region is attainable only through the dialogue of cultures. For this reason, it is the university that must play a special role in solving the problems of socio-cultural modernisation of the region on the basis of a synthesis of the values of modernity and the distinctive cultural traditions of the indigenous peoples of the region. The university should serve as a model for a modern – that is, an effective, multicultural, democratic and united – commonwealth. So, an important aspect of the university's activity is education of the public at large in the spirit of human rights, democracy, peace and tolerance.

The strategy to achieve these purposes should be related to establishing the mechanism of sustainable development of the regional education system. Universities of the classic type in the region can serve as a basis for a regional system of permanent education. Consequently, the regional system of education must be arranged in a specific way, to secure true participation of youth in the life of society, to secure the whole spectrum of social opportunities for self-realisation of every young person.

It is worth noting in this connection that the regional universities appear to be the most important social institutions for the promotion of human rights in north Caucasus. The reasons are twofold. On the one hand, the Universal Declaration of Human Rights proclaims in Article 26 that everyone has the right to education. And more than that, we can say that in the modern world the right to education is indispensable for the full realisation of other human rights, such as the right to work, the right to free choice of employment, the right to freely participate in the cultural life of the community, the right to equal access to public services, and others. There is no need to go into lengthy argument for the importance of these rights in the present economic condition of the north Caucasus region. One need only consider the meaning of the fact that in the Kabardino-Balkarian State University more than 10 000 students are educated in 15 professional fields and 24 specialties. On the other hand, Article 26 sets forth an explicit demand: "Education shall be directed to the full development of the human personality and to the strengthening of respect for human rights and fundamental freedoms. It shall promote understanding, tolerance and friendship among all nations, racial or religious groups, and shall further the activities of the United Nations for the maintenance of peace". So human rights will be universally secured only if they have an adequate cultural basis in every society throughout the world.

In accordance with this, our public activities are aimed at spreading and strengthening a modern outlook in contemporary Russian society, based on the values and principles of the culture of peace and human rights.

We are quite conscious of the fact that the main trends in modern world culture are related to the growing diversity of worldviews and lifestyles, to the spreading of individualism and multi-culturalism. One can question whether a single "modern outlook" actually exists, and even more the right of anybody to define and enforce it. Such a vision, however, ignores the simple fact that the individualisation and diversification in our ways of life are taking place within one and the same world.

The need for a rational and humane ordering of the life of people in family, community, nation, and obviously, all over the world, is ever growing. A modern world outlook unites our understanding of the rights and interests of the individual with those of the community, the nation and humankind. Undoubtedly, such an outlook is always personal, but hardly particularistic. It may be based on rational or scientific premises while also guided by humanitarian values. It must not be something given once and forever; it must always be open to dialogue and innovation.

Has dialogue contributed
to conflict management, conflict avoidance
or conflict resolution in the Lebanese crisis?

Michel Nehme

The general objective of my article is to specify the indirect role and responsibility of universities in general and Lebanese universities in particular. As units in their own societies, Lebanese universities in my opinion have de facto responsibility for creating conditions that will allow the promotion and construction of a civilisation based on intercultural dialogue and respect of cultural diversity; they also have a responsibility to contribute to the creation of conditions favouring the prevention of violent conflicts, the management and control of conflicts and post-conflict reconciliation. This objective should be reached by means of cultural action programmes involving all generations and aiming to bring cultures closer. This could be done through constructive dialogue and cultural exchanges in all their tangible and intangible components, in such sub-fields of sciences or arts as the archaeological, architectural, artistic, economic, ethnic, historical, linguistic, religious and social. What is important is that universities take steps to expand on the deep meanings of the concepts of communication and dialogue not only through classroom work but also by creating institutions that may be used as channels of communication with the different units of society.

In an attempt to explain the relativity theory of Einstein, Professor John A. Vasquez posed the following question: If the whole universe and every single thing in it and on it is to expand five time its size, can the eyes of human beings detect such an enlargement? All answers to this question were negative. No one would be able to see the difference (Vasquez 1999).

My question now is: what if the world, meaning our planet Earth, were to shrink ten times in size, would we notice such a decrease? The answer to that is yes because the fast acceleration of technological innovation and use are causing the world to shrink in terms of geography, distance and time, but not yet in multiplicity of culture, convictions and interests. The globe has truly shrunk to become one diversified global village.

In a global village of different concoctions of human societies there will always be disparity of views and interests. But the reality today is that we are all interdependent and have to co-exist on this small planet. Therefore, the only sensible and intelligent way of resolving differences and clashes of interests, whether between individuals or nations, is through dialogue. The promotion of a culture of dialogue and non-violence for the future of mankind is thus an important task of the international community and specifically of universities.

A co-intelligent culture

In a speech to the Forum 2000 Conference in Prague on 4 September 1997, the Dalai Lama said that the task of building a co-intelligent culture is different from many other kinds of social change and utopian vision because there is no arrival point, not even in our dreams (Dalai Lama 1997). The final result is a culture that can keep on going, a sustainable, co-evolutionary culture that can learn from its experience and adapt and create in harmony with its circumstances. This means that such a culture will be always changing.

Of course, our culture is already changing but those changes are not coming from people learning and looking ahead together, as a culture, as whole communities. That is what we need to change most: the amount of conscious, collective intelligence at work. And we can start doing that right now, right here, wherever we are. Mostly this involves creating what the Dalai Lama calls "a culture of dialogue". Who is better at doing this than universities? A culture of dialogue is one in which people habitually gather to explore their lives, their differences, their dreams. Every facet of such a culture would contribute to people learning together, building healthy relationships with each other and the natural world, and co-creating better prospects for their shared future.

I wonder if a culture of dialogue can be one of mass-consumption such as the one that dominates our world today. Co-intelligence requires community, some sort of stable interconnection, people knowing each other and committed to each other. These are exactly the conditions that are undermined by anonymous, temporary global market relationships that ask only "what is the price?" and steady erode the local, the inter-personal, the mutually answerable, the ecologically and culturally responsive.

This is a gigantic subject which I can only hint at here. But at least I want to raise this issue before I proceed to more direct efforts to assess the possibility a co-intelligent culture of dialogue in Lebanon. The creation of that culture will probably require a change in our material conditions, and a change in such conditions will probably only come about through our efforts to build a culture of dialogue. The two are necessary conditions for each other and so they are likely evolve together, step by step.

Cultural diversity or division

Awareness of the vital importance of culture – as a primary vehicle of meaning and a tool for understanding, a democratic agent, an instrument of individual and collective human development and a forum for rapprochement and dialogue between all men and women – and awareness that new forms of conflict may increase the difficulties of dialogue between cultures has led certain groups to use culture with the avowed or unstated aim of fuelling hatred, xenophobia and confrontation between different communities.

At the outset there is a need to emphasise the fact that nobody should be harassed on account of his or her lawful opinions and that every individual therefore enjoys an inalienable right to define and choose his or her cultural and/or religious affiliation and identity. There is an increasingly strong tendency academically and intellectually to imply that cultural impoverishment and marginalisation, on the one hand, and prejudice and ignorance, on the other, are among the prime causes of increasing violence and stereotyping of others, thus altering the nature of peaceful and constructive relations between different cultural communities. There is also an emerging consensus that it is appropriate to ensure that better understanding between cultures and intercultural dialogue becomes a mean of conflict prevention at every level and in all its contexts and components.

In the past, religions and cultural diversity have been responsible for wars, or have at least shared responsibility for them, and we cannot say that this is no longer the case today. The wider picture contains both light and shadow. On more than one occasion in the course of history the religious and cultural factors have prevented or moderated violence. One thinks, for example, of 'the truce of God' during the Christian Middle Ages, the strict conditions that Islamic Law attached to a 'just war' or the care for prisoners of war and innocent victims called for by various religions. However, the main reason for the so-called wars of religion and cultural diversity was not so much hostility between the religions and value-oriented cultures themselves, but much more the pursuit of power by individuals and human groups (empires, dynasties and nations), in the course of which religion and culture were used in the service of personal or collective ambition.

As regards contemporary conflicts, it is important to examine information critically before alleging simple religious or cultural motivation. It would, for example, be simplistic to designate as merely "religious" or "cultural" the conflicts in Lebanon or comparable situations in places like Northern Ireland, the Balkans, the Philippines and Afghanistan. On the contrary, in many of these cases the religious authorities and / or cultural elite, far from having incited these conflicts, have been passionately committed to peace and reconciliation.

Cultural and religious pluralism contribute to the mystery and richness of Lebanon. At times this pluralism is explosive. For 15 years, from 1975 to 1990, Lebanon was plunged into a civil war that violently divided the country into regions controlled by religious and ethnic factions, including Sunni, Shiite and Druze Muslims and Maronite Christians. The diverse interests of the Lebanese, Palestinians and other national groups fuelled the war, even though they each form part of the country's make-up. Seventeen religious communities inform people's religious consciousness. Social discontinuity is also a major factor in Lebanon's pluralism, pitching the poor (Christians and Muslims) against the rich (Christians and Muslims). On the fringes of this diverse, even fragmented social order, where stands the future of Lebanon?[19]

---

19. For more information on the topic, read "Dialogue at times of war?" Message by the executive director of the Anna Lindh Euro-Mediterranean Foundation for the Dialogue between Cultures – Alexandria, Egypt, 27 July 2006; see www.funci.org/en/2006/issues/dialogue-at-times-of-war/.

How to define Lebanon?

Lebanon is vital for the existence of democracy in the Middle East, because the destiny of democratic processes is profoundly bound up with Lebanon's destiny and its particular mission (John Paul II 1997: 10).[20] Geographic Lebanon, according to the Exhortation, comprises the existing state with its internationally recognised boundaries. It is a Lebanon threatened by occupation in the south and by the presence of non-Lebanese armed forces on its territory (ibid: 26). Lebanon's human capacity is composed of several communities, which are "at the same time its fortune and its uniqueness" (ibid: 4). Because it is composed of several different communities, Lebanon is regarded by its own intellectuals as an exemplary land. In fact, today as yesterday, these diverse religious and cultural communities endeavour to live together on the same land in order to build a nation of dialogue and conviviality,[21] and to co-operate in matters of state and nation building (ibid: 186-197).

The cultural value of Lebanon lies in being the cradle of an ancient culture and one of the beacons of the Mediterranean. No one could ignore the name of Byblos, which reminds us of the origins of the alphabet. In his address to the patriarchs and bishops of the Catholic Church on 1 May 1984, Pope John Paul II confirmed that Lebanon has a "valuable cultural worth" and that Lebanon is "more than a country: Lebanon is a message and an example for the East as well as for the West." The pope said that "Lebanon's historical message" is a "message of freedom," of democracy, and that it is "a land of dialogue and conviviality among diverse religions and cultures" (Al Khoutout 1993: 77, Arabic). Pope John Paul II reiterated the same idea during the opening of the synod, saying "Lebanon, this small country, is larger than its size in what it represents in terms of values. Lebanon is grand in its history, comprehensiveness, esteem and message" (Journal 1996: 280, Arabic).

Therefore, Lebanon represents the sum of its geographic position, its human capacity and its cultural value, with all three attributes organically intertwined. These three intertwined attributes lie at the core of the concern for the autonomy of Lebanon. It is from this base that Lebanese intellectuals resolutely object to any division of Lebanon and categorically reject any partial or total occupation or annexation of Lebanon by any state. The army, as it symbolises the unity of Lebanon, demands that Lebanon regain its full independence (territorial integrity), total sovereignty and unambiguous freedom.

Living together in Lebanon

If we are to envisage a new formula for living together in Lebanon, this indicates that the existing formula does not conform with the requirements and expectations for a New Hope for Lebanon and consequently does not serve the ideal aspirations for Lebanon.

---

20. Ideas developed in this part of the article closely follow Najm (2007).
21 'Conviviality' is used in Lebanon to convey the idea of different groups living together in a spirit of common and peaceful understanding.

In carefully reading and examining history, it becomes obvious that every time emphasis is placed on the issues of dialogue, patriotism, politics, society and the like, it is accompanied by calls for the establishment of new conditions and new structures. In this respect, the pivotal idea of any intellectual contribution is to arrive at a proposed national political structure based on living together in harmonious interaction.

However, if the Lebanese people – meaning the holders of Lebanese nationality – believe that they form a homogeneous society, is there any need to discuss the issue of living together? Yes, there is a need. The reality is that Lebanese society is not homogeneous. It is a heterogeneous society which has been and still is incompatible in social identity. There is a need to acknowledge that Lebanon's society is heterogeneous, that is, plural.

Understanding the terminology of plurality

Some of the terms related to diversity, such as pluralism and multiplicity, co-existence, living together and conviviality, are often interchangeable in common use. Their use in the case of Lebanon, however, calls for clarification of the true meaning of each.

Pluralism *versus* diversity

There is a need to understand the distinction between the two terms "pluralism" and "diversity" and the two expressions "living together" and "conviviality". Many Lebanese object to the term pluralism, which is often used by political and social scientists, and request that it be replaced by the term diversity. Although the term pluralism is often misinterpreted, I see no reason to yield it to the will of the opposition and use of the term diversity, because I believe that pluralism and diversity can be used synonymously.

The prefix "pluri" comes from the Latin *plures*, meaning "plural", while "diverse" and "varied" are derived from *diversus*. However, Arabic does not make this distinction. Dr Henri Kremona, in defining the terms "diversity" and "pluralism", stated:

> Diversity is quite different from pluralism. According to most social scientists, diversity is mentioned in the framework of diversity of cultural heritage. Diversity supposes a fundamental unity on the level of social commitment, which exists in the dogma of belief. As for the unity in pluralism, it remains a difficult task, because it tries to unify elements that are fundamentally and dogmatically different and culturally separate. Unity in one religion is realized through confessional diversity, and unity in the nation is realized through religious pluralism. (Kremona 1997: 15)

The Imam Sheikh Mohammed Mehdi Shamseddin, who previously had categorically opposed the use of the term pluralism, then seemed to change his position. He announced in an interposition [introduction of a remark or opinion during a debate or conversation] at the Beirut Book Fair that "either we believe in dialogue, which inwardly encompasses an acknowledgement of pluralism. Or we can pretend that we are not pluralist or diverse, and thus we have no need for dialogue" (Shamseddin 1997).

Kamal Salibi in *A House of Many Mansions* speaks in his introduction about the different confessions in Lebanon whose historical roots are of a religious nature (Salibi 1993: 19-37). These religious roots are the roots of Lebanon's national identity and politics. This makes the connection between religious pluralism and cultural pluralism a totally organic one. In this regard, Lebanon has its own specificity. It is the fruit of its own history; it is inter-communal. It is our formula for conviviality and respect for the cultural identity of each of our communities. Each religion, because it is incarnated, manifests itself culturally. Therefore, our religious affiliation, whether Christian or Muslim, has necessarily a sociological and communal dimension; it shapes our family, social and spiritual life.

Many works of Lebanese literature talk about cultural presence and its distinctiveness, as well as about connecting culture with religion. In their discussion of the life of fraternity and solidarity, many authors consider it to be based on the affirmation that each person has the right to his or her own role in the social, political and cultural life without compromising fidelity towards her or his spiritual and cultural tradition.

UNESCO in its communiqué in Mexico in 1982 stated that "Culture is a series of distinctive characteristics, spiritual, material and intellectual, which describes a society or a social group. It encompasses, in addition to arts and literature, formulas of living and the fundamental rights of the human being, as well as value systems, traditions and beliefs" (Journal 1996: 66). In this sense, the term "culture" surpasses its pure meaning and embodies the living group characteristics of a particular societal identity. Accordingly, pluralist culture in our society is not defined by the skin colour of the Lebanese or by their appearance, their language, their origin or their race. It is rather a religious-cultural pluralism reflected in the group's concepts, views, values and formulas of living. It rarely leads to a difference in education, traditions or behaviours.

Is 'conviviality' possible in Lebanon?

"Living together" may be limited to cohabitation, being neighbourly, or to frequenting and interacting among people without the existence of co-operation, collaboration, harmony, affection and conviviality. "Living together" may be governed by collision, as has been the case in Lebanon during periods of crisis. In other words, "living together" may be overshadowed by a basic sense of passive reality, of being in the same neighbourhood without effectively living together. This is not bad, but it is not sufficient. This might lead to a confrontational situation. "Conviviality", on the other hand, elevates common living to a level of sociability and affection. "Conviviality", as viewed in the social studies, is what should govern people's relations, whoever they are, wherever they may be and however they may differ.

Diverse social groups provide a positive, convincing and definitive answer to the possibility of "conviviality" in Lebanon. The Catholic Church sees the Islamic-Christian "living together" as divine will in the sense of being neighbourly, cohabiting and interacting with people. In its pastoral letter, the Council of the Eastern Catholic Patriarchs declared in 1992 that "God in His wisdom wanted us [Christians and Muslims] to live together in this land of the world and we do accept His will with tolerance" (Al Khoutout 1993: 82).

How to attain 'conviviality'?

Social scientists are aware that intention by itself is not enough to attain "conviviality", though it is a fundamental requirement. Real conviviality requires the existence of suitable circumstances, conditions, systems, regulations and institutions, without which it cannot exist. Once these requirements materialise, conviviality can take shape. An undeclared author[22] lists the five most important conditions for conviviality to be realised as: a just social and political system, rejection of secularisation, true dialogue, common destiny and fidelity to cultural pluralism.

A just social and political system

It is easy to be symbolic and principle-oriented, like those thinkers who ask the Lebanese people to build a just and equitable social and political system, one that respects every individual and all the currents that form Lebanon, in order to build their common home together. These thinkers would not have called for the establishment of a just and equitable social and political system if the existing system were effective. The system is inappropriate simply because since independence it has not succeeded in preventing protracted severe crises, the last of which culminated in the 2008 political deadlock and a strife manifesting itself in bloody confrontations.

For optimum results, conviviality should come to life, become incarnate, within a political system. An un-incarnated conviviality remains sweet rhetoric, which does not become part of the conscience of people and remains a delusion. In working towards establishing such a political system, respect for all currents (political, social, ethnic, ideological) is essential. These currents are the inclinations and desires of the Lebanese communities, rooted in their cultural formation. The correlation between the social and political system, all the political and societal currents, and the realisation of complete acceptance of pluralism, form the symbol which unties the knot in the Lebanese dilemma over a future political system. Otherwise, each group will fail to consider the needs and legitimate aspirations of the other.

Social scientists assert that an equitable sharing of responsibilities – the idea that sharing of responsibility is a powerful tool to create commitment to the decision-making process – ought to develop in the heart of the nation and its system. Researchers of social stability believe that the legitimate authorities have a duty to ensure that all communities and individuals enjoy the same rights and are subject to the same obligations according to the principles of equity, equality and justice, this is a requisite to stability.

---

22. Tools for Conviviality, www.opencollector.org/history/homebrew/tools.

This is another confirmation of the importance of conviviality in a political system. We notice that social scientists repeat the term "community rights" in addition to "individual rights", in order that no one will suppose that the Lebanese population is only composed of individuals. That is to say, unity is the responsibility of each individual and each cultural and religious group.

Rejection of immediate secularisation

The Lebanese as a people and Lebanon as a state in the region are called upon to reject immediate secularisation. A secular system, if it is to happen by imposition in the Lebanese system and society, in its various aspects has the tendency to organise itself in the absence of common values and this leads to a dictatorship of an unclear majority coalition with dispersed values whose members will, as soon as they subdue the rest of the communities, themselves fight against one another, taking Lebanon back to civil strife. This means that the values of authority, legislation, justice and even life itself should derive their criteria from the existing world of communities and not from the proclaimed Eminent One.

Laicism is considered today as a system that places the government in a neutral position in regard to the beliefs of citizens, allowing them to live their beliefs the way they want and allowing religious institutions to perform all their functions. It also allows for the establishment of religious schools and other schools belonging to the diverse religious communities. Lebanon at this stage of its history should consider laicism as a fundamental principle in its development. It is therefore misleading and confusing to equate the word laicism with secularisation. Some Lebanese unwisely refuse the wise attitude to secularisation, considering that "living together and / or "conviviality" cannot happen except by severing the umbilical cord of the right of religion to guide and advise people. They also call for the concerns of religious leaders to be confined to houses of worship. They promote the secularisation of various pieces of legislation and give absolute priority to a value-free endeavour that does not exist in true reality.

True dialogue

The state of Lebanon should call for the formation of a constitutional committee whose job is to work for a true dialogue, which respects the sensibility of individuals and various communities. This committee should be instructed to note that the Muslim-Christian dialogue aims in the first place at promoting living together between Christians and Muslims in a spirit of openness and collaboration, which is indispensable for each person if they are to flourish and determine choices dictated by a conscience of citizenship.

This committee should connect the essential conditions for true dialogue with encouraging the Lebanese to know each other better and fully accept pluralism. With this, the committee would acknowledge that avowing pluralism is the door to all solutions, and without it solutions remain unattainable (Najm et al. 1993: 55).

Common destiny

According to its constitution, Lebanon is an integral part of the Arab world, and the same destiny links Christians and Muslims to Lebanon and to the other countries of the region. The Christians of Lebanon should maintain and strengthen their ties of solidarity with the Arab world without losing their distinctive values. The Christians are called upon to consider their further involvement in Arab culture, most of which is enriching in a global world where old social values are diminishing. The Lebanese should know that by committing themselves to such a step, especially the Muslim-Christian dialogue, collaboration in Lebanon can help those in other countries in applying the same approach (John Paul II 1997: 149-150).

Lebanon is fortunate to have its Christians open to dialogue. They have also always been part of the Arab world and have invariably contributed to Arab culture. There was rarely a dispute between the Christians and Muslims on such matters. The dispute has been and will remain about what is called the Islamisation of Lebanon. The Islamists, whether Sunnis or Shiites, aspire to one of two objectives in this: either to annex Lebanon to what is called "The Greater Nation of Islam", or to establish an Islamic or quasi-Islamic system in Lebanon. The majority of the Lebanese reject both these aspirations.

Fidelity to cultural pluralism

The Lebanese are called on to be faithful to their history and the continuity of their cultural and religious pluralism. "Conviviality" does not cause pluralism to melt away or become diffused, which would in turn lead to loss of identity, culture and character in each group. Only dialogue, with the process of mutual learning which it involves, can open the religions up to each other so that people can learn to live together in diversity and get to know and understand each other better. Religious pluralism is a mystery. It has something to do, on the one hand, with God's respect for human freedom, and, on the other hand, with the natural conditions of human religious and cultural development.

For thousands of years the main human groups lived in isolation from each other, in Europe, in Africa, in Asia and in America. Today, in contrast, the world is characterised by a diversity of interconnections and by a consciousness of mutual dependence. Of course there are still various tensions and violent conflicts between human groups. The religions have an important role to play here; they share in responsibility for the achievement of greater justice and harmony in relations between the nations, economic blocs and cultural groupings of our world. All conflict between religions – such as polemics and insensitive proselytism – should be avoided, as should syncretism, which destroys the originality and authenticity of religion. This is not a matter of denying differences but rather of grasping what these differences really amount to. Neither does dialogue in any way exclude witnessing at times to one's own faith and inviting others to recognise what one has oneself come to know as true and valuable. Believers of different religions should try to

145

identify those issues on which a shared, believing witness is possible, together with a genuine search for unity, in humble submission to God's will.

It is a fact that Islam and Christianity both claim to be universally valid. There is no reason why either should give up this claim. Everything depends on the methods used as the two religions seek to express and live out their universal claims. Today there should be no place for methods that rest chiefly on individual or collective ambition: violence; war; coercion in all its forms and manifestations, whether subtle or otherwise. The only way that is acceptable to humanity and worthy to obtain universal recognition for the values one holds to be true and valid is through frank dialogue, along with the necessary respect for free decision of the human conscience.

Religious freedom is an inalienable right of every human person. To suppress it, or even just to limit it, is to ridicule humanity. It is the union between essential values and the state. Any abuse of such a union would empty the responsible administration of its significant and symbolic power of decision-making. All religions have the right to liberate themselves from such systems of value emptiness.

All people, whether Christian or Muslim, are committed to living in solidarity with their own religious community or group and to seeking its peace and prosperity, whether this is the *Umma,* the Church or other groups. At the same time it is important to show full respect for free decisions made in good conscience in regard to faith and religious adherence. The one binding principle in this sphere is to follow the voice of one's own conscience, that is, a conscience that is genuinely seeking the truth. Faith and religion can only be genuine if people are totally free to choose or reject them.

Which political system would embody conviviality?

In their repeated use of the following terms and expressions, social scientists outline the elements required to assure a political system that would embody conviviality.

In which formula or pact would the following expressions, terms and sentences take on a meaningful life together?

- Living together or co-existence;
- Respect for every confession, fidelity of the Lebanese to their history and adherence to their plural cultural and religious heritage;
- Building a nation of dialogue;
- Lebanon's historical roots as it now stands are of a religious nature and are the basis of its national identity and politics;
- Elevate living together to a higher level, that is, to conviviality;
- Acceptance of pluralism;
- Teaching a just and equitable social and political system which respects individuals and all tendencies;
- Equitable sharing of responsibilities;

146

- Ensuring that all communities and individuals enjoy the same rights and are subject to the same obligations;
- Freedom of education and schooling;
- Guaranteed freedoms and rights of the individual; and
- Religious freedom.

The above requirements lead us to envisage the Lebanese state as a composed entity and its political system as a consensual democracy. Most Lebanese intellectuals explicitly state that the desired system should be based on a consensual democracy. At the Special Assembly of the Synod of Bishops for Lebanon, the Reverend Jean Ducruet, the late President Emeritus of Saint-Joseph University in Beirut, made clear the meaning of "consensual democracy". He believes that strengthening national unity requires a firmly established political system in which all confessions share in making national decisions and in which no one confession can impose on the nation what is not acceptable to the tradition of the other confessions.

This system cannot function at the mercy of the ideology of the majority. Numerical majority is not compatible with consensual democracy. It can only be conceivable in a country without fundamental diversity. Consensual democracy necessitates a coalition government and a mutual veto on decisions that are seen as contrary to the vital interests of any of the communities. Official posts should be distributed in a manner by which no one group will dominate positions of responsibility by virtue of its power and number. This system requires the self-autonomy of some departments, such as the departments of personal status, which would remain the prerogatives of the various groups (Slim 1997: 69; Assemblée Spéciale 1996: 65-66).

Composed in this manner, the state and a system of consensual democracy constitute what is called unity in diversity. In other words, the formula of living together or co-existence in Lebanon is a complex concept. It is a unity-in-diversity system, which is tailored to Lebanon's body and answers to its needs, that is to say, it is accepted willingly and is not forcibly imposed.

Constructive pluralism: international perspective

The colloquium Towards a Constructive Pluralism took place at the UNESCO Headquarters in Paris on 28-30 January 1999. There were 40 participants from 29 countries: politicians, academics and representatives of civil society. The colloquium was organised by the United Nations Educational Scientific and Cultural Organization (UNESCO) and the Commonwealth Secretariat. UNESCO, with its 186 member states, is dedicated to international intellectual co-operation to promote development for peace and peace for development. To this end, one of its key activities is the Culture of Peace Programme inspired by the universal values of liberty, justice, equality, solidarity and social and cultural dignity. The 54-member Commonwealth is united by a set of fundamental democratic and other values, as embodied in the 1991 Harare Commonwealth Declaration, and a commitment to sustainable development. Both of these intergovernmental organisations are committed to the promotion of unity in diversity.[23] Participants affirmed that ethnic, religious, cultural and other pluralism is a positive phenomenon, to be welcomed and celebrated. There was agreement that everything possible should be done to create conditions in which it can flourish within and between states.

At the same time, it was recognised that difference could be used to promote division and tension. It can be an excuse for marginalisation, exclusion and oppression, and all too often it can be the occasion for violent conflict and even warfare. Participants gave examples of campaigns of genocide, civil war and other violence, which had claimed millions of lives. It was pointed out that, according to one study, 79 of the 82 conflicts around the world between 1989 and 1992 were intra-state in nature and that most of them were linked to ethnic, religious or cultural differences. It was argued that 'divisive pluralism' will constitute one of the key threats to peace in the 21st century unless appropriate action is taken. This document suggests ways to prevent such conflicts by promoting the positive alternative.

We as Lebanese should recognise that approaches to this issue need to take account of the significant changes that have taken and are taking place in the world – in particular, the dual forces of globalisation and fragmentation, and the fact that the world is becoming increasingly homogeneous globally, but more and more hetero-geneous locally. This has important implications for attempts to accommodate the complexities and meet the challenges of pluralism.

In this context, the Lebanese should agree on the importance of appreciating our common humanity and the shared and universal values this entails. Lebanese should refer to the importance of respect for difference, equality and non-discrimination, the upholding of human rights, and the democratic legitimacy of institutions, accountability, participation and qualitative representation. Lebanese should, and this happens only through education and state propaganda, accept that the aim should be equality and inclusiveness, not uniformity. The recognition of difference can strengthen unity by allowing individuals to enjoy the security of particular identities within an accepted social and constitutional framework.

There should be recognition of the need to balance the affirmation of particular identities and the requirements of an increasingly interdependent world where we must all co-exist and co-operate. Identities can be mobilised or exploited for either negative or positive purposes. Finding ways to encourage positive uses of identity is important for all Lebanese, regardless of the minority they belong to or their socio-economic status. This issue is relevant to everyone, as all communities are vulnerable to division. It is the responsibility of universities and a prerogative of the Lebanese Government to take a dynamic and positive view of ethnic, religious, cultural and other pluralism as an invitation for people to interact, to celebrate and to learn from difference, rather than just passively accept the fact that pluralism exists. Speakers at the colloquium stressed that pluralism is enriching and can make

---

23. UNESCO Colloquium on The Role of NGOs in a Building Process of Constructive Pluralism in Contemporary Multicultural Societies, Paris, 28-30 January 1999.

an important contribution both to balanced development within particular countries and the building of positive relationships between countries. The UNESCO colloquium acknowledged that particular identities and society's means of dealing with cultural and other forms of difference involve arrangements and attitudes that can be made and unmade. Consequently, there is always the possibility of improvement and dynamic evolution, whether this involves building new forms of identity or working with existing ones.

This colloquium recognised that there are problems of terminology and vocabulary and that lack of clarity can impede understanding and the development of consensus. For instance, terms such as "facilitating", "implementing", "managing", "accommodating", "handling", "empowering" and "sustaining" were used and it was recognised that, while often relevant, each had its limitations. Participants in this UNESCO colloquium also recognised that terminology might be a problem so far as the interpretation of pluralism in different contexts is concerned. They agreed, however, that none of the formulations used should be taken to suggest that there should be any national or international efforts to contain pluralism. In this context, Lebanese ought to recognise that greater clarity is needed regarding our understanding of the past and its relationship to the development of a constructive pluralism for the future.

Fields for action

While increasing pluralism is recognised as a universal fact, Lebanese should also acknowledge that each community (minority) has its own particular character and history. Matters of pluralism within a state have to be seen in the context of a wider international environment.

How to respond to pluralism is an issue that concerns all Lebanese and needs to be addressed at the personal, social, cultural and political levels: the personal, because it is about who we are and how we define ourselves; the social, because it concerns how we interact with each other; the cultural, because it inevitably involves our beliefs, ideas and understandings; and the political because to accommodate pluralism involves the distribution of power and access to resources. For this reason, intellectuals need to consider the role of both the state and civil society.

The state

Social scientists have long recognised the important and positive role that the state can play – for instance, by promoting a sense of belonging and common citizenship in a democratic framework – and the continual need for the renewal of its role. But state institutions can play a negative role if, in a pluralistic society, they only reflect the priorities of one dominant group. In most states the ethnic and cultural composition of populations is changing and there is often an awakening of ethnic identities in these new demographic landscapes. There is no one model that can be applied in all circumstances, and social scientists usually stress the need for a flexible approach.

To help make ethnically, religiously and culturally plural societies work effectively, it is important to address the following:

- processes of participation that include all groups and ensure qualitative, not merely quantitative, representation (such processes should not exclude minorities in the name of majority rule);
- inclusive, flexible approaches to constitution-making – and the working of constitutions – to ensure proper representation of all groups and full representation and participation by minority, deprived and marginalised groups;
- decentralised or devolved structures, as appropriate;
- sustainable development and equitable resource allocation;
- codes of conduct for politicians and other leaders;
- recognition and implementation of indigenous peoples' rights;
- the development of educational processes that promote understanding of pluralism and positive attitudes to people in other communities;
- providing conditions in which public and other media can reflect the diversity of society;
- facilitating opportunities for intercultural contacts and equitable allocation of funding for cultural activities;
- a legal framework to safeguard rights;
- building up oversight institutions such as human rights commissions and ombudspersons, so that they become important role players in maintaining democratic governance.

Civil society

There is a key role for a vigorous democratic civil society in empowering pluralism, although it is, of course, possible for elements in civil society to exacerbate tensions and deepen divisions. Civil society organisations have the advantages of being flexible, creative and able to promote dialogue through their networks. The following parts of civil society merit particular attention:

- Community groups, and other NGOs which can bridge cross-community divisions;
- Local authorities, which can be effective in strengthening intra-communal harmony;
- The media, in encouraging increased understanding of the realities and issues involved in constructive pluralism;
- Professional associations, which can encourage communication and co-operation between members of different cultures;

- Businesses and trade unions, which can promote diversity in the workplace through inclusive working practices, diverse representation and culturally sensitive working arrangements;

- Religious groups, which can encourage mutual respect and understanding if they emphasise the inclusive aspects of their respective traditions;

- The academic community, by encouraging greater understanding of the nature of pluralism;

- Multicultural publications and media that provide for positive self-expression of particular communities while combating divisions;

- Increased cultural diversity in the marketplace.

International bodies

While aware that international interventions can sometimes be negative, NGO leaders recognise the important and sometimes decisive role of regional and international institutions and organisations in standing firm against the negative exploitation of pluralism and also promoting appreciation and respect for human rights and ethnic, religious and cultural pluralism.

Recommendations

We as Lebanese should organise our universities to be able to inject modern concepts in the minds of intellectuals and students, leading to the belief that all sections of society need to work in partnership to sustain policies that support, celebrate and popularise constructive pluralism. There is a particular need for positive leadership to make pluralism attractive and viable. Lebanese universities, in conjunction with appropriate organisations, should:

- promote further discussion on issues of pluralism, including at regional level and through the media;

- review the work of organisations already involved in this area and construct a database of those with technical expertise in the promotion and implementation of pluralism (e.g. in combating stereotypes);

- produce a manual of good practice, a code of conduct and normative guidelines;

- promote international recognition of the examples of states and institutions which are following good practice;

- encourage the creation of early warning mechanisms to detect incipient conflict in plural societies and combat divisiveness and ghettoïsation;

- distribute all positive information as widely as possible.

The Lebanese Government should stress that:

- religious, ethnic, linguistic and other groups should be encouraged to emphasise those aspects in their traditions that foster mutual respect and understanding;

- where appropriate and requested, assistance should be given to individuals and communities to reconstruct their identities when these have been disrupted by migration and urbanisation;

- a range of educational processes should be developed to support interaction and encourage respect between communities;

- academics, policy makers and practitioners should be encouraged to engage in dialogue with each other, to inform the debate on pluralism.

Finally, I would like to underline the importance of areas where further research should be undertaken. A number of bodies could assist in research work addressing:

- the implications of globalisation on issues of identity in Lebanon and on the capacity of groups to interact;

- the impact of technological change on various levels of pluralism;

- the affective as well as the rational dimensions of pluralism;

- the challenge of pluralism at rural, urban, regional and global level;

- the implications of cultural rights;

- the effect of existing measures to promote equality and respect for human dignity (Kaymakcan and Leirvik 2003).

References

Al Khoutout al 'Arida (1993): The Special Assembly of the Synod of Bishops for Lebanon, Vatican [Arabic].

Assemblée Spéciale pour le Liban du Synode des Evêques, Message de l' (1996): "Le Christ est notre espérance: Renouvelés par Son esprit, solidaires, nous témoignons de Son amour", 2nd edn, El-Metn, Lebanon: Centre Catholique d'Information.

H.H. the Dalai Lama (1997): speech to the Forum 2000 Conference in Prague on 4 September 1997, www.forum²000.cz/en/projects/forum-2000-conferences/1997/transcripts1/morning-session--sept--4/.

John Paul II (1987): *Christifideles laïci* ('Lay Believers in Jesus'), Vatican.

John Paul II (1997): *Une Espérance*, Exhortation Apostolique Post-Synodale, Vatican.

Journal du Synode des Evêques pour le Liban (1996): *Documents, Positions, Prospective*, Paris: Centre d'Etudes et de Recherches Pastorales.

Kaymakcan, Recep and Oddbjørn Leirvik (2003): *Teaching Tolerance in Muslim Majority Societies*, Istanbul: Centre for Values Education.

Kremona, H. (1997): "Al Irshad al Rasouly Raja Jadid Li Lubnan … Part II", *Al-Raiyat* (October), pp. 14-17.

Najm, A. et al. (1993): *Ajwibat 'ala As'ilat Sinodos al Asakifat*, Lebanon.

Najm, A. (2007): "Envisioning a formula for living together in Lebanon in the light of the apostolic exhortation", www.futuremovement.org/forum/showthread. php?t=4394.

Salibi, Kamal (1993): *A House of Many Mansions – The History of Lebanon Reconsidered*, London: I.B. Tauris.

Shamseddin, M.H. (1997): "'Anakeed al Ghadab", *Al-Marqab* (Fall), pp. 13-54.

Slim, S. (1997): "Synodos al Katholic men Ajl Lubnan", *Al-Marqab* (Fall), pp. 55-76.

Vasquez, John A. (1999): *The Power of Power Politics: From Classical Realism to Neotraditionalism*, Cambridge Studies in International Relations, Cambridge: Cambridge University Press.

Cultural pluralism as a challenge to the effectiveness of university education in fostering dialogue and understanding

Is-haq O. Oloyede

The contemporary world is increasingly multicultural and the identity crisis resulting from this sometimes threatens sustainable human development. This makes the promotion of understanding and dialogue a prime issue in the management of multiculturalism, global peace and security. What roles can and should higher education play in attaining this worldwide objective? How are such roles being played? What are the context-specific challenges being faced? This article attempts to answer these questions by taking a critical look at the situation in Nigeria – one of the most culturally-complex countries in the world.

The article is in three parts. In the first part, the nature of the social conflicts in the country, bordering on ethnic and religious contestations, is briefly considered. The impact of these conflicts on Nigeria generally, and the university system specifically, is discussed with a view to demonstrating how a national crisis could partly challenge the ability of the university system to maximise its potential to contribute to the fostering of national understanding and dialogue. The last part of the article makes the point that, these challenges notwithstanding, Nigerian universities (with the aid of the constitution and the dexterity of vice chancellors) still manage to make some outstanding contributions in the direction of promoting dialogue among the contending forces in the country. The Nigerian case study is therefore internationally instructive.

The Nigerian background

Nigeria is a plural society in terms of its multi-ethnic and multi-religious nature. The country has over 400 ethnic groups (Suberu 1998: 277) and two major religions, Islam and Christianity. Of all the federal democracies in the world, only India can match Nigeria's cultural complexity (Joseph 2006: 15). If well managed, this factor of unity in diversity would be a major asset to the Nigerian state, but the contrary is the case. Nigeria's cultural diversity is politicised and exploited by the elite in such a way that it slows down the nation's growth and progress. The problem affects all aspects of Nigeria's national life: federal (and even local) resource allocation, management of public institutions (Dudley 1973; Egwu 1993; Ake 1996; Anber 1967) and youth development (Akinyele 2001). The problem has fuelled several bloody clashes between ethnic neighbours across the country (see Albert 1993; Otite and Albert 1999; Uwazie, Albert and Uzoigwe 1991; Albert 2001), destabilised the country, especially at national level (Nnoli 1978; Mustapha 2002, 2004) and even produced a civil war in 1967-70 (Nafziger 1983).

The most threatening of the problems faced by the country is ethnicity. The problem of ethnicity in Nigeria is more easily understood in terms of competition between ethnic groups for the scarce resources available to the federation. Ethnicity can affect any aspect of a society, especially the ownership and management of national resources. Public institutions in multi-ethnic and multi-religious societies are usually micro-political systems and this can place heavy burdens on their management.

At national level, the ethnic conflicts in Nigeria are largely among the three dominant groups in the country: the Hausa/Fulani, Yoruba and Igbo. At local level, the conflicts are between ethnic neighbours and these vary from one state to the other. In each place, groups compete for the available economic, material and political resources and institutions, often in a manner that threatens national peace and stability.

Effects on the university system

The national crisis negatively affects higher education in terms of how ethnic groups compete, sometimes acrimoniously, for the location and management of federal universities, polytechnics, colleges of education and colleges of agriculture. Of these, the university system is one of the most contested by the contending groups.

The aggressive competition between the diverse groups in Nigeria for the control of universities derives from the assumption that these institutions have significant roles to play in elite formation and recruitment in addition to the fact that the institutions generate local employment and economic regeneration. Within this framework, ethnic and sub-ethnic groups in the country are sensitive to the location of universities, appointment of their vice-chancellors, staff recruitment and the admission of students. In most cases, the people of the states and communities where the federal and state universities are located see the institutions as their personal property and want them managed as such.

The most controversial issue is the vice-chancellorship. Ethnic groups in Nigeria come together to "fight" one another when a new vice-chancellor is to be appointed – there are several cases of this type of problem in Nigeria – and then the vice-chancellor comes under pressure when staff are recruited and students are to be admitted.

Interestingly, many of these conflicts started to occur in the late 1990s when the issues of ethnicity and religious fundamentalism became critical factors in Nigerian politics (Uwazie, Albert and Uzoigwe 1999). As groups fight among themselves over religious issues, land ownership and the need to reform the Nigerian state generally, they politicise the questions of who should head the universities, how staff should be recruited and how students should be admitted. Most vice-chancellors that were appointed before this period served outside their states of origin and did well. The list includes Professor Akinkugbe, a Yoruba man, who served as vice-chancellor of the Ahmadu Bello University, in a Hausa-Fulani enclave; Professor Adamu Baikie, a Hausa-Fulani who served successfully as vice-chancellor of the University of Benin and even got a second term; Professor J. Ezeilo, an Igbo and Christian who served as vice-chancellor of the Bayero University in Kano, a centre of Islamic civilisation; Professor Essien-Udom, an Ibibio was at the University of Maiduguri, the Kanuri heartland; Professor Tekena Tamuno, an Ijaw, was vice-chancellor of the University of Ibadan; Professor Onwuemechili, an Igbo, was at the University of Ife as vice-chancellor; and Professor Ayandele, a Yoruba, served as vice-chancellor of the University of Calabar.

Towards a culture of dialogue, understanding and tolerance

The foregoing makes the need for fostering the culture of dialogue and under-standing a major national project for Nigeria. What is "dialogue" and how do we want it applied to the issue of Nigeria's multiculturalism? Dialogue, as a social science concept, derives from two Greek words *dia* and *logos*. *Dia* means "through" or "with each other" while *logos* means "the word". To this end, the word "dialogue" is etymologically understood to mean a free flow of information or meaning between people. In a multicultural society, it refers to an organic exchange of information between and amongst peoples of diverse ethnic or religious orientations in a way that helps to break down stereotypes and poor understanding of how others think or perceive the world around them (Weimann 2004: 19).

The significance of dialogue in this respect is embedded in the fact that poor communication is a major cause of identity conflict around the world. Explaining how this type of conflict crystallises, Weimann argued that:

> Our interpretation of the message we have received from another person, as well as the decoding of the message, depends on our knowledge of this person. But, if the reality in which the message was formulated or encoded is too different from the reality it is interpreted in, or decoded, then the message received will not resemble the message emitted. (Weimann 2004: 23)

A Nigerian example suffices to support the above position. It has been clearly established at various meetings of the Nigeria Inter-religious Council (NIREC), which I co-ordinate, that the major cause of religious crisis in Nigeria is that many adherents of the two major religions in the country – Islam and Christianity – do not have sufficient information on what each other's religion preaches. The Muslims are poorly educated about Christianity and the Christians are poorly educated about Islam. The reason is that there is limited opportunity for exchange of information between the adherents of the two religions. NIREC was established to deal with this problem.

Dialogue is a collaborative exercise; it requires social actors to be ready to interact. It is also voluntary; it cannot be forced on anybody. It requires trust, sincerity and the willingness to accept diversity in human nature. It entails collective reflec-tions, learning and communication between groups and a tolerance of paradox (or opposing views), the suspension of judgment and empathic listening. Its main goal is to promote societal cohesion by making complex issues be collectively explored (Isaacs 1993; McGinn 2004).

Dialogue and the Nigerian university system

In the context of higher education in Nigeria, dialogue refers to two main situations: the extent to which Nigerian universities are able to facilitate healthy interaction among Nigerians, especially through capacity building; and the extent to which the university campus could be said to be a locus of intercultural exchange. The achievability of these two objectives depends very much on the extent to which the government (especially the federal government) is able to deal with the problem of the identity crisis at national level. This is because, as said earlier, the problems come from the top.

It is thus compelling for us at this point to examine a number of federal policies that promote the culture of dialogue, understanding and tolerance to the extent of having powerful impact on the functioning of the university system in Nigeria. The first such policy is contained in Section 14, sub-section 3 of the 1979 constitution, which provides as follows:

> The composition of the Government of the Federation or any of its agencies and the conduct of its affairs shall be carried out in such a manner as to reflect the federal char-acter of Nigeria and the need to promote national unity, and also to command national loyalty, thereby ensuring that there shall be no predominance of persons from a few states or combination of a few ethnic or other sectional groups in that Government or any of its agencies.

Section 277, sub-section 1 of the 1979 constitution defined "federal character of Nigeria" as "the distinctive desire of the people of Nigeria to promote national unity, foster national unity and give every Nigerian a sense of belonging to the nation as expressed in Section 14, sub-sections 3 and 4 of this Constitution".

Since 1979, the "federal character" principle and others deriving from it (e.g. Section 157, sub-section 5; Section 197, sub-section 2; Section 199) have provided the basis for location of universities, polytechnics, colleges of education and even federal secondary schools (high schools) in Nigeria, as well as the personnel to staff these institutions. This policy is aimed at promoting equity in Nigerian society and making all Nigerians feel a sense of belonging. A body known as the Federal Character Commission promotes, enforces and monitors compliance with the provisions of the "federal character" clauses of the Nigerian Constitution.

It is necessary to note however that the Nigerian Constitution – unlike those of Lebanon, Belgium, Cyprus, India and Malaysia, where comparable constitutional provisions and public policy exist – does not reserve or earmark any quotas for desig-nated ethnic groups. Thus, each group in the federation adopts its own peculiar self-help strategies to get what it considers to be its fair share of the "Nigerian national cake". The end product is widespread suspicion among groups and sub-groups in the country, which makes dialogue and understanding even more desirable at the national, state and communal levels, but even more difficult to attain in Nigeria. Higher education has significant roles to play in dealing with this problem.

Additionally, the Revised National Policy on Education, which came into effect in 1981, specified that the growth and development of the university system in the country should ensure "a more even geographical distribution [of universities] to provide a fairer spread of higher education facilities" in the country and that "admission of students and recruitment of staff into universities and other institutions of higher learning should be on a broad national basis" (FGN, quoted in Yoloye 1989: 75). This policy, in my opinion, is merely calling attention once again to the need to reflect "federal character". Ethnic and religious politics have made this policy a source of conflict in many Nigerian universities today.

The Nigerian state also has a system for promoting dialogue and understanding on issues relating to student admission to federal universities. The current regulation for the admission of students to the federal universities in the country was set out in a circular (Ref. No. FME/S/518/Vol. 1/99 of 2 September 1983) in which all universities in the country are enjoined to promote diversity in their admission policies. Similarly, the Association of American Universities (AAU), consisting of 62 leading North American research universities, adopted a statement on 14 April 1997 that expresses strong support for continued attention to diversity in university admissions. The US diversity scheme takes into account a wide range of considerations – including ethnicity, race, and gender (AAU 1997). The AAU statement, which is significant for putting the Nigerian policy in global perspective, provided the following as the rationale for the diversity policy:

> We believe that our students benefit significantly from education that takes place within a diverse setting. In the course of their university education, our students encounter and learn from others who have backgrounds and characteristics very different from their own. As we seek to prepare students for life in the twenty-first century, the educational value of such encounters will become very important, not less, than in the past.

> A very substantial portion of our curriculum is enhanced by the discourse made possible by the heterogeneous backgrounds of our students. Equally, a significant part of education in our institutions takes place outside the classroom, in extracurricular activities where students learn how to work together, as well as to compete; how to exercise leadership, as well as to build their consensus. If our institutional capacity to bring together a genuinely diverse group of students is removed – or severely reduced – then the quality and texture of the education we provide will be significantly reduced … In this respect, we speak not only as educators, but also as concerned citizens. As presidents and chancellors of universities that have historically produced many of America's leaders in business, government, the professions, and the arts, we are conscious of our obligation to educate exceptional people who will serve all of the nation's different communities.

The US statement on diversity in admissions contained a statement that requires us to shed more light on the equivalent policy in Nigeria. The AAU statement noted: "We do not advocate admitting students who cannot meet the criteria for admission to our universities. We do not endorse quota or 'set asides' in admissions. But we do insist that we must be able, as educators, to select those students – from among many qualified applicants – who will best enable our institutions to fulfil their broad educational purposes".

The Nigerian admission policy favours what the AAU refers to pejoratively as "quota" or "set asides". However, the policy is not to compromise meritocracy but rather provide opportunities for the best candidates from all regions of the country to be given access to university education. The first regulation is that all students to be admitted must have met the minimum standards of the affected universities.

The Nigerian circular mentioned above specified the following admission criteria: (a) merit, 40%; (b) catchment/locality, 30%; (c) educationally less developed states, 20%; (d) others, 10%. In other words if 100 students are to be admitted, the best 40 are admitted first, the next 30 are the best from the locality and catchment area, and the next 20 are the best from the states of the federation considered to be educationally less developed; the university uses its discretion to choose the final 10 on any criteria it considers best. Overall, the 100 students admitted are among the best qualified candidates. No unqualified students are admitted.

We need to throw more light on the admission criteria. "Merit" as used above is determined by each candidate's score in the competitive examination conducted by the Joint Admissions Matriculation Board (JAMB) or the Advanced Level Certificate Examination conducted by the West African Examinations Council, the University of London and other related examination bodies. Under this criterion, the higher the score of a candidate, the higher the chances of his/her being admitted. "Catchment area or locality" is determined on the basis of states contiguous to the states in which each federal university is located. The "Educationally less developed states" are the later starters in Western education. Candidates from these states are given special concessions in the admission policy to enable them catch up with their counterparts in the more advanced states. Most of these states are in northern Nigeria. "Discretion" is used to admit students who would not be admitted on the basis of the three earlier criteria but who in the opinion of the university administrators deserve consideration, usually on humanitarian grounds (Yoloye 1998: 65-68).

The role of universities in promoting dialogue and understanding

Federal policy in the appointment of vice chancellors and staff and in the admission of students has a positive impact on the promotion of a culture of dialogue, understanding and tolerance in Nigeria. It makes every Nigerian university into a microcosm of Nigerian society, in terms of a generous mixture of all the ethnic and religious groups. Students from different parts of the country are thus forced to live side by side in hostels; they do class assignments together and discuss the problems of Nigeria together. By the time many of these students return to their communities, they are a different species of Nigerians altogether, having towered above those ethnic and religious stereotypes that bedevil Nigerian society and retard the country's growth. Staff members go through the same experience. Their neighbours in the office, as a result of the "federal character" policy, are from other parts of Nigeria. Through the gossip and discussion of national issues in the office, they too are forced to understand the other groups in the country and to learn to work harmoniously with them.

The committee system in the university, the senate traditions and the wide ethnic and religious distribution of the teaching staff and principal officers of the university also constrain any vice-chancellor from being sectional in his or her admission. He or she has to consult very widely and get the approval of appropriate bodies for every step he or she takes. A good vice-chancellor, under the present system in Nigeria, cannot afford not to be a good social mixer, being daily invited by staff and even students to naming ceremonies, funeral rites and other social functions that could in some cases offend his or her beliefs. The vice-chancellor must demonstrate tolerance and understanding by attending many of these social functions.

Universities in Nigeria, like their counterparts elsewhere, have three important mandates: to produce high-quality individuals for promoting national and international development; to carry out cutting-edge research; and to engage in community service. Issues of fostering dialogue and understanding point to the university's "community service" responsibility. Equally, however, universities promote dialogue and understanding in the process of teaching and research. Some intervention projects of Nigerian universities can be mentioned to shed more light on this.

Peace as a GNS course

With a view to making Nigerian universities into places that promote dialogue, understanding and tolerance, there is now a standing policy in the country for all universities to teach Peace and Conflict Studies to all first- and second-year students. The goal of this project – which started in 2004 and is enforced by the National Universities Commission (NUC) – is to give all Nigerian university graduates a grounding in how to handle non-violently all forms of conflict they might encounter with other Nigerians. All students must take and pass the course, which is part of the compulsory General Nigerian Studies (GNS) programme.

Some PhD research on this GNS project reveals that it has gone a long way to positively change the attitude and behaviour of Nigerian university students towards other Nigerians and foreigners alike (see Albert 2009). One obvious snag in implementing the policy is that most lecturers teaching the course are themselves not properly trained in peace studies, and few institutions provide such hands-on training in West Africa. The significance of this finding – given the level of progress made so far – is that the Nigerian society would become more peaceful if more teachers were trained to facilitate the GNS course.

Peace Studies

The first Peace Studies programme to be established in any Nigerian university was at the University of Ibadan. The project started in 1994 in reaction to the political crisis generated by the administration of General Sani Abacha, who ruled Nigeria with an iron fist from 1994 to 1997. The high-handedness of the regime increased ethnic conflict (and, by implication, religious suspicion) among the Nigerian peoples. Indeed, Nigeria was on the verge of breaking up when General Abacha suddenly died in 1998 and was succeeded by General Abdulsalami Abubakar, who stopped the conflict situation by adopting reconciliatory policies towards the various aggrieved groups in the country.

The Ibadan Peace Studies programme was aimed at promoting dialogue and understanding among Nigerians at a time when the military dictators were actually tearing the country apart by the assassination of key political actors in the country, arrest of military officers and their civilian counterparts on account of phantom coups d'état, and other forms of state terrorism (Albert 2005a). The goal was to produce well-trained Nigerians who could engage in community work aimed at peacemaking, peacebuilding and preventive diplomacy. The project began as a British Council-supported academic link programme between the University of Ibadan in Nigeria and the University of Ulster in Northern Ireland.

Between 1996 and 2000, the two universities exchanged academic staff members. This enabled the Ibadan MA and PhD course in Peace and Conflict Studies to take off in 2000 (Albert 2005b). Since then, the course – at the university's Institute of African Studies – has produced several hundred well-trained peace workers in the West African sub-region, and not just Nigeria alone. Some of these peace studies graduates come from the security sector and non-governmental organisations engaged in various forms of humanitarian work. The latter spend the best of their time doing community-based conflict-transformation projects involving the promotion of dialogue and understanding among the diverse groups in the country.

The Society for Peace Studies and Practice

As part of its agenda to foster dialogue and understanding at the grassroots level, the Peace and Conflict Studies programme of the University of Ibadan championed the establishment of a professional body known as the Society for Peace Studies and Practice (SPSP), consisting of conflict-management scholars and practitioners brought together from different parts of Nigeria. The main aim of the society is to promote a synergic relationship between peace studies scholars and conflict-management practitioners who have hitherto worked on issues relating to dialogue and cultural understanding at different levels. Through the conflict-management scholars, the peace practitioners in the society draw some theoretical lessons, while the scholars learn about Track II Diplomacy from the peace practitioners. The society holds an annual conference and general assembly, during which the members discuss issues relating to the fostering of dialogue and understanding in Nigeria and far beyond. The author of this paper is a Fellow of the Society.

The Ilorin Peace and Strategic Studies programme

Following the example set by the University of Ibadan, and with the technical support of the SPSP, the University of Ilorin decided in 2008 to establish a Centre for Peace and Strategic Studies (CPSS) to award MA and PhD degrees in Peace and Development Studies. The academic programmes of the centre took off in December 2009 with 30 MA students and three PhD students. The PhD students included graduates of the MA course in Peace and Conflict Studies from the University of Ibadan. The goal of the Ilorin Peace Studies programme is to link peace and development work and produce students with hands-on experience in peace work. To this extent, the Ilorin programme focuses more on peace practice and most of the students are people with practical field experience in conflict management, especially from the Middle Belt region and the northern parts of Nigeria, which were hitherto not well reached by the Ibadan course in Peace and Conflict Studies.

In addition to producing world-class students for peace work at local level, the University of Ilorin has adopted three interesting strategies for fostering dialogue and understanding in Nigeria. It has instituted a Distinguished Personality Lecture series, which makes it possible for a prominent Nigerian leader to be invited (on a quarterly basis) to address a topic bordering on national conflict or peace. Two such lecturers have been invited so far. The first is the Governor of Niger State, Dr Mu'azu Babangida Aliyu, and the second is the Governor of Rivers States (one of the hottest sites of youth militancy in Nigeria), Mr Rotimi Amaechi. In addition to the interesting debates generated by the lectures within the university, the issues raised by the invited speakers are often discussed and debated by the media for weeks. This helps to widen the opportunities for dialogue and understanding in the country.

The second strategy adopted by the Ilorin Peace and Strategic Studies programme is to reach out to the security sector, not only as a way of supporting the security-sector reforms in the country but more importantly to introduce the officers of the Nigerian Army, State Security Services and Nigerian Security and Civil Defence Corps to non-violent conflict-management strategies. The university has made significant strides in achieving this objective.

The third strategy adopted by the University of Ilorin is to institute a biennial conference series in peace theory and practice as part of the grand strategy for enabling the CPSS to make significant contributions to the promotion of dialogue in Africa. The first such conference – on the theme Peace Processes in West Africa – took place on 3-5 August 2009 and was attended by over a hundred peace scholars and practitioners across the West African sub-region. The conference enabled us to discuss issues relating to conflicts in the University of Ilorin, Nigeria, West Africa, Africa and the larger world, and to identify solutions to some of these problems. The proceedings of the conference are being published by a leading Nigerian publisher and will be distributed far and wide with a view to making it another channel for promoting dialogue and understanding in Africa.

Conclusion

This article has made the point that Nigerian society is divided by factors of ethnicity and religion, and this works against the smooth running of universities in the country, especially in terms of staff appointments, management of the institutions and recruitment of students. All of these limit the extent to which the university system in the country can effectively foster a culture of dialogue and understanding. This article has defined the problem but also attempted to underscore some modest efforts that some universities are making to reach out to people, most of all by making significant contributions to peace building in the country.

Nigerian universities are merely a microcosm of the larger Nigerian society. Within this framework, I have argued, the problems of ethnicity and religiosity in our universities will not go away until these two problems are played down at national level by instituting the policy of true federalism and a culture of tolerance – most notably by the elite who exploit ethnicity and religiosity for personal gain. This does not mean that the universities themselves cannot help to solve the problems besetting them through in-house activities. These include the need for vice-chancellors to begin to see themselves as not representing any particular ethnic or religious group, as often happens, but as being the "mothers/fathers of all".

The management of the universities must place emphasis on meritocracy rather than mediocrity. This would make both staff and students begin to see their future as being a function of how hard-working they are, rather than how sycophantic they can be, tied to ethnicity and religiosity. Universities must also organise regular seminars, workshops and conferences that build bridges across ethnic and religious divides. The lesson of the Peace Studies programmes at Ibadan and Ilorin is that universities can silently contribute to the fostering of dialogue and understanding by training high-quality individuals for these activities at the grassroots level.

Bibliography

AAU (1997): "AAU Statement on the importance of diversity in university admissions", Washington, DC: The Association of American Universities.

Adekanye, B. (1983): "'Federal character' provisions of the 1979 constitution and the composition of the Nigerian armed forces", *Plural Societies*, Vol. 14.

Ake, C. (1996): "The political question", in O. Oyediran (ed.), *Governance and Development in Nigeria: Essays in Honour Billy Dudley*, Ibadan: Agbo Areo.

Akinyele, R.T. (2001): "Ethnic militancy and national stability in Nigeria: a case study of the Oodua People's Congress", *African Affairs*, Vol. 100, pp. 623-640.

Albert, I.O. (1993): *Inter-Ethnic Relations in a Nigerian City: A Historical Perspective of the Hausa-Igbo Conflicts in Kano 1953-1991*, Ibadan: IFRA.

Albert, I.O. (ed.) (2001): *Building Peace, Advancing Democracy: Third Party Intervention in Nigeria's Conflicts*, Ibadan: PETRAF/John Archers Books.

Albert, I.O. (2005a): "Terror as a political weapon: reflections on the bomb explosions in Abacha's Nigeria", *IFRA Special Research Issue*, Vol. 1, pp. 37-56.

Albert, I.O. (2005b): "General introduction", in I.O. Albert (ed.), *Perspectives on Peace and Conflict in Africa: Essays in Honour of General (Dr.) Abdulsalami Abubakar*, Ibadan: Peace and Conflict Studies Programme, University of Ibadan.

Albert, O. (2009): "An assessment of the NUC policy on the teaching of Peace Studies as a GES course", PhD thesis submitted to the University of Ibadan, June 2009.

Anber, P. (1967): "Modernization and political disintegration: Nigeria and the Ibos", *Journal of Modern African Studies*, Vol. 5, No. 5, pp. 163-179.

Dudley, B.J. (1973): *Instability and Political Order: Politics and Crisis in Nigeria*, Ibadan: University Press.

Egwu, S (1993): "Ethnicity, economic crisis and national development in Nigeria" in O. Nnoli (ed.), *Dead-end to Nigerian Development: An Investigation on the Social Economic and Political Crisis in Nigeria*, Dakar: CODESRIA Book Series, pp. 44-78.

Isaacs, W. (1993): "Dialogue: the power of collective thinking", *The Systems Thinker* (April).

Jinadu, L.A. (1985): "Federalism, the consociational state and ethnic conflict in Nigeria", *PUBLIUS: The Journal of Federalism*, Vol. 15, pp. 71-100.

Jinadu, L.A. (2002): "Ethnic conflict and federalism in Nigeria", ZEF-Discussion Papers on Development Policy. Bonn, Germany: Center for Development Research.

Jinadu, L.A. (2006): "Nigerian university and the problem of cultural diversity: policy responses and consequences", in W.R. Allen, M. Bonous-Hammark and R.T. Teranishi (eds), Higher Education in a global society: Achieving diversity, equity and excellence, *Advances in Education in Diverse Communities: Research, Policy and Praxis*, Vol. 5, pp. 7-32.

Joseph, R. (2006): "Mis-governance and the African predicament: can the code be broken?" Faculty Distinguished Personality Lecture Series 1, Delivered 30 November, Faculty of the Social Sciences, University of Ibadan.

Materu, P. (2007): *Higher education quality assurance in sub-Saharan Africa: Status, challenges, opportunities, and promising practices*, New York: The World Bank.

McGinn, N.F. (2004): "An argument for dialogue in definition of national policies for education", *Journal of International Cooperation*, Vol. 7, No. 1, pp. 15-25.

Mustapha, A.R. (2002): "Ethnicity and democratization in Nigeria", in D. Eyoh, B. Berman and W. Kymlicka (eds), *Ethnicity and Democracy in Africa*, Oxford: James Currey.

Mustapha, A.R. (2004): "Nigeria: ethnic structure, governance and public sector reform", paper presented at UNRISD Conference on Ethnic Structure, Governance and Public Sector Reform, March 2004.

Nafziger, E.W. (1983): *The Economics of Political Instability: The Nigerian-Biafran War*, Boulder CO: Westview Press.

165

Nnekwu, D.A. (2007): "A comparative survey of the impact of ethnicity and religious affiliation on the alienation of staff from their work environment in Nigerian universities", *Research in Education*, Vol. 78, pp. 35-53.

Nnoli, O. (1978): *Ethnic Politics in Nigeria*, Enugu: Fourth Dimension Publishers.

Otite, O. (1990): *Ethnic pluralism and ethnicity in Nigeria*, Ibadan, Nigeria: Safari Books.

Otite, O. and I.O. Albert (eds) (1999): *Community Conflicts in Nigeria: Management, Resolution and Transformation*, Ibadan: Spectrum Books.

Suberu, T.R. (1998): "States creation and the political economy of Nigerian federalism", in Kunle Amuwo et al. (eds), *Federalism and political restructuring in Nigeria*, Ibadan: Spectrum Books.

Uwazie, E.U., Albert, I.O and Uzoigwe, G.N. (eds) (1999): *Inter-Ethnic and Religious Conflict Resolution in Nigeria*, Lanham, MD: Lexington Books.

Weimann, G. (2004): "Openness to dialogue and the limits of intercultural dialogue", in *Conflict: What has religion go to do with it?*, Accra: Woeli Publishing Services.

Yoloye, F.A. (1989): "Federal character and institutions of higher learning", in P. Ekeh and E. Osaghae (eds), *Federal Character and Federalism in Nigeria*, Ibadan: Heinemann Educational Books (Nigeria), pp. 47-49.

For a culture of dialogue and mutual understanding: a Lebanese case

Georges N. Nahas

The objective of this article is to show, based on the case of a particular university in Lebanon, the role that universities can play in creating an atmosphere of multi-cultural understanding. The rise of religiously driven political speech all over the world created a rupture in society, and the universities in Lebanon immediately suffered from the fallout.

Lebanon's multi-confessional reality and the political tension that underlies it together create a real challenge to the tolerance and mutual understanding that universities have to champion. This article, illustrated by a real-life example, aims to support the thesis that a new approach to academic curricula, an approach that emphasises knowledge of the other and the creation of activities of collaboration, will enhance the establishment of a new paradigm for conviviality[24] in a multicultural and multi-confessional society.

This article (i) presents Lebanon as an example of a multi-confessional country, open to all the risks that this entails, (ii) states the specific case of a university which has tried to make in-depth changes in its approach by preparing its students to live in a dialogue perspective, and (iii) ends by making some proposals to be discussed within the framework of an international forum.

The global context

Globalisation is making the world more permeable to the exchange of ideas and making people more aware of changes, wherever and whenever they may occur. At the same time the media, a major communication tool, propagates information, thoughts and events by groups and individuals as fast as they happen. Use of the media is increasingly considered a must, but people are not always aware that media is often a subject of controversy.

In the evolution of civilisation these two vectors, globalisation and media-driven communication, cannot be subjected to the wishes or the control of local decision makers. Universities have to deal with these facts, and with their technological and human dimensions, by making the best use of their positive potential and creating a mechanism of defence to avoid any type of alienation.

In contrast, rightly or wrongly, religion is involved in politics in many countries as a factor in discord and tension. This seems to be true at international and local levels,

---

24. 'Conviviality' is used in Lebanon to convey the idea of different groups living together in a spirit of common and peaceful understanding.

especially in multi-confessional environments. Religion is called on to be a source of tolerance and a place to meet the Other who is different; the use of religion as a determining factor in politics and international relations is distorting debate by presenting religion as an element of cultural discord.

At the same time, people's positive everyday life experiences of conviviality in several countries are underestimated and replaced by negative images, which are reported daily in the media with a lot of subjective analysis of the facts. The question is then: How will universities react in the short and medium term to this negative trend, which uses religion as a driver for discord? What solutions will universities develop to stop the fatal evolution of such a trend and to establish an adequate atmosphere for co-operation and a common contribution to the future of human kind?

Lebanon and its multi-confessional structure

The Lebanese political profile

At the eastern limits of the Mediterranean Sea and the western borders of the Middle East, the geopolitical position of Lebanon has conferred upon this small country a particular importance at the political and economic levels. Being witness to a number of wars and demographic changes, Lebanon experienced along the centuries a very particular status that made it a place for rich and important cultural exchanges.

Lebanese political life from the 16th century onwards exposed the country to the impact of Western influences, which took advantage of the fact that Lebanon's population belonged to different religious communities. Successive 20th-century changes in the demographic profile of the Lebanese population, mainly due to various political interference, were reflected in political life and the tensions that ensued. Naturally, this impact was mirrored at the level of the student body in universities: conviviality and tolerance became more and more at risk on campus.

The Lebanese population

The Lebanese population is composed of 18 different religious confessions. The political system is based on this multiplicity and, from 1922 until now, has been unable to overcome difficulties driven by the misuse of what we call confession-alism.[25] This confession-driven system is based on two important articles of the Lebanese Constitution: one of these makes belonging to a religious confession compulsory in order to be able to get involved in political life and ask for civil rights, and the other gives the religious confessions political and educational rights.

Because of this compulsory membership and the rights given to the religious confessions, any kind of inflexible religious speech forces citizens to make a fatal choice of

---

25. In two successive volumes of the journal *Al-Markab* (UOB Publications), researchers from different fields emphasised the drawbacks for the Lebanese population and political life in Lebanon of such a political system.

priorities. Nevertheless, the political system claims that the principle of conviviality is the philosophical basis of the country, and all the confessions are urged by the constitution to work for a mutual understanding and a national co-operation that goes beyond religious affiliation.

Confessionalism and democracy in Lebanon

Lebanon went through a civil war in 1975. This war ended in 1992 with the adoption of a new constitution, which introduced a new paradigm into Lebanese political life, based on the following declaration: to establish a harmony between Confessionalism and Democracy (Kheir 2003). For Lebanese thinkers, the question was and still is: Is this possible? If yes, how?

Democracy, ultimately, means equality among citizens as individuals; a confession-driven political system gives priority to the religious affiliation of citizens. If we want to go deeper and question how sound is this politically – how can we have harmony between these two principles? – we will notice that the semantic field of the democratic approach is also challenged. Confessions are trying to take advantages and privileges to strengthen their political status, claiming for themselves a special type of democracy. At the same time, citizens searching for equality under the law find themselves deprived of some of their civic rights. Asking for a civic status outside a confession may even be considered to be an evil claim (Moukhayber 1997). The main question for a number of citizens is this: In a constructive vision of conviviality and tolerance, and taking into consideration this unhealthy atmosphere of confessionalism to which citizens are exposed, can universities be a factor for positive change?

Universities in Lebanon

Higher education in Lebanon was established in the middle of the 19th century. This academic activity, which was (and still is) one of the Lebanese achievements in the region, did not stop even during the wars that the region and the country went through in the 20th century. The university tradition in Lebanon be proud of this positive achievement before 1968. That was a turning point because the important political changes that occurred in the region that year[26] had a direct impact on political life in Lebanon because of the country's religious fragmentation.

Until 1955, the private universities, even though established on a religious basis, had a very positive impact on the cultural and religious life of Lebanon and the Middle East in general. These institutions helped to develop a spirit of liberty, democracy and openness. They influenced not only Lebanese citizens but also students coming from all the Middle Eastern countries. Between 1955 and 1968, new universities were established in Lebanon, among them the only public university of the country and the first private institutions not belonging to a religious entity. Nevertheless,

---

26. The Arab-Israeli war and the launching of the Palestinian Resistance.

until 1968, all the universities in Lebanon were places of tolerance, spaces of intercultural dialogue and foyers of emergence of new political and social ideas.

After 1968, things changed in Lebanon. From 1968 to 1975 a new atmosphere gradually took over, as confessional tensions began to prevail. Between 1975 and 1990, due to the civil war, the era of democratic debates, conviviality and tolerance became a thing of the past. Some Lebanese thinkers (Salem 2009) consider that universities in Lebanon, particularly between 1943 and 1975, did not act adequately to prepare future generations to become catalysts of the kind of change that goes towards creating a democracy free from any confessional stench. Proof is seen in the positions and speeches of a number of politicians who had attended or taught in these universities before 1975 and all through the civil war.

Between 1996 and 2008, the number of universities and institutions of higher education grew drastically.[27] Many of these institutions are microcosms of the country, exposed to the crossfire of political movements and driven by a loss of conviviality and tolerance. Administrators of such universities therefore have to act appropriately in managing the everyday life of their institutions. The question remains: Do universities carry any responsibility for this deterioration because they did not and do not know how to prepare for the future and face the crisis?

Answering such a question is hazardous for several reasons. Firstly, the persons in charge were not prepared for the changes that took place so suddenly. The universities were run by academics trained mainly in Western countries and were managing their institutions as if they were living in a democratic Western environment. Secondly, the university curricula were very classic ones. Students were not formed to adopt critical attitudes nor to be able to counter politicised religious speech. The learning outcomes of the programmes were driven by the needs of a region that was made up mainly of developing countries. The political elite that came from these universities were looking at the political arena as a continuum of their academic know-how. Thirdly, the political situation was deteriorating very rapidly, making room for religious speech to become the reference frame, replacing the civic one. This helped establish a profound cleavage within the student body, while the faculty and the administrators were dealing with the emerging burning issues through means that were no longer adapted to circumstances.

During the civil war the status of the universities was a very challenging one, and universities and academics in Lebanon were not ready to let the higher education system in Lebanon sink because of the political turmoil. The launching of the University of Balamand was one of the actions taken in this spirit of renewing university life in Lebanon.

---

27. Lebanon now has 47 higher education institutions, of which 22 are universities. Only one is a public institution (the Lebanese University). Religious bodies founded 31 of the 47; the others are mainly family businesses.

The University of Balamand

The University of Balamand (UOB) was founded in 1988 by merging several institutions of higher education that were already in existence. This merger took place under the auspices of the Orthodox Antiochan Church, one of the 18 religious communities officially recognised in Lebanon, a community known for its openness and for the role it played on many occasions during the war in bridging the gap between different factions. This strategic merger, decided on by one Lebanese community in the midst of the civil war, was fully supported by persons from various confessions and backgrounds who believed in the future of Lebanon, and who were willing to help prepare for a new Lebanon through such institutions.

The specificity of UOB

Many aspects make UOB almost unique. Established in the northern part of the country, UOB is the first fully-fledged Lebanese campus so far from the larger Beirut area. Even though some higher education activities did exist in north Lebanon, it was the first time that a university with all its programmes, its cultural activities and its university life was launched there, thus creating a totally new environment. It is worth mentioning that this part of Lebanon was not exposed as severely to the civil war (1975-92) as the larger Beirut area. At the same time, for demographic reasons, an atmosphere of conviviality prevailed within UOB despite the war. This atmosphere helped UOB to adopt non-discrimination as the basis for recruitment at all levels. This explains the diversity of confessional belonging in the UOB faculty, staff and student body.

On the other hand, the Board of Trustees of UOB made a strategic decision from the very beginning. UOB officers were to have a single priority: to aim for excellence in their administrative and academic planning. Having this main objective as the ultimate goal, UOB worked hard to implement strategies to fulfil this commitment. Because of its strategic choices, UOB gained the support of all the surrounding communities with their variety of confessional affiliation. This support helped UOB to overcome many difficulties that threatened the process of establishing an atmosphere of tolerance and conviviality.

The vision and the role

UOB officers, together with the Board of Trustees, worked to elaborate a vision for the institution that would reflect its identity as an institution of higher education functioning in a specific multi-confessional human environment. This vision stresses what the founders considered as the cornerstone of the new institution. On one hand, UOB has to become a place for multi-confessional conviviality to testify what can be the future of Lebanon, when the war ends and a peaceful atmosphere reigns again in the country. On the other hand, adopting and applying a policy of non-discrimination at all levels is a must, to show that institutions in Lebanon can become places where only skills and performance are recognised, independently of the religious background of the students or the faculty and staff members. Finally,

171

UOB has to make nation-building its first priority, by emphasising the quality needed to reach a high level of excellence in order to help society overcome all the problems of the post-war period.

Strategic decisions and actions

Three strategic decisions were adopted to implement this vision, on three complementary levels: academic planning, institutional rules and regulations, and national and international relations. To follow up UOB's objectives, action plans were adopted at all three levels.

On the academic level

A four-course programme of Culture and Civilisation was established. Within this programme students take a course on Christianity and Islam. Its objective was to help students to better know one another, thus overcoming preconceived negative ideas and misconceptions. By refusing to avoid dealing with religious issues, UOB gave its students the occasion to discuss and deliberate on hot subjects in a spirit of openness and tolerance. UOB is still the only institution in Lebanon where students are exposed to such a course.

A graduate study programme in Christian-Muslim Studies was established with the objective of developing research that would promote and adopt approaches emphasising points of convergence and mutual understanding of national and cultural problems from the Christian and Muslim points of view. A summer school gathering of professors and researchers now meets annually to deliberate intercultural themes as an integral part of this master's degree curriculum.

On the institutional level

A research institute focusing on History, Archaeology and Oriental Heritage was founded. Its objective is to improve knowledge and understanding of the region's history and the conditions of conviviality and tolerance that have reigned there. This institute calls regularly for international academic seminars in co-operation with sister institutions; it finances research and publishes books as well as a peer-reviewed journal, *Chronos*.

A research centre for Christian-Muslim Studies was also founded. Its objective is to highlight the elements of mutual understanding between Christianity and Islam. In addition to a master's degree programme, the centre launched a Conviviality Observatory and regularly organises academic seminars; it aims to become a reference centre for all researchers interested in working within a non-conflictive atmosphere.

On the national and international relations level

UOB led, very efficiently, concerted efforts with other institutions to organise international seminars and to launch concerted initiatives in intercommunity and intercultural dialogue, in supervising research, and in publishing books and reviews on topical subjects.

An open policy for exchange of professors and students was implemented.[28] This policy aimed to attract faculty and students to Lebanon to study the evolution of intercultural dialogue in an atmosphere of social conviviality and to be able to evaluate the impact that world challenges are having on our human environment.

Evaluating the results

After 20 years, one may question whether UOB has managed to realise, even partially, its ambitious objectives. It is difficult to give an answer by Yes or No. We can underline certain successes that we may be proud of. It is clear to any external observer that a healthy atmosphere reigns among the students, particularly at the level of potential inter-confessional tensions; UOB is one of the few universities in Lebanon where decisions to avoid conflicts within the student body for political reasons (driven by religious means) were welcomed by the students.[29]

Open-mindedness at the level of debate takes place regularly in classrooms, where an academic atmosphere prevails; faculty members and administrators are aware of the sensitivity of the issue and always adopt a scientific approach that respects the beliefs of the students.

UOB has gained international recognition as a reference place for research and intercultural studies. This is clear in its participation in several multicultural international dialogues that take place all over the world. UOB issues many original publications that have worldwide recognition; these contributions of scholars from different backgrounds are peer-reviewed to ensure their scientific credibility. UOB also has a rather wide local audience in this domain.

At the same time, we have to admit that UOB has encountered some failures too. The atmosphere that prevails among the students has not had, till now, a solid social impact on the community at large. The students need to be encouraged to have a more engaged attitude towards conviviality and openness in their respective milieus.

Apart from the compulsory Culture and Civilisation programme mentioned earlier, few students follow the Christian-Muslim Studies programme offered by the university, while the need for specialists in the field is very high. This raises a double-edged question: How do we explain the low interest in Christian-Muslim studies among students? But also, why do other disciplines fail to introduce courses debating Christian-Muslim relations? We at UOB think there is much to do in order to establish a trend that will fill this existing gap.

---

28. UOB has signed seven different agreements with universities from France, USA and Australia, dealing with issues related to intercultural dialogue. UOB has hosted three international conferences on intercultural dialogue and received four visiting professors to give courses and supervise master's theses in its academic programmes.
29. An example of such decisions is the adoption by the University Council of a new form of student participation in the UOB decision-making process. Another example is the organisation of activities driven by the student body, where clubs are becoming the forum of interaction in areas of common interest.

From time to time, representatives of fundamentalist tendencies try to disrupt and disturb the positive atmosphere that prevails in our academic seminars and research meetings. Finally, the political instability in the country does not help in establishing exchange programmes for faculty and students as much as we would like and expect.

Based on these facts, how do we assess our experience at UOB? All in all, it is a positive one, though we are still faced by challenges that universities need to face together: (i) we must better target some of our adopted policies to ensure a stronger social impact for their outcomes, (ii) we must plan new actions to create among students, and the community at large, growing interest in inter-confessional and intercultural dialogue, and (iii) we need to involve new actors in civil society to widen the audience of universities within the framework of intercultural dialogue.

Conclusion

We may say that the efforts of UOB show clearly that universities play an important role in creating a healthy and constructive atmosphere, one that enables them to be an effective forum for debating all the thorny problems of civil life. In this regard, the adoption of programmes based on problem solving and critical thinking and the development of courses related to intercultural and inter-confessional dialogue are effective means to encourage conviviality and to create in younger generations a self-defence system against politicised religious fundamentalism. On the other hand, in their day-to-day life, universities can be model microcosms where students can experience the positive impact of dialogue and better knowing the other. Universities can be an ideal place for conviviality and tolerance. Finally, we think the case of UOB is just an illustration that should incite other institutions to launch programmes and adopt policies that encourage inter-confessional and intercultural dialogues.

Bibliography

Kheir, Wael (2003): "Confessionalism and democracy: the case of Lebanon", in God in Multicultural Society: Religion and Politics/Religion and Globalization, Notre Dame University and Lebanese American University Joint Research and Value Philosophy Seminar. Beirut, Lebanon.

Moukhayber, Ghassan (1997): "A minority searching for its place within the Lebanese confessional system", in *Al-Marqab*, No. 1. Center for Christian-Muslim Studies. Balamand, Lebanon: Publications of the University of Balamand. [in Arabic]

Salem, Elie (2009): "The university and scope of responsibility", in the 29th Conference for Deans of Admissions and Registration in the Arab World. Beirut, Lebanon.

Tueni, Ghassan (1993): "Democracy in Lebanon: anatomy of a crisis"; in *Beirut Review*, No. 6, Beirut, Lebanon: Lebanese Center for Policy Studies' Publications.

Internationalisation and intercultural understanding through higher education: the Chinese experience

Zixin Hou and Qinghua Liu

At the outset of the 21st century, conflicts between countries are continually escalating and intensifying on the background of globalisation, a combination which presents new and bigger challenges to education. As globalisation touches on more and more questions, so education for international understanding needs to cover new issues like global education, peace education, human rights education, multicultural education and environmental education. In this article we make use of the experience of Chinese higher education to explore methods and a possible system for teaching international understanding, and we look for moral support from education to promote the harmonious development and joint progress of the peoples of the world.

International understanding is neither new nor static

Education for international understanding is in fact a kind of quality education of human beings. It aims to promote peaceful co-existence through education and it is initiated and pushed forward by international peace organisations and UNESCO. Its ideal is international understanding – a long-term bilateral understanding implying exchange and interaction, the goal of which is to understand the politics, economics and culture of other countries as well as to actively seek understanding from other countries. Its essence is to uphold life, dignity and equality, to identify common denominators of human nature, to respect the diversity of human values and to live with each other, so that conflicts between countries will decrease, especially in the fields of ideology, political regimes and religious belief.

Many cultures and civilisations co-exist and this is a fact that education for international understanding needs to face. Different cultures make the world rich and colourful and we should respect the cultural traditions of each country and understand their cultures and national spirit. In his 1996 book *Clash of Civilizations* (based on a 1993 article), Samuel P. Huntington suggests that all the international violence and clashes after the end of Cold War were derived from cultural and religious differences (Huntington 1993). However, the international situation and historical reality show that differences of culture or civilisation do not necessarily cause conflict. As a matter of fact, the basic causes of such conflicts are not cultural, but political and economic. So we need to accept the diversity of cultures to maintain world security. In 2001, the 31st UNESCO ministerial conference adopted the Universal Declaration on Cultural Diversity, which points out that cultural diversity is humanity's common heritage. Culture has different forms of expression in different times and regions, and that cultural diversity is formed by the uniqueness and specificity of different groups and societies (Wan and Li 2006).

International understanding works through international exchange and co-operation. Over their long history, each culture goes through a process of birth, rise and fall. If there is no intercultural exchange and interaction, there will be no development. Exchange between different cultures is inevitable and no one can resist it. From ancient times to the present, there is no culture that has not been influenced by foreign cultures (Cai 2001).

For instance, for more than one thousand years from the 7th to the 17th centuries AD, China's material culture and system of civilisation affected South Korea, Japan, Ryukyu and Vietnam extensively. They formed a Cultural Circle of Ancient Chinese Characters or a Cultural Circle of an East Asian Imperial Examinations System. After the Sino-British Opium War in 1845, intellectuals from China and indeed the whole of eastern Asia began to learn from Western countries. For another example, after the Pre-Qin period, Buddhism, Christianity and Islam began to spread in China and finally completed their process of integration and adaptation, namely sinoisation. Buddhism, which began to spread in China during the Eastern Han Dynasty, had a particularly important impact on Chinese culture over a long period of mutual exchange during which it assimilated with and influenced Chinese culture. Along with Confucian and Taoist culture, Buddhism constituted one of the three pillars of Chinese traditional culture. When Buddhism was introduced in China, on the one hand we selected its essence from a good number of Buddhist documents and identified its doctrine and practical method in accordance with Chinese conditions; on the other hand, we merged these with Chinese culture and then broadened them into popular culture, forming Buddhism with Chinese characteristics (Luo 2005).

Universities should take new responsibility for training world citizens

Universities of the 21st century need to accept the moral and legal obligations of educating world citizens. Higher education of course should shoulder responsibility for the public product which it is. Education needs to actively promote citizens' understanding of their duties and commitment to social solidarity. The international community has common interests and universal values, which form the basis of the spirit of world citizenship, whereas ever greater cultural diversity in the 21st century means that the peoples of the world have far from homogeneous values and ideals. With the rapid development of network technology, more and more convenient transport and tourism, and the continual deepening of economic globalisation, the relationships of interdependence and mutual competition become more evident. A global civil society has developed, amd the higher education of each country urgently needs to recognise the importance of education for international under-standing and its moral and legal responsibility for educating citizens of the world.

Higher education must help citizens to be guided by global civil society, avoid as much as possible the vulnerability and absence of economic ethics among business managers, to avoid the extreme disparity, even polarisation of the economic condi-tions of the peoples of the world and avoid the depletion of natural resources, environmental deterioration and strained human relations. Otherwise, the global economy will fade and social crises will follow. A political response to globalisation, suggested by Beck, is to establish and extend education and the knowledge-based society, and to make the educational process aim at developing critical abilities, such as social skills, team capacity, conflict-resolving skills and cultural understanding (Yang and Xie 2006: 141). In 1998, UNESCO released a public statement advocating that 21st-century higher education, along with other actors, should work to meet the world's demands and engage in creating a more just, tolerant and responsible society (UNESCO 1998).

To foster a humanistic spirit among citizens, it is necessary for each country's higher education system and institutions to consciously absorb the insights and achievements of each other's culture. At present, education for international understanding faces the extreme development that leads to antagonism between countries, while the concept of cosmopolitanism implies a Western-centric hegemony, so that students from the rest of the world, including China, have taken learning from the West more as their only way to international recognition than as a method of absorbing knowledge (Yang Tian and Deng Lei 2009: 26). To solve these dilemmas, it is no wonder that we need to draw on the insights and achievements of all the cultures in the world and to have a broader humanistic spirit. At present, with the background of globalisation, to build a harmonious world we obviously need the traditional Chinese Confucian cultural spirit of kindness, harmony without uniformity, humanitarianism and peace; we need the natural idea of harmony between man and nature, which is a significant contribution to the world's civilisation in Islamic ecological thought; we need the philosophy of the modern citizen, which cares about civil affairs, politics, social rights and contracts; and we need the cultural spirit of freedom, equality and legality of the Western world. Of course, emphasising the humanistic spirit of citizens does not deny universities the right to educate citizens with a national consciousness. Actually, there is no education in the world that produces potentially straying citizens; all these citizens have their own national identity and cultural base. With European economic integration, today European education is also promoting a sense of European citizenship and there is a desire for their universities to play a leading role in protecting and advocating those moral values.

Strengthen education for international understanding as part of the internationalisation of universities

Internationalisation is inherent in the character of universities. Since the founding of universities in medieval Europe, their most laudable characteristics have turned out to be World Spirit and Transnationalism. Latin was the common language of education and used for international communication, while the universalists managed to integrate the world in an atmosphere of learning without borders (Yang Tian and Deng Lei 2009: 25). In essence, science is universal and internationalism is based on its universality. Universities should be at the forefront of international communication and improvement of international understanding.

In terms of its content, the internationalisation of universities includes the flow of students and teachers across borders, participation in international conferences and congresses, and even the participation in co-operative studies and international research projects. All of those projects can help universities play an essential role in establishing a harmonious world. Research has shown that, on the basis of international co-operation, scientific progress would promote the cause of peace. Universities are important places for cultivating leaders who have international concepts and intercultural knowledge. A German student who studied abroad in different universities for many years wrote: "The greatest influence on me from my study-abroad experience is that it has made me learn to be tolerant, to consider questions in a comparative perspective, and to accept another way of life while doubting that I am always absolutely correct" (Martins Roméo, 2003). Daisaku and Du pointed out that to pay more attention to foreign students is, indeed, to attach importance to the future of the world, for foreign students are likely to attain positions of leadership in their own countries (Daisaku and Du 2007).

Chinese higher education attaches great importance to the internationalisation of universities, adhering to the principle that "Education should be oriented towards modernisation, the world and the future". Since the policy of reform and opening up was launched in 1978, China has strongly encouraged and supported international exchanges and co-operation in higher education. Agreements on mutual recognition of academic degrees have been signed between China and 34 countries; and over 40 international organisations maintain co-operation with China. On the issue of overseas education, we not only put emphasis on sending our own students abroad but also believe it is important to bring foreign students to China. Table 1 shows the numbers of study-abroad and visiting overseas students in 1978 and from 1999 to 2008.

Table 1: Students studying abroad or visiting China (1978, 1999 to 2008)

year	1978	1999	2000	2001	2002	2003	2004	2005	2006	2007	2008
	number of students (in thousands)										
Chinese students studying abroad	0.86	24	39	84	125	117.2	114.6	118.6	133.6	144.5	179.8
Overseas students studying in China	1.2	44.7	52.2	61.9	85.8	77.7	110.8	141.1	162.7	195.5	223.5

Source: China Education Yearbook, "Work and study abroad".

From 1978 to the end of 2008, 1 391 500 Chinese students were sent to foreign countries, increasing from 860 students in 1978 to 179 800 in 2008, in other words by a factor of almost 210 (Miao 2009). From the research by Tsinghua University and Beijing University, we can see that, though an imbalance exists in higher education communication and co-operation between China and foreign countries – for example, less than 40% of students return home and few of the students choose to study humanities – those who do return home have become an important bridge for international exchange, playing an important role in advancing international communication and co-operation between universities and helping to improve the academic standards of colleges and universities. Furthermore, they are not only practitioners in domestic education reform but form the backbone of the personnel building the domestic economy (Tian Ling 2003).

China was host to 1 236 overseas students in 1978 and 223 500 in 2008, a factor of increase of 180. Those overseas students came from 189 countries and regions, and they studied in 592 higher education institutions throughout the country (Xiao 2009). In fact, international communication and co-operation not only make citizens understand the economy as a global phenomenon, but also educate world citizens who can understand foreign cultures, systems and thinking.

The Nankai-Aichi pattern

In the wave of internationalisation of universities, Nankai University has tried hard to find new ways to strengthen education for international understanding and has set up the "Nankai-Aichi pattern" in co-operation with Aichi University of Japan, a peaceful university with a deep Chinese background; its predecessor was the East Asia College, founded in Shanghai in the 1920s. At the beginning of the 1980s Nankai established communication with Aichi. In the mid- and late 1990s, in order to meet manpower demands brought about by economic globalisation, Aichi University founded the Department of Modern China, which aims to cultivate talents doing communication work related to Sino-Japanese economic affairs, politics and culture.

To better acquaint the students with modern China, Nankai University and Aichi University worked together and designed a four-month on-site teaching programme especially for students from Aichi University. In the meantime, students from the Department of Modern China at Aichi began taking some courses, such as Chinese culture, history, economy and law, that were taught by professors from Nankai University. What is more, they were able to participate in some relevant social activities and develop contacts with Chinese students and ordinary people. In order to support the co-operation programme, both universities collaborated to build an Aichi Guild Hall for the use of visiting Japanese students at Nankai University.

So far, the programme has run for ten years and has brought more than 2 000 students to study at Nankai University. The students have not only acquired some useful knowledge as required by their study programmes but have also acquainted themselves with China and understood China better from first-hand experience. According to a survey of students from Aichi University, over 80% of the students who have studied in China are willing to go back again to study or communicate. More and more universities give attention to this kind of co-operation, and several – like Kokugakuin University – have organised similar co-operation programmes with Nankai.

Confucius institutes: strengthening education for international understanding

In order to strengthen education for international understanding, we wish to find more and better ways to promote conversation, communication, mutual recognition and respect between different cultures, to maintain universal human values, to show the unique value of one's own culture and to promote harmony all over the world.

China has established Confucius institutes in other countries as a new approach to strengthening education for international understanding. We aim to advance dialogue between different cultures, further mutual understanding, enhance understanding of Chinese language and culture, defend our firm relationship with foreign countries, promote multicultural development and dedicate ourselves to building a harmonious world.

The Confucius Institute is a non-profit educational and cultural institution which aims to promote Chinese language and culture. The first overseas Confucius Institute was set up in Seoul in 2004. By 2010, China plans to establish 500 Confucius institutes around the world. By 11 December 2008, China had already founded 249 Confucius institutes and 56 Confucius classrooms in 78 countries and regions. These have provided more than 6 000 Chinese language courses at all levels, with an enrolment of 120 000 students, and they have organised cultural exchanges with a total of 1.2 million participants. The Confucius institutes have a combined staff of 2 100 teachers and administrators, and occupy office and teaching space of about 4.6 million square metres. Furthermore, over 40 countries and 100 universities and institutions were awaiting the approval of the National Office for Teaching Chinese as a Foreign Language (Chen and Wu 2009).

In addition, China's first Radio Confucius Institute was established in Beijing on 6 December 2007. It teaches Chinese to learners all over the world, in 38 languages, by radio and online radio, in order to disseminate Chinese culture. Organised by Confucius Institute Headquarters, the Confucius Institute Network began operating on 20 March 2008, providing online courses to Chinese language learners, teaching resources to teachers of Chinese, online management and press releases to the Confucius institutes, and other functions (Confucius Institute Headquarters 2007). At the time of writing, in co-operation with foreign universities, Nankai University has established five overseas Confucius institutes: the first such institute in the United States, at the University of Maryland; the Confucius Institute of Aichi University in Japan; the first in Colombia, at the Andean University; the first in Portugal, at the University of Minho; and the Confucius Institute of the University of South Florida.

Depending on the host country, regional circumstances and people's language-learning requirements, the Confucius Institute has launched a series of Chinese courses, covering academic and non-academic qualifications, from kindergarten to university, and carried out various activities and services for local people (Xu 2008). For example, the Confucius Institute organised by Nankai University and the University of Maryland in November 2004 increased overseas interest in and understanding of China, initially by going out to recruit students, and has since adapted its teaching methods – for example, by providing off-campus classes according to need, taking full advantage of time during the evening, weekends and summer vacation to conduct Chinese language teaching, arranging two or more cultural activities almost every month, including "Chinese Bridge" competitions for college students, Chinese celebrity lectures, Chinese Film Week, Confucius Reading Council and academic conferences (Zhang 2009).

Confucius's Golden Mean implies that being impartial as a man, then being generous as a government, is the way to make interpersonal relationships friendly and firm, make society harmonious and peaceful, and bring about co-existence among nations. Whether a theory – the Golden Mean of Confucius, or Samuel P. Huntington's clash of civilisations – works or not is tested by practice (Wang 2009). That the Confucius Institute is welcomed by the world shows that the development of world peace needs Confucianism alongside an active role for higher education, which needs to plunge into international cultural exchange and to further education for international understanding.

China, with a civilisation 5 000 years old, prides itself on a tremendous accumu- lation of culture. From the 16th to the 19th centuries, Westerners who came to China discovered that no European book could be compared with Chinese books, based on the number of words. The China scholar John King Fairbank demonstrated in his book *The United States and China* (Fairbank 2003) that the amount of books printed in Chinese before 1750 is larger than all the books printed in all other languages worldwide. Under the guidance of "the pursuit of harmony", "harmony without uniformity" and "the golden mean", in the positive and innovative exchange of cultures around the world, Chinese higher education will play a more effective role in the future of education for international understanding.

References

For the references in Chinese, please contact the authors at: lqh7110@163.com.

Beck, Ulrich, transl. Patrick Camiller (1999): *What is Globalization?* Cambridge: Polity Press.

Cai Degui (2001): "Mr. Ji Xianlin's theory of the complementation of Eastern and Western cultures" [in Chinese], *Journal of China Youth College for Political Sciences*, April.

Chen Juewan and Wu Duanyang (2009): "Analysis of the course, causes and characteristics of the development of overseas Confucius Institute" [in Chinese], *Journal of National Academy of Education Administration*, No. 4.

Confucius Institute Headquarters and National Office for Teaching Chinese as a Foreign Language (2007): Annual Report for 2007, China: Renmin University Press.

Daisaku, Ikeda and Du Weiming (2007): *Civilization of Dialogue* [in Chinese], Sichuan People's Publishing House.

Fairbank, John King (2003): *The United States and China*, 4th Chinese edn, Beijing: World Knowledge Publishing House.

Huntington, Samuel P. (1993): "The clash of civilizations", *Foreign Affairs*, Vol. 72, No. 3, pp. 22-49.

Luo Yingguang (2005): "On the spreading and localization of Buddhism, Christianity and Islam in China" [in Chinese], *Journal of Sichuan University (Social Science Edition)*, No. 6, p. 80.

Martins Roméo, José Raymundo (2003): "Higher education in Latin America", *Journal of Higher Education in Europe*, April. Bucharest: UNESCO-CEPES.

Miao Danguo (2009): "Analysis of the discussion and research for the facts and data relevant to study abroad" [in Chinese], China: World Education Information, No. 4.

Tian Ling (2003): *Research on foreign exchange in Chinese higher education* [in Chinese], Nationalities Publishing House, pp. 137-171.

Tomlinson, John (1999): *Globalization and Culture*. Cambridge: Polity Press.

UNESCO (1998): "Higher education in the twenty-first century: vision and action", October, Paris: UNESCO.

Wan, Ming gang and Li, Yanhong (2006): "Educational ideal and practice of learning to live together" [in Chinese], *Journal of Educational Research*, Vol. 12.

Wang Dao (2009): "Huntington outmoded, Confucius in mode" [in Chinese], in *Hong Kong DaKung Daily*, 4 January.

Xiao Chunfei (2009): "Overseas students increased 180 fold over 30 years", *China Youth Daily* [in Chinese], 2 April.

Xu Lihua (2008): "The development of status, problems and trends of Confucius Institute" [in Chinese], *Zhejiang Normal University Journal (Social Science Edition*, No. 5.

Yang Shanhua and Xie Zhongli (2006): *Sociological theory of West* [in Chinese], Beijing: Beijing University Publishing House.

Yang Tian and Deng Lei (2009): "The characteristics of universities and the educating of world citizens in China" [in Chinese], *Journal of International Education*, No. 2.

Zhang Zhiguo (2009): "Field study of Confucius Institute of University of Maryland in U.S." [in Chinese], *Co-operation and Communication*, No. 3.

Intercultural dialogue as an element of the internationalisation of education

Alf Rasmussen

This article, drawing on a government report on this matter to the Norwegian Parliament, aims to present how Norway deals with the internationalisation of education, emphasising intercultural dialogue. I would like to have chosen, as the title of my article, our favourite proposal for the title of the report the ministry had been working on since 2008, "Should I Stay or Should I Go?" – a song title from 1981 by the British punk-rock group The Clash – accompanied by a picture of a group of penguins who are wondering if they dare to cross over to join the other penguins on the next ice floe. I think this illustrates almost everything about internationalisation. We have to decide whether to stay as we are, remain cut off and try to make the best of it or dare to jump and join the others. But, as you see, instead of being funny, we ended up – as usual – using a bureaucratic, descriptive and not very exciting title.

The Norwegian background

Norway is almost equally divided north and south by the Arctic Circle and it is on the outskirts of northern Europe, so it goes without saying: we could not stay – we had to go! Therefore, historically, we have always been well connected to the outside world when it comes to trade and political alliances. But Norwegian society itself was relatively homogeneous until thirty or forty years ago. In the early 1970s, the first large group of non-European immigrants came to Norway, seeking employment. Since then, the number of immigrants has grown rapidly and is still increasing. In parallel with globalisation of the economy, trade, labour market, education and research, our society has changed significantly.

For Norway, international success in education, research collaboration and competition depends on how successful we are in intercultural dialogue and understanding. The Norwegian policy is to prepare everyone to be intercultural citizens in this society from early childhood, and this has consequences for our schools and universities. The reason for this is of course a significant change in the demographic profile with an increasing number of immigrants to Norway and the growth of globalisation and internationalisation.

Immigrants from different parts of the world form 10% of the inhabitants of Norway. In our capital Oslo, they are 25%. In primary schools in Oslo, more than 120 languages are spoken and in some cases up to 80 languages are represented in a single school. One third of the pupils have a minority background and the number of immigrants is increasing, especially from countries outside Western Europe. This rapidly growing mix of cultures is a challenge to our society, our minds and our way of living. That is why it is important to integrate the international and inter-cultural perspective in our education system. On the other hand, our enterprises are more international than ever and we need a workforce that knows how to work internationally, in Norway as well as abroad. So far, we have done a lot but we still have work to do.

Norway today is a welfare state and we are doing well in many areas. However, our future prosperity will be based less on oil, fish and other commodities, more on skills and know-how. To survive, we have to compete and co-operate with relevant actors abroad. As a small country, we just have to recognise that most of the world's knowledge production takes place outside Norway, and it is vital for the development of Norwegian society that we are able to benefit from knowledge that is generated elsewhere. Therefore, we must be an interesting partner for other countries and our education institutions must be of interest to institutions abroad. In some areas, we believe that we really are a good and equal partner, even for countries bigger than ourselves. In some areas we are genuinely excellent, with expertise that makes our institutions highly attractive partners for highly prestigious institutions abroad.

We Norwegians have historically collaborated mostly with our Nordic neighbours, a few other European countries and North America. But, as the world is changing when it comes to trade patterns, education and research, we must constantly ask ourselves: Should we stay – or should we go? New and strong economies are emerging and a key to "the good life" lies in excellent education and superior research. Maybe we have good connections already, but like most other countries we have to rethink opportunities and measures, strategies and partnerships.

Norway has participated in the Bologna Process from the very beginning, we have followed up the Lisbon Recognition Convention actively and our institutions participate in numerous European programmes and projects. But our involvement in activities in other countries and areas of the world is also rapidly increasing. The Ministry of Education and Research has contributed to this development by signing a memorandum of understanding for collaboration on education and research with a growing number of new strategic partner countries around the world. Since 2007, we have signed such agreements with China, India, Brazil, Argentina and Chile, and we hope to sign one with Russia in the near future. The change of perspectives and measures in our international relations is quite extensive. In parallel with pan-European processes, Norway has changed much of the organisation and content of its education and research since the late 1990s. It was about time we summed up and evaluated the situation.

The Norwegian White Paper

As I mentioned, the Norwegian Government submitted a report to the Norwegian Parliament (the Storting) on internationalisation of education in February 2009. One of the main goals with the White Paper was to present and discuss the full picture of internationalisation in education, and to make some strategic choices about where to go next. In accordance with the Norwegian tradition of broad involvement in important processes, the document is based on research and research literature, a large number of meetings and written contributions from education institutions at all levels, student organisations, social partners and other stakeholders in Norway, along with seminars and visits to a selection of European organisations and countries.

The report describes the current situation and proposes new measures to ensure that the Norwegian education system provides pupils and students with the necessary skills to act and interact in an increasingly globalised world. It covers the whole education system, from primary and secondary education and training to non-university tertiary education and higher education, including research education. It is the first time the Norwegian Government has produced a report with this holistic approach to the topic.

International perspectives, languages and cultural awareness are increasingly important competences for those seeking employment. The internationalisation of education must therefore not only focus on students and staff spending semesters or years abroad, but also ensure that the education offered in Norway is international in character and internationally competitive in its quality standards. To do so, we must evaluate study programmes in Norway and make sure they are attractive for both international and Norwegian students. Over 80% of Norwegian students do not study abroad at all and they must be provided with high-quality education at home. But in our internationalisation policies, we must emphasise quality of education in addition to the overall value of visiting foreign countries and institutions. And last, but not least our new strategic partner countries make it even more important to focus on foreign languages and cultural awareness.

The main measures in the report will, as we see it, give the following results once the policies have been implemented:

–   Improved quality in the Norwegian education system
    -   Quality is a guiding principle for the internationalisation of education in Norway, both with respect to studies abroad and in the development of provision in Norwegian education institutions.
–   Norway more attractive to foreign students and academics
    -   We have over 200 master's programmes taught in English (the number increases every year) and they are important both in attracting international students and academics and in offering international study programmes to Norwegian students.
–   Benefits at all levels
    -   Internationalisation will affect all pupils, students and staff, not just those who may go abroad. Administrative and technical staff must also be prepared and trained for the internationalisation of their institution.
–   International campus
    -   Students coming to Norway will find an international campus, with foreign students, teachers and researchers, and international perspectives on the

curriculum. Master's and doctorate students will participate in international research co-operation.

– Increased co-operation
  - Co-operation between Norwegian education institutions and with similar institutions abroad will be even more strongly emphasised, notably co-operation with developing countries.

Schools

In primary and secondary education, the international perspective is important for many of the qualification targets in the Norwegian curriculum. There are, however, significant variations between schools when it comes to other internationalisation indicators, for example student and staff mobility. Measures to enhance the international dimension in primary and secondary education include:

– ensuring a better overview of what schools do already, sharing best practice and emphasising international perspectives in the local curriculum;

– increased participation in international programmes, improved access to information and guidance on studying abroad for schools and school owners.

– a broader mandate for the Norwegian Centre for International Co-operation in Higher Education (SIU), an administrative agency under the Ministry of Education and Research, providing knowledge and services with the aim of promoting and facilitating co-operation, standardisation and mobility, overcoming cultural barriers to communication and exchange in higher education at international level and co-ordinating national measures according to official Norwegian policy in the field of internationalisation.

– assessment of measures to promote study abroad for certain groups of pupils in order to ensure greater geographical dispersion and better representation of vocational education, and to examine how further groups could be given opportunities to study abroad.

Non-university tertiary education

There are considerable variations, but these institutions are supposed to be a real alternative to higher education and provide courses or programmes which range from six months' to two years' duration. We need to collect more statistical information about these study programmes, rates of course completion, drop-out rates and mobility, and plans are in hand to do so in the near future. The reason for this lack of information is that the laws and regulations for this type of education are rather new in Norway. Therefore, we need some more systematic knowledge about these schools before we can advise on and stimulate internationalisation.

We propose to:

– improve the statistical knowledge base in the area of non-university tertiary education (the Ministry of Education and Research will be in charge of this project);

–   set up a National Qualifications Framework for non-university tertiary education adapted to the European Qualifications Framework for lifelong learning, with the intention of making it easier to communicate with international partners and stimulating our institutions to collaborate with institutions abroad.

Universities

We launched a Quality Reform in higher education in 2003. The first evaluation of this reform shows that Norwegian higher education institutions have made significant progress in internationalisation at home, establishing a more international campus and improving student and staff mobility. The Quality Reform – inspired by and including the Bologna action lines – gave all Norwegian students the right to a study visit abroad as part of a degree at their home institutions. We are proud to say that more than 30% of Norwegian students completing a degree in Norway have included a study visit abroad. To further stimulate student mobility, Norwegian institutions are entitled to a minor sum of money from the ministry for each incoming and outgoing student.

From now on, it will be important to focus even more on structure, involvement and collaboration with institutions abroad and to associate internationalisation with strategic development of the institutions. Among the main new measures are:

–   projects to develop joint degrees and study programmes at master's and doctorate levels
    -   Some academics are quite experienced in this kind of project, whereas others are not. We want to initiate more joint projects. We have seen successful examples in the Erasmus Mundus programme and under the auspices of the Nordic Council of Ministers.

–   projects to transfer training and common improvements across national borders
    -   These Tuning-like projects are, like the projects for joint degrees and joint study programmes, most demanding for all partners involved. For such projects to be successful, participants must collaborate and evaluate each others' qualifications, expectations, study content, results, learning outcomes and structures. This is one very important kind of co-operation when it comes to uncovering your own thinking and choice of values. And it greatly helps all participants to improve.

–   pilot projects for internationalisation in short professional degree studies
    -   First and foremost we plan pilot projects in study programmes for engineers, nurses and teachers. This is where we have found most difficulty in introducing mobility exchange possibilities. We will initiate projects to show how this can be done while making the study programme more international.

–   gathering knowledge and experience of how education and research can benefit from closer co-operation
    -   We want to give a group of experts the mandate to explore opportunities and models for this. One important issue is how students can be involved

in research projects before they finish their master's degree. This is important in order to recruit more researchers and to show students that a research career is an option. This could be a win-win situation.

- researching effects, best practice and other issues in internationalising higher education

    - We simply need to know more and to systematise what we already know for everyone to use. We have to encourage our institutions to collaborate more closely, to share international experiences and to share best practice on internationalisation at home. Some of our universities and university colleges are strong enough to attract high-quality partners abroad without any help. Other institutions have neither the ability nor the resources, and would benefit from closer co-operation with other Norwegian institutions, and from financial help. Smaller institutions might, if they co-operate and find a sensible division of labour and responsibility, be attractive as a network to quality institutions abroad.

As I stated earlier, Norway has quite a few students who participate in mobility programmes as part of their academic degree. Both to these Norwegian mobility students and to Norwegian degree students studying abroad (bachelor, master's and doctorate), we can offer some of the best state funding in the world. They are entitled to loans and grants for general living expenses, in fact to the same amount of money whether they study in Norway or abroad. They are free to choose whatever university or study programme they like, as long as the education is equivalent to a bachelor or master's degree in Norway. In addition, the state will give loans and grants to cover a fair part of any tuition fees. Even more support can be granted to cover expenses in connection with study visits at high-quality institutions. Students are also entitled to reimbursement of travel costs.

Mobility

The mobility of students is important and it must be based on quality when it comes to choice of institution and study programme. The number of Norwegian students in high-quality exchange programmes or seeking degrees at foreign universities must increase, which will require a high standard of information and guidance about high-quality opportunities to study abroad.

Studies abroad will continue to have high priority, especially student exchange and degree studies at master's level. The government will ensure that students are motivated to choose studies of high quality by:

- adjusting its financial support for tuition fees;

- maintaining financial support for subsistence and travel grants at current levels;

- maintaining financial support for study at institutions without tuition fees throughout the world at current levels.

188

It must be made economically more attractive to study at foreign institutions of high quality. The four main actions of the new scheme will be phased in gradually, from the academic year 2011/12 at the earliest.

- An advisory group will be assigned the task of proposing quality criteria and drafting lists of high-quality institutions and programmes. These lists will be considerably more extensive than the current supplementary grant lists, which will be discontinued.

- Support will be given for the first year of bachelor degree courses offered by institutions and within programmes included in the new high-quality lists.

- Larger grants will be given to cover tuition fees at institutions of high quality.

- We plan to assess whether the level of grants to cover tuition fees for exchange students should be associated with institutional agreements.

Conclusion

The 40 measures listed in the report reflect what we identified as the most important ones, after extensive hearings among stakeholders and actors within education in Norway. And it is most interesting to see that many other countries have a similar situation when it comes to internationalisation of education. However, the point is not to make all education systems similar but to make them more transparent; and we do not wish all study programmes to be like copies of each other but for all to be of high quality. That includes most definitely an international perspective and intercultural understanding. So if we work hard and smart, the question will not any longer be: "Should I stay – or should I go?" but rather "Where do I go – and when?"

The Norwegian White Paper on internationalisation of education focuses on four aspects:

- High quality in international collaboration and in all education institutions at home;

- Co-operation between institutions to secure the best possible relations and results in education and research;

- Attractiveness to international partners and students;

- Relevance to every student and employee, to the labour market and to trade and industry.

Every country and every education institution must find its own way of dealing with internationalisation in education and research. This article will, I hope, be a small contribution to continuing the valuable work for better intercultural dialogue in international co-operation and competition. The International Association of Universities and the Council of Europe deserve credit for putting this crucial but often neglected issue on the table, from their different perspectives as an inter-university body and intergovernmental organisation respectively. I hope this article will inspire others by showing how a national government has sought to place intercultural dialogue within its overall internationalisation policies.

The editors and authors

Editors

Sjur Bergan is Head of the Council of Europe's Department for Higher Education and History Teaching. He is Series Editor of the Council of Europe Higher Education Series, author of *Qualifications: Introduction to a Concept*, editor or co-editor of several volumes in the Higher Education series and author of numerous articles on higher education policy. He is a member of the Bologna Follow Up Group, chairs the Working Group on Qualifications Frameworks and contributes frequently to debates on education policy.

Hilligje van't Land is Director, Membership and Programme Development, at the International Association of Universities (IAU), Paris. She studied in France, the Netherlands and Canada. She holds a PhD from Groningen University and a post-doctoral degree from Laval University in Canada. Her research and teaching focused on contemporary Francophone literatures; she taught at Groningen University, the Netherlands, Université Laval, Canada and l'Université d'Avignon et des Pays du Vaucluse, France. She has spoken at many conferences and has published in refereed journals and books internationally. Among other things, at the IAU, she is Chief Editor of the association's magazine *IAU Horizons*, is in charge of membership development strategies and project developments, leads projects in the fields of higher education, sustainable development and intercultural learning and dialogue and runs a study and research project on the changing nature of doctoral programmes in sub-Saharan Africa.

Authors

Edward J. Alam is Secretary-General, Council for Research in Values and Philosophy, Lebanon and Associate Professor in the Faculty of Humanities, Notre Dame University – Louaize, where he has taught philosophy and theology since 1996. As the university's Director of International Academic Affairs (1999-2004), he had several notable actions there on international relations linked with his name. He also initiated and directed a project devoted to the interface between religion and science, which was awarded a supplementary grant in 2004 for its outstanding accomplishments. Dr Alam has delivered several speeches on metaphysics and mysticism. He has travelled extensively, giving lectures and chairing seminars in Iran, Korea, India, China, Thailand, Africa, Vietnam, Taiwan, Cambodia, Spain, Sweden and the United States, where he conducted a five-week philosophy seminar at the Catholic University of America in Washington, DC. Alam was elected Secretary/Treasurer of the World Union of Catholic Philosophical Societies in 2008 and has since become General Secretary of the Council for Research in Values and Philosophy, CUA/NDU.

Gabriella Battaini-Dragoni is Director General, Education, Culture and Heritage, Youth and Sport, Council of Europe. She was the first woman ever to be nominated to the rank of Director General in that organisation when in 2001 she was appointed Director General of Social Cohesion. In November 2005, Mrs Battaini-Dragoni was appointed Co-ordinator for Intercultural Dialogue, responsible for monitoring all activities of the Council of Europe in the area of intercultural dialogue and for co-ordination with external partners. In this capacity, she was responsible for preparation of the Council of Europe White Paper on Intercultural Dialogue – adopted on 7 May 2008 at ministerial level, the first international document of its kind – and the Council of Europe Speak Out against Discrimination campaign. Her objective is modernising the European social model with due regard to cultural factors, citizenship issues, diversity policies and the potential of intercultural dialogue. Gabriella Battaini-Dragoni is a frequently invited guest speaker at UN, OECD, OSCE and EU meetings.

Andrea Blättler is a member of the Executive Committee of the European Students' Union (ESU) and she studies Political Science and Philosophy at the University of Luzern. As an ESU Executive Committee Member she co-ordinates the Academic Affairs Committee and thus focuses on issues such as implementation of the Bologna Process, quality assurance, student participation, financing of higher education and higher education governance. Andrea Blättler is one of ESU's two representatives in the Bologna Follow Up Group and participated in both the UNESCO Forum on Higher Education in the Europe Region: Access, Values, Quality and Competitiveness and the UNESCO World Conference on Higher Education 2009 on behalf of the European Students' Union. She chaired the international co-operation working group of ESU for one year and as such co-organised two global student meetings around the UNESCO World Conference. Within the Executive Committee of ESU, Andrea now continues this work with the aim of strengthening the global student movement.

Yazmín Cruz is Project Manager, Global University Network for Innovation (GUNI). From 2003 to 2005 she worked for the Environmental Planning Office of Universitat Politècnica de Catalunya (UPC) and the UNESCO Chair on Sustainability at UPC, co-ordinating projects linking higher education with sustainable development. Previously, she worked at the Environmental Centre as well as the Virtual University and the Sustainable Development Centre of the Instituto Tecnológico y de Estudios Superiores de Monterrey (ITESM); at the Business Council for Sustainable Development, Latin-American Chapter as eco-efficiency programme co-ordinator; as a consultant on issues related to quality and environment and auditor on ISO 14001. Yazmín Cruz holds a PhD in Industrial Engineering from the Universitat Politècnica de Catalunya with a thesis on accreditation as a mechanism for ensuring the social commitment of universities. She also holds a master's degree in Environmental Engineering from ITESM and also a master's degree in Industrial Waste Management from UPC.

Darla K. Deardorff is Executive Director, Association of International Education Administrators (AIEA), a national professional organisation based at Duke University, where she also teaches cross-cultural courses. In addition, she is an adjunct professor at North Carolina State University (NCSU) and the University of North Carolina-Chapel Hill, and is on the faculty of the Summer Institute for Intercultural Communication in Portland, Oregon. With nearly twenty years of experience in the field, she has published widely on topics in international education, including her recent book, *Handbook of Intercultural Competence* (Sage, 2009). Dr Deardorff holds master's and doctorate degrees from NCSU, where she specialised in international education. Her dissertation, on the definition and assessment of intercultural competence, has drawn national and international attention and her intercultural competence models developed through that research are used by organisations and educational institutions worldwide.

Germain Dondelinger is *premier conseiller de gouvernement* and co-ordinator for higher education in the Luxembourg Ministry of Culture, Higher Education and Research. He has been a member of the Bologna Follow Up Group since its founding (2001) and was its vice-chair in 2007-2009. In 2005, during the Luxembourg Presidency of the Council of the European Union, he was heavily engaged in the negotiation of the Bergen Declaration. In conjunction with playing a fundamental role in the creation and implementation of the University of Luxembourg, he has also been engaged in the development of Campus Europae. He is Vice Chair of the Steering Committee for Higher Education and Research of the Council of Europe and holds board positions in a number of research institutes. Germain Dondelinger chairs the administrative board of Fonds Belval, a development company dealing with research and university infrastructure as well as industrial heritage on a brownfield site in Luxembourg. Throughout the 1990s, he was heavily involved with European educational affairs at council level.

Eva Egron-Polak is Secretary-General, International Association of Universities (IAU), Paris. She was educated in the Czech Republic, Canada and France. Having studied French literature, political science and international political economy, she focused her postgraduate research on higher education policy. She has had extensive experience in international co-operation in higher education, having served for more than 15 years in various senior positions at the Association of Universities and Colleges of Canada (AUCC) prior to becoming the Secretary-General of the IAU in 2002. At the IAU, she is engaged with many policy issues in higher education – among others the internationalisation of higher education and intercultural learning, the quality of cross-border higher education and equitable access to and success in higher education. She has focused on expanding the IAU's convening role, consolidating the association's capacity as a clearing house of information, and launched a number of projects, including the LEADHER grants programme for professional development and North-South collaboration. She is a member of a large number of committees at UNESCO, the OECD and the EU, and has expanded IAU partnerships to include many new organisations.

193

Cristina Escrigas is a social psychologist from the Autonomous University of Barcelona (UAB) and holds degrees of Master in Business Administration from the Universitat Politécnica de Catalunya (UPC), Master in Training of Trainers, Methodology and Management, also from the UPC, and Master in Organisational Development from the GR Institute, Israel. Her specialism is organisational development and strategic management. She worked on strategic management and institutional change at the UPC for several years and was Director of the Seminar on Strategic University Management for five years. She was also Director of the UNESCO Chair of Higher Education Management. She has worked on strategic planning for several universities in Spain. She has also worked in the Universal Forum of Cultures, as Director of Participation, encouraging civil society organisations to become involved in promoting the Forum and its programme related to intercultural understanding, sustainability and peace at global scale. She also contributed to the creation and development of the knowledge bank where the Forum's main ideas and contents have been published. She is currently Executive Director of the Global University Network for Innovation (GUNI).

Zixin Hou is Director of the Chinese Association of Higher Education. He is the former President of Nankai University (1995-2006) in China and Director of the Chinese Association of Higher Education. He sits on the German and American Editorial Board of the journal *Mathematical Reviews*.

Barasby S. Karamurzov was born in the Kabardino-Balkarian Republic, Russia. He undertook higher education studies in physics at the Kabardino-Balkarian State University (Nalchik, Russia) in 1964-69. He obtained a Candidate of Sciences (*kandidat nauk*) degree in physics in 1975 and a Doctor of Sciences (*doktor nauk*) degree in 1990. He is Professor at the Kabardino-Balkarian State University and has been its rector since 1994. He has held the UNESCO Chair in Education for a Culture of Peace and Human Rights since 1999. Barasby S. Karamurzov has carried out research in the fields of physics and the development of the higher education system, particularly in relation to the role of the university as a regional centre of scientific, educational and cultural activities.

Qinghua Liu is Assistant Professor at the higher education institute of Nankai University. He is Secretary of the National Guidance Committee on Vocational Education of the Ministry of Education of the People's Republic of China.

Federico Mayor Zaragoza is President, Culture of Peace Foundation, former Director-General of UNESCO and Co-Chair of the High Level Group of the United Nations Alliance of Civilizations. Federico Mayor holds a Doctorate in Pharmacy, became Professor of Biochemistry and from 1968 to 1972 was Rector of the University of Granada. He was a co-founder of the Severo Ochoa Centre of Molecular Biology at the Universidad Autónoma of Madrid and the High Council for Scientific Research. Among other political posts Professor Mayor has held are those of Undersecretary of Education and Science in the Spanish Government (1974-75), Deputy in the Spanish Parliament (1977-78), Adviser to the President of the Government (1977-78), Minister of Education and Science (1981-82) and Member of the European Parliament (1978). In 1978 he became the Deputy Director-General of UNESCO, and in 1987 he was elected Director-General of that organisation. During his twelve years as head of UNESCO (1987-99), Professor Mayor Zaragoza gave new life to the organisation's mission to "build a bastion of peace in the minds of all people". Under his guidance, UNESCO created the Culture of Peace Programme, whose objectives revolve around four key themes: education for peace, human rights and democracy; the fight against isolation and poverty; the defence of cultural diversity and intercultural dialogue; and conflict prevention and the consolidation of peace. In 1999, the United Nations General Assembly adopted the Declaration and Programme of Action on a Culture of Peace, which embodies Professor Mayor Zaragoza's greatest aspirations from both a conceptual and practical standpoint.

Georges Nahas is Vice-President, University of Balamand, Lebanon. After a study period in Lebanon, he obtained a D.E.A. in Mathematics from Université de Paris and a PhD in Educational Sciences from Université René Descartes – Paris V. He has been Vice-President, University of Balamand, since 1996 and Dean, Saint John of Damascus Institute of Theology at the same university, since 2005. Previously, he taught at the Lebanese University, then at St Joseph University and now at the University of Balamand. He also acted as Director of the Collège Notre Dame du Balamand (1975-93) and Dean of the Faculty of Arts and Social Sciences at the University of Balamand (1988-95). He has been a Member of the Lebanese Association of Educational Sciences since 1995; Member of the National Committee of the Ministry of Education and Higher Education since 1999; and Member of the Société Européenne pour la Formation des Ingénieurs since 2008. His research focuses on cognitive psychology in the field of conceptualisation and the development of conceptual fields theory.

Michel Nehme is Professor of Political Science and International Affairs and Director of the International Affairs Office, Notre Dame University – Louaize, Lebanon. He obtained his PhD in Political Science from Rutgers University, New Jersey, in 1983. His dissertation focused on Saudi Arabia: Political Implications of the Development Plans. He specialised in Comparative Politics, International Relations and Political Theory. Before becoming Director of University International Affairs, Notre Dame University – Louaize and as a Professor of Political Science, NDU since 2001, he was Dean of the Faculty of Political Science, Public Administration and Diplomacy, Notre Dame University – Louaize (2001-06). During his academic career he has lectured about political change in the Middle East in different universities and educational institutions in the USA and Canada. He is the author of *Fear and Anxiety in the Arab World* (Florida University Press) and has published chapters in several other books, articles on the Bitterlemons website (www.bitterlemons.org) and articles in international refereed journals.

Is-haq O. Oloyede is Vice-Chancellor of the University of Ilorin, Nigeria; President of the Association of African Universities, IAU Deputy Board Member, Executive

Secretary of the Nigeria Inter-Religious Council and former Co-Secretary of the National Political Reform Conference. He became a Professor of Islamic Studies in 1995 and vice-chancellor in 2007. Professor Oloyede has received several awards and honours, and is also a member of many professional bodies. He is a recipient of the Arab League Prize for the Best Certificate Student in Arabic and Islamic Studies, University of Ibadan; Recipient of Merit Award by the Islamic Mission of Africa; Fellow of the Islamic Academy of Cambridge, United Kingdom; Fellow, Academy of Religion; Fellow, Society for Peace Studies and Practice; Member, Nigerian Institute of Management; Board Member, African Centre for Religions and the Sciences; and Member, Nigerian Association for the Study and Teaching of Religion and the Natural Sciences.

Olav Øye is a former member of the Executive Committee of the European Students' Union (ESU), where he was responsible for student union development. He is currently responsible for communications within ESU. Øye was ESU's representative in the Mobility Co-ordination Group in the Bologna Process in 2008-09. He is a former president of the Norwegian Association of Students (StL) and represented students as a member of the Board of Volda University College and the Board of the Norwegian Association of Higher Education Institutions (UHR). Øye currently studies economics at Oslo University College. He holds a Bachelor of Journalism degree from Volda University College and has studied history at the University of Trondheim and journalism at the University of Queensland.

Alf Rasmussen holds a Master's degree in Political Science and is currently working in the Norwegian Ministry of Education and Research, Department of Higher Education. His main areas of responsibility are the global perspectives of the Bologna Process, co-operation with Latin America and the follow-up to the Norwegian White Paper on internationalisation of education, of which he was also the key author. From 1997 to 2005 he was engaged as Senior Adviser at the Nordic Council of Ministers in Copenhagen, Denmark, responsible for Higher Education Co-operation. From 1988 to 1997 he was working in the Norwegian Ministry of Culture and Science and also in the Ministry of Education and Research, Department of Higher Education and Department for Lifelong Learning.

Bernd Wächter is Director of the Academic Co-operation Association. His previous positions included Head of the European Programmes' Section in the German Academic Exchange Service (DAAD) and Head of Department for Erasmus in the Socrates & Youth for Europe Technical Assistance Office. He is an internationally recognised expert on academic mobility and the internationalisation of higher education, and is a member of the Bologna working group on the global dimension of the European Higher Education Area. His publications include *English-Taught Programmes in European Higher Education: The Picture in 2007* (with Friedhelm Maiworm; Bonn 2008: Lemmens) and Bernd Wächter (ed.), *Higher Education in a Changing Environment: Internationalisation of Higher Education Policy in Europe* (Bonn 2004: Lemmens).

Publications in the Council of Europe Higher Education series

No. 1:   *The university as res publica: higher education governance, student participation and the university as a site of citizenship* (2004), ISBN 978-92-871-5515-3

No. 2:   *The public responsibility for higher education and research* (2005), ISBN 978-92-871-5679-2

No. 3:   *Standards for recognition: the Lisbon Recognition Convention and its subsidiary texts* (2006), ISBN 978-92-871-5903-8

No. 4:   *Recognition in the Bologna Process: policy development and the road to good practice* (2006), ISBN 978-92-871-6007-2

No. 5:   *Higher education governance between democratic culture, academic aspirations and market forces* (2006), ISBN 978-92-871-5957-1

No. 6:   *Qualifications: introduction to a concept* (2007), ISBN 978-92-871-6125-3

No. 7:   *The heritage of European universities*, 2nd edn (2007), ISBN 978-92-871-6121-5

No. 8:   *Higher education and democratic culture: citizenship, human rights and civic responsibility* (2008), ISBN 978-92-871-6274-8

No. 9:   *The legitimacy of quality assurance in higher education* (2008), ISBN 978-92-871-6237-3

No. 10: *New challenges in recognition* (2008), ISBN 978-92-871-6331-8

No. 11: *Intercultural dialogue on campus* (2009), ISBN 978-92-871-6503-9

No. 12: *Improving recognition in the European Higher Education Area: an analysis of national action plans* (2010), ISBN 978-92-871-6648-7

No. 13: *Developing attitudes to recognition: substantial differences in an age of globalisation* (2010), ISBN 978-92-871-6697-5

No. 14: *Advancing democratic practice: a self-assessment guide for higher education* (2010), ISBN 978-92-871-6663-0

No. 15: *Higher education for modern societies: competences and values* (2010), ISBN 978-92-871-6777-4

Sales agents for publications of the Council of Europe
Agents de vente des publications du Conseil de l'Europe

BELGIUM/BELGIQUE
La Librairie Européenne -
The European Bookshop
Rue de l'Orme, 1
BE-1040 BRUXELLES
Tel.: +32 (0)2 231 04 35
Fax: +32 (0)2 735 08 60
E-mail: order@libeurop.be
http://www.libeurop.be

Jean De Lannoy/DL Services
Avenue du Roi 202 Koningslaan
BE-1190 BRUXELLES
Tel.: +32 (0)2 538 43 08
Fax: +32 (0)2 538 08 41
E-mail: jean.de.lannoy@dl-servi.com
http://www.jean-de-lannoy.be

BOSNIA AND HERZEGOVINA/
BOSNIE-HERZÉGOVINE
Robert's Plus d.o.o.
Marka Marulíça 2/V
BA-71000, SARAJEVO
Tel.: + 387 33 640 818
Fax: + 387 33 640 818
E-mail: robertsplus@bih.net.ba

CANADA
Renouf Publishing Co. Ltd.
1-5369 Canotek Road
CA-OTTAWA, Ontario K1J 9J3
Tel.: +1 613 745 2665
Fax: +1 613 745 7660
Toll-Free Tel.: (866) 767-6766
E-mail: order.dept@renoufbooks.com
http://www.renoufbooks.com

CROATIA/CROATIE
Robert's Plus d.o.o.
Marasoviçeva 67
HR-21000, SPLIT
Tel.: + 385 21 315 800, 801, 802, 803
Fax: + 385 21 315 804
E-mail: robertsplus@robertsplus.hr

CZECH REPUBLIC/
RÉPUBLIQUE TCHÈQUE
Suweco CZ, s.r.o.
Klecakova 347
CZ-180 21 PRAHA 9
Tel.: +420 2 424 59 204
Fax: +420 2 848 21 646
F-mail: import@suweco.cz
http://www.suweco.cz

DENMARK/DANEMARK
GAD
Vimmelskaftet 32
DK-1161 KØBENHAVN K
Tel.: +45 77 66 60 00
Fax: +45 77 66 60 01
E-mail: gad@gad.dk
http://www.gad.dk

FINLAND/FINLANDE
Akateeminen Kirjakauppa
PO Box 128
Keskuskatu 1
FI-00100 HELSINKI
Tel.: +358 (0)9 121 4430
Fax: +358 (0)9 121 4242
E-mail: akatilaus@akateeminen.com
http://www.akateeminen.com

FRANCE
La Documentation française
(diffusion/distribution France entière)
124, rue Henri Barbusse
FR-93308 AUBERVILLIERS CEDEX
Tél.: +33 (0)1 40 15 70 00
Fax: +33 (0)1 40 15 68 00
E-mail: commande@ladocumentationfrancaise.fr
http://www.ladocumentationfrancaise.fr

Librairie Kléber
1 rue des Francs Bourgeois
FR-67000 STRASBOURG
Tel.: +33 (0)3 88 15 78 88
Fax: +33 (0)3 88 15 78 80
E-mail: librairie-kleber@coe.int
http://www.librairie-kleber.com

GERMANY/ALLEMAGNE
AUSTRIA/AUTRICHE
UNO Verlag GmbH
August-Bebel-Allee 6
DE-53175 BONN
Tel.: +49 (0)228 94 90 20
Fax: +49 (0)228 94 90 222
E-mail: bestellung@uno-verlag.de
http://www.uno-verlag.de

GREECE/GRÈCE
Librairie Kauffmann s.a.
Stadiou 28
GR-105 64 ATHINAI
Tel.: +30 210 32 55 321
Fax.: +30 210 32 30 320
E-mail: ord@otenet.gr
http://www.kauffmann.gr

HUNGARY/HONGRIE
Euro Info Service
Pannónia u. 58.
PF. 1039
HU-1136 BUDAPEST
Tel.: +36 1 329 2170
Fax: +36 1 349 2053
E-mail: euroinfo@euroinfo.hu
http://www.euroinfo.hu

ITALY/ITALIE
Licosa SpA
Via Duca di Calabria, 1/1
IT-50125 FIRENZE
Tel.: +39 0556 483215
Fax: +39 0556 41257
E-mail: licosa@licosa.com
http://www.licosa.com

MEXICO/MEXIQUE
Mundi-Prensa México, S.A. De C.V.
Río Pánuco, 141 Delegacíon Cuauhtémoc
MX-06500 MÉXICO, D.F.
Tel.: +52 (01)55 55 33 56 58
Fax: +52 (01)55 55 14 67 99
E-mail: mundiprensa@mundiprensa.com.mx
http://www.mundiprensa.com.mx

NETHERLANDS/PAYS-BAS
Roodveldt Import BV
Nieuwe Hemweg 50
NE-1013 CX AMSTERDAM
Tel.: + 31 20 622 8035
Fax.: + 31 20 625 5493
Website: www.publidis.org
Email: orders@publidis.org

NORWAY/NORVÈGE
Akademika
Postboks 84 Blindern
NO-0314 OSLO
Tel.: +47 2 218 8100
Fax: +47 2 218 8103
E-mail: support@akademika.no
http://www.akademika.no

POLAND/POLOGNE
Ars Polona JSC
25 Obroncow Street
PL-03-933 WARSZAWA
Tel.: +48 (0)22 509 86 00
Fax: +48 (0)22 509 86 10
E-mail: arspolona@arspolona.com.pl
http://www.arspolona.com.pl

PORTUGAL
Livraria Portugal
(Dias & Andrade, Lda.)
Rua do Carmo, 70
PT-1200-094 LISBOA
Tel.: +351 21 347 42 82 / 85
Fax: +351 21 347 02 64
E-mail: info@livrariaportugal.pt
http://www.livrariaportugal.pt

RUSSIAN FEDERATION/
FÉDÉRATION DE RUSSIE
Ves Mir
17b, Butlerova ul.
RU-101000 MOSCOW
Tel.: +7 495 739 0971
Fax: +7 495 739 0971
E-mail: orders@vesmirbooks.ru
http://www.vesmirbooks.ru

SPAIN/ESPAGNE
Mundi-Prensa Libros, s.a.
Castelló, 37
ES-28001 MADRID
Tel.: +34 914 36 37 00
Fax: +34 915 75 39 98
E-mail: libreria@mundiprensa.es
http://www.mundiprensa.com

SWITZERLAND/SUISSE
Planetis Sàrl
16 chemin des pins
CH-1273 ARZIER
Tel.: +41 22 366 51 77
Fax: +41 22 366 51 78
E-mail: info@planetis.ch

UNITED KINGDOM/ROYAUME-UNI
The Stationery Office Ltd
PO Box 29
GB-NORWICH NR3 1GN
Tel.: +44 (0)870 600 5522
Fax: +44 (0)870 600 5533
E-mail: book.enquiries@tso.co.uk
http://www.tsoshop.co.uk

UNITED STATES and CANADA/
ÉTATS-UNIS et CANADA
Manhattan Publishing Company
468 Albany Post Road
US-CROTON-ON-HUDSON, NY 10520
Tel.: +1 914 271 5194
Fax: +1 914 271 5856
E-mail: Info@manhattanpublishing.com
http://www.manhattanpublishing.com

Council of Europe Publishing/Editions du Conseil de l'Europe
FR-67075 STRASBOURG Cedex
Tel.: +33 (0)3 88 41 25 81 – Fax: +33 (0)3 88 41 39 10 – E-mail: publishing@coe.int – Website: http://book.coe.int